Lecture Notes in Computer Science　　12723

More information about this subseries at http://www.springer.com/series/7407

Jinyun Xue · Fumiko Nagoya · Shaoying Liu ·
Zhenhua Duan (Eds.)

Structured Object-Oriented Formal Language and Method

10th International Workshop, SOFL+MSVL 2020
Singapore, March 1, 2021
Revised Selected Papers

 Springer

Editors
Jinyun Xue
Jiangxi Normal University
Nanchang, China

Fumiko Nagoya
Nihon University
Tokyo, Japan

Shaoying Liu
Hiroshima University
Hiroshima, Japan

Zhenhua Duan
Xidian University
Xi'an, China

ISSN 0302-9743   ISSN 1611-3349 (electronic)
Lecture Notes in Computer Science
ISBN 978-3-030-77473-8   ISBN 978-3-030-77474-5 (eBook)
https://doi.org/10.1007/978-3-030-77474-5

LNCS Sublibrary: SL1 – Theoretical Computer Science and General Issues

This Springer imprint is published by the registered company Springer Nature Switzerland AG
The registered company address is: Gewerbestrasse 11, 6330 Cham, Switzerland

Preface

The Structured Object-Oriented Formal Language (SOFL) has been developed to address the challenge of how to transform formal methods principles and techniques into practice by providing a comprehensible specification language, a practical modeling method, various verification and validation techniques, and tool support through effective integration of formal methods with conventional software engineering techniques. SOFL integrates Data Flow Diagrams, Petri Nets; and VDM-SL to offer a visualized and formal notation for specification construction; a three-step approach to requirements acquisition and system design; specification-based inspection and testing methods for detecting errors in both specifications and programs; and a set of tools to support modeling and verification. The Modeling, Simulation and Verification Language (MSVL) is a parallel programming language. Its supporting toolkit, MSV, has been developed to enable us to model, simulate, and verify a system in a formal manner. Following the success of previous SOFL+MSVL workshops, this workshop aimed to continuously promote the development and combination of the SOFL formal engineering method and the MSVL formal method, as well as the applications of their fundamental principles and specific techniques for developing other formal engineering techniques.

The workshop attracted 24 submissions on formal modeling, formal verification, model checking, metamorphic testing, natural language processing, and geometric modeling. Each submission was rigorously reviewed by two or more Program Committee members on the basis of technical quality, relevance, significance, and clarity, and 13 papers were accepted for publication in the workshop proceedings. The acceptance rate was 54%.

We would like to thank ICFEM 2020 for supporting the organization of the virtual meeting and all of the Program Committee members for their great efforts and cooperation in reviewing and selecting the papers. We would also like to thank all the participants for attending presentation sessions and actively joining discussions at the workshop. Finally, our gratitude goes to the editors, Anna Kramer and Guido Zosimo-Landolfo at Springer, for their continuous support in publishing the workshop proceedings.

March 2021

Jinyun Xue
Fumiko Nagoya
Shaoying Liu
Zhenhua Duan

Organization

General Chairs

Shaoying Liu   Hiroshima University, Japan
Zhenhua Duan   Xidian University, China

Program Co-chairs

Fumiko Nagoya   Nihon University, Japan
Jinyun Xue   Jiangxi Normal University, China

Program Committee

Busalire Emeka   Hosei University, Japan
Colin Fidge   Queensland University of Technology, Australia
Huaikou Miao   Shanghai University, China
Kazuhiro Ogata   JAIST, Japan
Shengchao Qin   Teesside University, UK
Shin Nakajima   National Institute of Informatics, Japan
Wuwei Shen   Western Michigan University, USA
Xinfeng Shu   Xi'an University of Posts and Telecommunications, China
Yuting Chen   Shanghai Jiao Tong University, China
Zhen You   Jiangxi Normal University, China
Zhuo Cheng   Jiangxi Normal University, China

Contents

Testing and Formal Verification

Modeling and Specification

An MSVL-Based Modeling Framework for Back Propagation Neural Networks

Liang Zhao[1], Zhe Feng[1], Xiaobing Wang[1(✉)], and Xinfeng Shu[2(✉)]

[1] Institute of Computing Theory and Technology, ISN Laboratory,
Xidian University, Xi'an 710071, People's Republic of China
lzhao@xidian.edu.cn, xbwang@mail.xidian.edu.cn
[2] School of Computer Science and Technology, Xi'an University of Posts
and Telecommunications, Xi'an 710061, People's Republic of China
shuxf@xupt.edu.cn

Abstract. With the rapid development and wide application of artificial neural networks, formal modeling and verification of their security become more and more significant. As a basic step towards the direction, this work proposes a comprehensive modeling framework for back propagation (BP) neural networks based on the formal language MSVL. In this framework, the structure and behavior of a BP neural network are formalized as specifications of data structures and operations, and they are in turn implemented as MSVL structs and functions, respectively. Based on the formalization, models of BP neural networks can be constructed and trained according to the requirements of users. Experimental results show that these models have good performance in terms of metrics concerning training and prediction such as loss and accuracy.

Keywords: Formal modeling · MSVL · Artificial neural network · Back propagation · Formal verification

1 Introduction

In recent years, with the advancement of computer software and hardware and the development of machine learning technology, artificial intelligence, especially artificial neural network, has become a hot topic in computer science. Different artificial neural network models have been proposed, such as convolutional neural networks and recurrent neural networks, with excellent abilities of data computing and classification. In the meantime, various systems based on artificial neural networks have been developed, and they have been successfully applied to areas of our daily life including transportation, medical treatment, social network and electronic commerce.

This research is supported by National Natural Science Foundation of China Grant Nos. 61972301, 61672403 and 61732013, National Natural Science Foundation of Shaanxi Province under Grant No. 2020GY-043, and Shaanxi Key Science and Technology Innovation Team Project Grant No. 2019TD-001.

J. Xue et al. (Eds.): SOFL+MSVL 2020, LNCS 12723, pp. 3–22, 2021.
https://doi.org/10.1007/978-3-030-77474-5_1

With their rapid development and wide application, the security of artificial neural networks has been paid more and more attention. Systems of artificial neural networks may contain defects or leaks, or may be vulnerable to different malicious attacks, and such situations are not rare. In March 2018, a Uber self-driving vehicle collided with a pedestrian in Arizona, US and caused his death unfortunately, which became the first pedestrian death accident caused by automatic driving systems in the world. In December 2019, an artificial intelligence company named Kneron claimed to have used 3D masks to break through the face recognition systems of Alipay and WeChat, and successfully enter the railway station by face swiping.

So, it is vital to verify the security of artificial neural networks, especially those to be applied in safety-critical situations. Verification is a kind of formal methods, using techniques such as model checking [2] and theorem proving [11] to validate whether a system satisfies or violates expected properties. The basis of verification is to construct a model of the system with formal languages and notations, which enables strict mathematic and logic reasoning of the system and the properties. Nevertheless, formal modeling and verification of artificial neural networks is far from an easy job, since their behavior is somewhat opaque and unexplainable, depending on a huge number of parameters obtained through machine learning.

As far as we know, there is some work on formal modeling and verification of artificial neural networks. Huang et al. [10] study a kind of robustness properties of deep neural networks. By defining a set of manipulations to discretize the neighborhood space of certain standard sample, they establish a set of logic constraints and then use a solver of satisfiability modulo theory (SMT) to check whether there are adversarial samples in the neighborhood space. Katz et al. [12] extend the simplex method of linear programming by considering the rectified linear unit (ReLU) function. Based on this, they formalize and verify linear properties of neural networks with only ReLU as the activation function. Singh et al. [16] model feedforward neural networks and convolutional neural networks with an abstract domain of floating-point polyhedra and intervals that supports different transformation functions. Based on the abstract domain, certain properties of these networks, such as robustness and pre/post conditions, can be verified with certain precision. Ghodsi et al. [7] propose a verification model for neural network systems deployed in the cloud, using certain interactive proof protocols. They make a few restrictions on the structure of the neural network, e.g. the data should be in a finite domain and the activation functions should be quadratic. It can be observed that these studies consider different aspects of different neural networks, make different simplifying assumptions, and aim at different properties. They cannot form a systematic modeling and verification method for general neural networks.

To improve this situation, we are going to develop a comprehensive framework that models and verifies various aspects of various neural networks. This work is the first step towards this direction, proposing a fundamental framework for the modeling of general aspects, including details of the layered structure, the prediction behavior and the learning behavior, of back propagation (BP) neural networks, the most basic category of neural networks. As for the underlying formal language, we adopt Modeling, Simulation and Verification Language (MSVL) [6]. MSVL has a C-like syntax which is convenient to use, but it is actually defined based on Projection Temporal Logic (PTL) [4], a temporal logic with strong expressive power [17]. With the logic basis, the language is suitable for modeling, simulating and further verifying various computer systems and programs [5,22].

In this work, we propose a systematic modeling framework based on MSVL for BP neural networks. On the one hand, the structure of a BP neural network is modeled hierarchically. Entities of different levels, such as matrix, fully connected layer and network-level parameters, are characterized as specific data structures and implemented as MSVL structs. On the other hand, the behavior of the network is modeled. Behavior patterns of different levels, such as matrix operations, forward propagation and BP, are characterized as specific operations and implemented as MSVL functions. Based on these data structures and operations, we formulate a process for constructing and training a BP neural network according to the user's customization. We carry out an experiment using the framework to generate various instances of BP neural networks for the classification task of handwritten font recognition. The instances show good performance in terms of standard metrics such as loss and accuracy. Especially, the convergence of the loss and the increase of the accuracy during the training turn out to be more stable, compared with Python implementations of the same network structure.

The rest of this paper is organized as follows. Section 2 introduces basic notions of MSVL and BP neural network. Then, Sects. 3 and 4 specify the design and implementation of the modeling framework, respectively. After that, Sect. 5 presents the experiment which applies the framework to handwritten font recognition. Finally, conclusions are drawn is Sect. 6 with a discussion on future work.

2   Background

This section introduces basic notions of the language MSVL and back propagation neural network.

2.1   The Language MSVL

Modeling, Simulation and Verification Language (MSVL) [6,18] is a temporal logic programming language that supports formal modeling and verification of computer systems. Specifically, it is an executable subset of projection temporal logic (PTL) [4] with more succinct notations.

MSVL has a C-like syntax that is easy to use. It supports various data types such as integer, float, array types, pointer types and struct types. The syntax of arithmetic expressions e, l-value expressions le and boolean expressions b of MSVL is given as follows.

$$e \; := \; le \mid c \mid \bigcirc x \mid \ominus x \mid e_1 \text{ aop } e_2 \mid \&x \mid (T)e$$
$$le \; := \; x \mid e_1[e_2] \mid *e \mid e.a \mid e{\text{-}}> a$$
$$b \; := \; \texttt{true} \mid \texttt{false} \mid \neg b \mid b_1 \wedge b_2 \mid e_1 = e_2 \mid e_1 < e_2$$

Here, x denotes a variable, c denotes a constant, and a denotes an attribute name of a struct. Besides, $\bigcirc$ (next) and $\ominus$ (previous) are temporal operators, aop denotes an arithmetic operation such as addition and multiplication, while (T) represents a cast operation to a type T.

A statement of MSVL, generally represented by p or q, takes the form of one of the following constructs. Actually, each construct is defined by a PTL formula, which is interpreted over an interval of states. Readers may refer to [18] for the definition and semantics of the statements.

(1) Termination: `empty` (2) Unit Interval: `skip`

(3) Assignment: $le \Leftarrow e$ (4) Unit Assignment: $le := e$

(5) Variable Declaration: $T\ x$ (6) Interval Frame: `frame(x)`

(7) Conjunction: p `and` q (8) Selection: p `or` q

(9) Next: `next` p (10) Always: `alw` p

(11) Chop: $p; q$ (12) Parallel: $p \parallel q$

(13) Conditional Choice: `if` b `then` p `else` q (14) While Loop: `while` b `do` p

(15) Projection: $(p_1, ..., p_m)$ `prj` q (16) Function Call: $f(e_1, ..., e_n)$

The statement `empty` represents an interval of length 0, i.e., the current state is the last state, while `skip` represents a unit interval, i.e., the next state is the last state. A unit assignment $le := e$ indicates le is assigned by e over a unit interval. A frame statement `frame(x)` indicates the value of x is preserved at every state of the current interval, unless it is assigned explicitly. A projection statement $(p_1, ..., p_m)$ `prj` q represents a special form of parallel execution. It indicates $p_1, \cdots, p_m$ are executed sequentially, while q is executed "in parallel", over their projected interval. The intuition of the other statement constructs is straightforward.

MSVL has a compiler MC [20] based on LLVM. The compiler accepts a well-formed MSVL program as its input, and through the process of the lexical analysis, syntactic analysis and semantic analysis, generates the result of executable binary code. In this way, MC is suitable to realize modeling and verification tasks with MSVL.

2.2   Back Propagation Neural Network

Back propagation (BP) neural network [3] is a basic category of neural network composed of fully connected layers and trained through propagating the loss backwardly. A BP neural network may have multiple hidden layers between the input layer and the output layer. Each layer has several neurons, and neurons of adjacent layers are fully connected by weights.

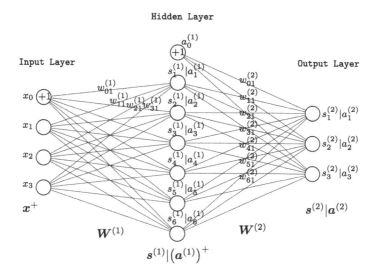

Fig. 1. An example BP neural network

We use bold lowercase letters, such as $\boldsymbol{a}$ and $\boldsymbol{\delta}$, to represent row vectors, and bold uppercase letters, such as $\boldsymbol{A}$ and $\boldsymbol{\Delta}$, to represent matrices. For a vector $\boldsymbol{a} = (a_1, \ldots, a_n)$, the notation $\boldsymbol{a}^+$ represents the extension of $\boldsymbol{a}$ with a bias 1 at the front, i.e. $\boldsymbol{a}^+ = (1, a_1, \ldots, a_n)$. Besides, σ and $\mathcal{L}$ represent the activation function and loss function, respectively.

We introduce the calculation behavior of BP neural networks through an example, shown in Fig. 1. The network has an input layer with three neurons, one hidden layer with six neurons and an output layer with three neurons, indicating there are three result categories. They are also called the 0-th, first and second layers, respectively.

The main behavior of a BP neural network is prediction and training. Prediction calculates the category of an input sample, which is a vector of features whose size equals the number of neurons of the input layer. In this example, an input sample $\boldsymbol{x} = (x_1, x_2, x_3)$ has three features. It is extended with the bias, and then multiplied by the matrix $\boldsymbol{W}^{(1)} = (w_{ij}^{(1)})_{4 \times 6}$ of weights of the first layer, obtaining the summation value vector $\boldsymbol{s}^{(1)} = \boldsymbol{x}^+ \boldsymbol{W}^{(1)}$. Then, it is activated by certain activation function, obtaining the activation value vector $\boldsymbol{a}^{(1)} = \sigma^{(1)}(\boldsymbol{s}^{(1)})$ of the layer. The calculation is the same for the second layer. $\boldsymbol{a}^{(1)}$ is extended with the bias, multiplied by the weight matrix $\boldsymbol{W}^{(2)} = (w_{ij}^{(2)})_{7 \times 3}$ as $\boldsymbol{s}^{(2)} = (\boldsymbol{a}^{(1)})^+ \boldsymbol{W}^{(2)}$, and then activated, obtaining the activation value vector $\boldsymbol{a}^{(2)} = \sigma^{(2)}(\boldsymbol{s}^{(2)})$ of the second layer. Such a calculation process is called forward propagation. $\boldsymbol{a}^{(2)}$ of size 3 is regarded as the probabilities that the input $\boldsymbol{x}$ belongs to the three categories. Thus, $\boldsymbol{x}$ is predicted to belong to the category with the highest probability.

To make the prediction accurate, the network should be trained so that the weights are set to proper values. The input of the training is a set of sample vectors $\boldsymbol{x}$ whose category is known and labelled by one-hot vectors $\boldsymbol{y}$. Each sample $\boldsymbol{x}$ is processed through forward propagation, obtaining the activation value vector $\boldsymbol{a}^{(2)}$. Then, the loss is calculated between $\boldsymbol{a}^{(2)}$ and $\boldsymbol{y}$. If we adopt mean square error as the loss function, the calculation is $\mathcal{L}(\boldsymbol{a}^{(2)}, \boldsymbol{y}) = 1/2 \sum_{i=1}^{3} (a_i^{(2)} - y_i)^2$.

After that, the gradient of the loss with respect to each weight parameter $w_{ij}^{(k)}$ is calculated. Suppose the activation functions of both layers are the sigmoid function. The calculation is performed backwardly: from the output layer to the first layer. Such a calculation process is called BP, sketched as follows.

$$\delta_k^{(2)} = \left(a_k^{(2)} - y_k\right) a_k^{(2)} \left(1 - a_k^{(2)}\right) \qquad \frac{\partial \mathcal{L}}{\partial w_{ik}^{(2)}} = \delta_k^{(2)} \left(a_i^{(1)}\right)^+$$

$$\delta_j^{(1)} = a_j^{(1)}(1 - a_j^{(1)}) \sum_{k \in K} \delta_k^{(2)} w_{jk}^{(2)} \qquad \frac{\partial \mathcal{L}}{\partial w_{ij}^{(1)}} = \delta_j^{(1)} \left(x_i^{(0)}\right)^+$$

Finally, to make the loss decrease effectively, each weight parameter is updated based on its corresponding gradient. At this stage, different optimization methods can be used to accelerate the decrease of loss, such as batch gradient descent (BGD) [19], mini-batch gradient descent (MBGD) [13] and Adam [14]. The training generally involves a large number of batched samples, and is repeated for multiple iterations.

3   Design of the Modeling Framework

This section presents the design of the modeling framework for BP neural networks. We first introduce a few principles based on which we carry out the design.

3.1   Design Principles

For designing the modeling framework, we take into account three general principles: portability, extensibility and training efficiency.

Portability refers to the ease with which software or applications can be transferred from one environment to another, and it is a necessary condition that models can be widely used. From an engineering point of view, portability indicates lower development costs. An application may be coded once and applied to different platforms, and developers pay more attention to the logic of the application itself. From the perspective of software and hardware development, portability enables software and hardware to be developed independent of each other. For good portability, the design of our framework is for an MSVL implementation. MSVL is a general modeling language that supports compilation with LLVM.

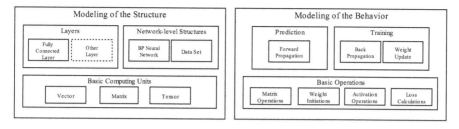

Fig. 2. Sketch of the modeling framework

Extensibility refers to the ability for software models or systems to extend. It considers the future growth of the a system by adding new functions or modifying existing functions. Generally, extensibility can be achieved through dynamically loaded plug-in, carefully designed hierarchical structure with abstract interfaces at the top, useful callback function construct, as well as functionally extensible code structure. For good extensibility, we carry out a hierarchical design and process-like construction according to the natures of neural networks and the characteristics of MSVL.

Training efficiency is a general principle for developing a machine-learning model, which may refer to the time cost for the model to be well trained, or more detailedly the speed that some loss metric converges. As one kind of machine-learning models, a neural network is usually trained by a large data set for many iterations, involving frequent calculation of losses and gradients in terms of operations of large matrices or tensors. For good training efficiency, our design supports general optimization strategies for gradient calculation and weight update. We also consider methods that improve single-point computing efficiency, such as sparse-matrix optimization [21].

3.2   Sketch of the Modeling Framework

The design of the modeling framework follows the above principles and considers the modeling of both the structure and behavior of BP neural networks, sketched as Fig. 2.

The modeling of the structure is a hierarchical design. At the first level, basic computing units of a BP neural network are specified, including vector, matrix and tensor. Among these basic computing units, matrix is the most important data structure. In fact, a vector can be regarded as a special matrix, while a three-dimensional tensor can be expressed in the form of a matrix array. Based on the first level, the second level involves the modeling of layers and network-level structures. For a model of BP neural networks, it is enough to consider only fully connected layers in this work. However, the modeling of other layers, such as convolutional layers, is also supported so that the framework is extensible to other types of neural networks. Network-level structures include the whole BP neural network and the sample data set. Notice that the data set is needed to model the training behavior.

FCLayer
NeurionNum: int   // the number of neurons
ActiFunc: int   // the activation function
ActiMat: Matrix   // the activation value matrix
SumMat: Matrix   // the summation value matrix
WeightMat: Matrix   // the weight matrix
WeightBiasMat: Matrix   // the weight bias matrix
DeltaMat: Matrix   // the intermediate temporary matrix for BP
NablaWbMat: Matrix   // the weight gradient matrix
ActiDeriMat: Matrix   // the activation derivation matrix

Matirx
row: int
// the number of rows
col: int
// the number of columns
element: float**
// the pointer referring to the data values

Fig. 3. Data structures: matrix and layer

The modeling of the structure of a BP neural network enables the modeling of its behavior. At the first level, we formalize a series of basic operations upon the matrix data structure, including matrix operations, weight initiations, activation operations and loss calculations. Based on the first level, the second level models the two major behavior patterns of a BP neural network: prediction and training. The main operation of prediction is forward propagation, while the main operations of training involves BP and weight update.

3.3   Modeling of the Structure

The modeling of the structure of a BP neural network involves the modeling of basic computing units, layers, and network-level structures.

Basic Computing Units. The basic computing units of a BP neural network generally indicate the one-dimensional row vector, the two-dimensional matrix and the three-dimensional tensor. We model the two-dimensional Matrix as a data structure shown in Fig. 3. It is the most basic data structure of this framework. Specifically, a matrix has three properties: the number of rows, the number of columns, and the pointer referring to the data values. Then, a vector is represented as a matrix with just one row, and a tensor can be represented as an array of matrices.

Layers. The layered structure is an important part of hierarchical modeling. Here, we only model fully connected layers that are enough to constitutes BP neural networks. Nevertheless, with the data structures of matrix and tensor, it is also feasible to model other kinds of layers, e.g. convolutional layers, so that different types of neural networks, e.g. convolutional neural networks, can be further characterized.

A fully connected layer is formalized as a data structure named FCLayer, shown in Fig. 3. Specifically, it has the following properties: the number of neurons, the activation function, the activation value matrix, the summation value matrix, the weight matrix, the weight bias matrix, the intermediate temporary matrix for BP, the weight gradient matrix, and the activation derivation matrix.

BPNN
CurrentSampleNum: int
// the current number of samples to deal with
SampleDimensionNum: int
// the number of data features
HiddenLayerNum: int
// the number of hidden layers
WeightInitWayNum: int
// the weight initialization method
Layers: FCLayer*
// the pointer referring to the structure of all layers
OnehotMat: Matrix
// the labels with one-hot encoding
ClassificationNum: int
// the number of categories
LossFunc: int
//the choice of loss function

DataSet
FeatureDataSet: Matrix // the set of features
LabelDataSet: Matrix // the set of labels
TrainFeature: Matrix // the training features
TrainLabel: Matrix // the training labels
BatchTrainFeature: Matrix // the batched training features
BatchTrainLabel: Matrix // the batched training labels
TestFeature: Matrix // the test features
TestLabel: Matrix // the test labels
SampleNum: int // the number of samples
TrainSampleNum: int // the numbers of training samples
TestSampleNum: int // the numbers of test samples
DimensionNum: int // the number of features
ClassificationNum: int // the number of categories
BatchSize: int // the batch size
BatchNum: int // the number of batches
Remainder: int // the size of the last data block

Fig. 4. Data structures of network level

Network-Level Structures. We consider two structures of network level: the BP neural network and the data set. By combining the fully connected layers and related parameters, we formalize a BP neural network as a data structure named BPNN, shown in Fig. 4. Specifically, its properties involve the current number of samples to deal with, the number of data features, the number of hidden layers, the weight initialization method, the pointer referring to the structure of all layers, the labels with one-hot encoding, the number of categories, and the choice of loss function.

Besides, we model a sample data set as a data structure named DataSet, also shown in Fig. 4. It has the following properties: the set of features, the set of labels, the training features, the training labels, the batched training features, the batched training labels, the test features, the test labels, the numbers of training and test samples, the number of features, the number of categories, the batch size, the number of batches, and the size of the last data block which may be smaller than the batch size.

3.4   Modeling of the Behavior

With the data structures designed in the previous subsection, we are able to model the behavior of a BP neural network. This involves the modeling of basic operations, the prediction behavior and the training behavior.

Basic Operations. Basic operations lay the foundation of specific behavior modes. As is shown in Fig. 5, we utilize the matrix data structure to formalize four categories of basic operations: matrix operations, weight initiations, activation operations and loss calculations.

Here, we introduce a few notations. For a matrix X, X^T represents the transposition of X, while the *plus* notation X^+ represents the extension of X

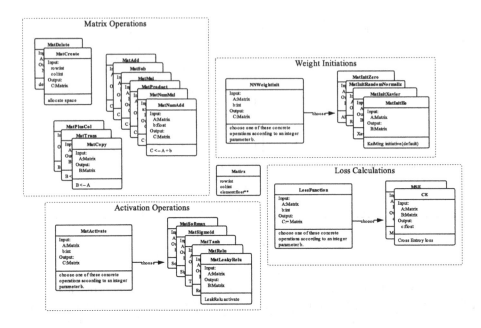

Fig. 5. Basic operations

with one bias column of all 1 to the left side. For two matrices X and Y of the same size, $X \circ Y$ represents the *product* of X and Y *by position*. For example,

$$\begin{pmatrix} a_1 \ a_2 \\ a_3 \ a_4 \end{pmatrix}^+ = \begin{pmatrix} 1 \ a_1 \ a_2 \\ 1 \ a_3 \ a_4 \end{pmatrix} \quad \text{and} \quad \begin{pmatrix} a_1 \ a_2 \\ a_3 \ a_4 \end{pmatrix} \circ \begin{pmatrix} b_1 \ b_2 \\ b_3 \ b_4 \end{pmatrix} = \begin{pmatrix} a_1b_1 \ a_2b_2 \\ a_3b_3 \ a_4b_4 \end{pmatrix}.$$

We formalize a group of matrix operations. MatCreate is for the creation of a matrix, while MatDelete is for its deletion. MatAdd, MatSub, MatMul and Mat-Product are for the addition, subtraction, multiplication and product by position (◦) of two matrices, respectively. Besides, MatNumMul multiplies a matrix by a constant number, i.e., each element of the matrix is multiplied by the number. The meaning of MatNumAdd is similar. In addition, MatCopy is for matrix copy. MatPlusCol and MatTrans calculate the plus X^+ and transposition X^T of a matrix X, respectively.

There are four main ways of weight initialization for neural networks: random initialization [1], all zero initialization, Xavier initialization [8] and HeKaiMing initialization [9]. We formalize them as four operations MatInitRandomNorm, MatInitZero, MatInitXavier and MatInitHe, respectively. We also model a general operation NNWeightInit of weight initialization that chooses one of these concrete operations according to an integer parameter.

We formalize five activation operations: MatSoftmax, MatSigmoid, MatTanh, MatRelu and MatLeakyRelu. They characterize the widely used activation functions softmax [15], sigmoid, tanh, relu and leaky relu, respectively. We also model a general activation operation MatActivate that chooses one of the five

```
NNForward
Input:
  featureMat: Matrix
  bpnn: BPNN*
Output:
  NULL (In-place update)

  if (CurrentSampleNum == feature.row) then pass
  Otherwise reallocate the parameter space of neural networks

  (bpnn->layers[0].ActiMat) <-- featureMat
  bpnn->Layer[0].ActiMatPlus <-- MatPlusCol(bpnn->Layer[0].ActiMat)

  for (i=0; i<bpnn->(HiddenLayerNum+1); i=i+1):
    bpnn->layers[i+1].SumMat <-- bpnn->layers[i].ActiMat * bpnn->layers[i+1].WeightBiasMat
    bpnn->layers[i+1].ActiMat <-- MatActivate(bpnn->layers[i+1].SumMat)
    if (i==bpnn->HiddenLayerNum) then pass
    Otherwise bpnn->layers[i+1].ActiMatPlus <-- MatPlusCol(bpnn->Layer[i+1].ActiMat)
```

Fig. 6. Operation of forward propagation

operation referring to an integer parameter. Similarly, for loss calculation, we formalize two operations CE and MSE that calculate the well known cross entropy loss [15] and mean square error loss, respectively. One of the two is chosen in a general operation LossFunction, according to a specific parameter.

Prediction. The core operation of the prediction behavior of a BP neural network is forward propagation. Given a vector of size M as the input, the output of forward propagation is a vector of size K indicating the probabilities that the input belongs to the K categories. Usually, the input vector is predicted to belong to the category with the highest probability.

Forward propagation can be generalized in that the input can be a matrix of size $N \times M$, representing a set of N vectors of the same size. They are dealt with at the same time, and the output is also a matrix, of size $N \times K$.

Suppose a BP neural network has H hidden layers. We call the input layer the 0-th layer and the output layer the $(H{+}1)$-th layer. Let $\boldsymbol{W}^{(i)}$, $\boldsymbol{S}^{(i)}$, $\boldsymbol{A}^{(i)}$ and $\sigma^{(i)}$ denote the weight matrix, the summation matrix, the activation matrix and the activation function of Layer i $(0 \leq i \leq H{+}1)$, respectively.

Inspired by the example presented in Sect. 2.2, we outline the calculation of forward propagation as follows. For consistency, the input matrix is denoted as $\boldsymbol{A}^{(0)}$.

$$
\begin{aligned}
&\left(A^{(0)}\right)^{+} W_{b}^{(1)} = S^{(1)} \xrightarrow{\sigma^{(1)}} A^{(1)} \xrightarrow{b} \left(A^{(1)}\right)^{+} \\
\Rightarrow&\cdots \\
\Rightarrow&\left(A^{(H-1)}\right)^{+} W_{b}^{(H)} = S^{(H)} \xrightarrow{\sigma^{(H)}} A^{(H)} \xrightarrow{b} \left(A^{(H)}\right)^{+} \\
\Rightarrow&\left(A^{(H)}\right)^{+} W_{b}^{(H+1)} = S^{(H+1)} \xrightarrow{\sigma^{(H+1)}} A^{(H+1)}
\end{aligned}
$$

Here, $\xrightarrow{b}$ indicates the extension with a bias column, while $\Rightarrow$ means entering the next layer. The calculation is formalized as an operation NNForward, shown in Fig. 6.

Training. Generally speaking, the training behavior is more complicated than the prediction behavior. The key of training is to calculate the gradients of the

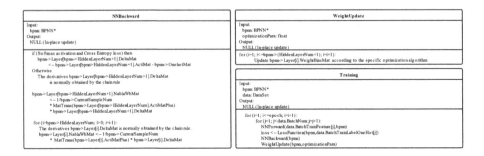

Fig. 7. Operations of training

loss with respect to the weights through BP. After that, all the weights are updated referring to the corresponding gradients.

Let $\boldsymbol{Y}$ be the label matrix, which may be composed of a set of one-hot vectors. Recall that $\mathcal{L}$ denotes the loss function. Assume $(\cdot)'$ calculates the derivative of a function, while $\nabla_{\boldsymbol{W}}$ calculates the gradients of a function with respect to the weights in a matrix $\boldsymbol{W}$.

Inspired by the example presented in Sect. 2.2, we outline a general calculation of BP in terms of matrix operations. First, for the output layer, i.e. the $(H+1)$-th layer, the gradients are calculated as follows.

$$\nabla_{\boldsymbol{W}_b^{(H+1)}}\mathcal{L}(\boldsymbol{A}^{(H+1)}, \boldsymbol{Y}) = \frac{1}{N}(\boldsymbol{A}^{(H)^+})^T\boldsymbol{\Delta}^{(H+1)}$$

$$\boldsymbol{\Delta}^{(H+1)} = \frac{\partial\mathcal{L}(\boldsymbol{A}^{(H+1)}, \boldsymbol{Y})}{\partial\boldsymbol{A}^{(H+1)}} \circ (\sigma^{(H+1)})'(\boldsymbol{S}^{(H+1)})$$

Here, we use an auxiliary matrix $\boldsymbol{\Delta}^{(i)}$ to record certain intermediate results of each layer i $(1 \leq i \leq H+1)$. Then, the calculation of the i-th hidden layer $(1 \leq i \leq H)$ depends on the results of its next layer. The calculation is actually performed backwardly, from Layer H to Layer 1.

$$\nabla_{\boldsymbol{W}_b^{(i)}}\mathcal{L}(\boldsymbol{A}^{(H+1)}, \boldsymbol{Y}) = \frac{1}{N}(\boldsymbol{A}^{(i-1)^+})^T\boldsymbol{\Delta}^{(i)}$$

$$\boldsymbol{\Delta}^{(i)} = \boldsymbol{\Delta}^{(i+1)}(\boldsymbol{W}^{(i+1)})^T \circ (\sigma^{(i)})'(\boldsymbol{S}^{(i)})$$

We formalize this calculation as an operation NNBackward, shown in Fig. 7.

The operation of BP calculates the gradients of the loss with respect to all the weights in the neural network. After that, the weights are updated according to the gradients, also in terms of matrix operations. In this phase, different optimization strategies, such as BGD, MBGD and Adam, can be used in order to improve the training efficiency. We specify this process as an operation WeightUpdate, shown in Fig. 7.

The training of a BP neural network is generally performed for multiple iterations, and each iteration is called an *epoch*. In each epoch, by utilizing the data set, we carry out forward propagation, calculate the loss, back-propagate the gradient, and finally update the weights. The whole process is formalized as an operation Training, shown also in Fig. 7.

4   Implementation of the Modeling Framework

This section introduces issues on implementing the modeling framework by MSVL, including the implementation of the data structures, the implementation of the operations, and a detailed process of constructing a BP neural network.

4.1   Implementation of the Data Structures

We have implemented all the data structures of the modeling framework by MSVL structs. Three representative ones, Mat, FCLayer and BPNN, are shown in Listing 1.

Listing 1. Representative Structs

```
1    struct  Mat {
2        int  row and
3        int  col  and
4        float  **element
5    };
6
7    struct  FCLayer {
8        Mat ActiMat and
9        Mat ActiMatPlus and
10       Mat SumMat and
11       Mat WeightMat and
12       Mat WeightBiasMat and
13       Mat DeltaMat and
14       Mat NablaWbMat and
15       Mat ActiFunDerivationMat and
16       int  NeuronNum and
17       int  AcitFuncNum
18   };
19
20   struct  BPNN {
21       int  CurrentSampleNum and
22       int  SampleDimensionNum and
23       int  HiddenLayerNum and
24       int  WeightInitWayNum and
25       FCLayer *Layer and
26       Mat OnehotMat and
27       int  ClassificationNum  and
28       int  LossFuncNum
29   };
```

As is shown in Line 4, the attribute element of the struct Mat is a pointer referring to a two-dimensional array of float numbers. The use of two-dimensional array instead of one-dimensional array is to balance the time and space consumption. In Line 17, the attribute AcitFuncNum of the struct FCLayer represents the choice of activation function of the layer. It is simply a zero-based integer: 0 for inactivation, 1 for sigmoid, 2 for tanh, 3 for relu, 4 for leaky relu and 5 for softmax. Similarly, in Lines 24 and 28, the attributes WeightInitWayNum and LossFuncNum of the struct BPNN represent the choices of weight initialization methods and loss functions, respectively. Supporting various selections, the framework has good expressiveness and extensibility.

4.2   Implementation of Operations

We have implemented all the operations of the modeling framework by MSVL functions. Two representative ones, MatMul and NNBackward, are shown in Listings 2 and 3, respectively. Notice that in an MSVL function, RValue represents the return value.

Listing 2. Function MatMul

```
 1   function MatMul (Mat *src1, Mat *src2, Mat *dst, Mat* RValue)
 2   {
 3        frame(row,col,i,temp1,temp2,temp3,temp4,return) and (
 4        int return<==0 and skip;
 5        int row,col and skip;
 6        int i and skip;
 7        MatZeros(dst,RValue);
 8        float temp1<==0.0 and skip;
 9        float temp2<==0.0 and skip;
10        row:=0;
11        while( row<src1−>row )
12        {
13            col:=0;
14            while( col<src1−>col )
15            {
16                temp1:=(src1−>element[row])[col];
17                int temp3 and skip;
18                temp3:=equal(temp1,0,RValue);
19                if(temp3=0) then
20                {
21                    i:=0;
22                    while( i<src2−>col )
23                    {
24                        temp2:=(src2−>element[col])[i];
25                        int temp4 and skip;
26                        temp4:=equal(temp2,0,RValue);
27                        if(temp4=0) then
28                        {
29                            (dst−>element[row])[i]:=(dst−>element[row])[i]+temp1*temp2
30                        }
31                        else
32                        {
33                            skip
34                        };
35                        i:=i+1
36                    }
37                }
38                else
39                {
40                    skip
41                };
42                col:=col+1
43            };
44            row:=row+1
45        };
46        return<==1 and RValue:=dst;
47        skip
48        )
49   };
```

Among the basic operations, matrix multiplication is the most direct factor affecting the training efficiency of the framework. To accelerate the calculation of matrix multiplication, we adopt three kinds of optimizations in this framework: register optimization, multi-level cache optimization, and sparse optimization. The idea of sparse optimization is that a lot of matrices, e.g. the activation value matrices of deep layers, become sparse, with most elements to be 0, as the number of training epochs increases. For this kind of matrices, the multiplication can be simplified by ignoring many 0 factors. The key code of sparse optimization is presented in Lines 17–41 of Listing 2. It can greatly improve the efficiency of matrix multiplication.

Listing 3. Function NNBackward

```
1   function NNBackward (FCNN *fcnn, Mat* RValue)
2   {
3       frame(i,TransM,ActiM,MulM,ProdM,TAM,return) and (
4       int return <==0 and skip;
5       NNOuputLayerBackward(fcnn,RValue);
6       int i <==fcnn->HiddenLayerNum and skip;
7       while( i>0 )
8       {
9           Mat TransM and skip;
10          Mat ActiM and skip;
11          Mat MulM and skip;
12          Mat ProdM and skip;
13          Mat TAM and skip;
14          MatCreate(&TransM,fcnn->Layer[i+1].WeightMat.col,fcnn->Layer[i+1].WeightMat.row,RValue);
15          MatCreate(&ActiM,fcnn->Layer[i].SumMat.row,fcnn->Layer[i].SumMat.col,RValue);
16          MatCreate(&MulM,fcnn->Layer[i+1].DeltaMat.row,fcnn->Layer[i+1].WeightMat.row,RValue);
17          MatCreate(&ProdM,fcnn->Layer[i].SumMat.row,fcnn->Layer[i].SumMat.col,RValue);
18          MatCreate(&TAM,fcnn->Layer[i-1].ActiMatPlus.col,fcnn->Layer[i-1].ActiMatPlus.row,RValue);
19          TransM(&fcnn->Layer[i+1].WeightMat,&TransM,RValue);
20          ActiFunDerivation(fcnn->Layer[i].SumMat,&ActiM,fcnn->Layer[i].AcitFuncNum,RValue);
21          MatMul(&fcnn->Layer[i+1].DeltaMat,&TransM,&MulM,RValue);
22          MatProduct(&MulM,&ActiM,&fcnn->Layer[i].DeltaMat,RValue);
23          TransM(&fcnn->Layer[i-1].ActiMatPlus,&TAM,RValue);
24          MatMul(&TAM,&fcnn->Layer[i].DeltaMat,&fcnn->Layer[i].NablaWbMat,RValue);
25          MatNumMul(1.0/fcnn->sampleCapacity,&fcnn->Layer[i].NablaWbMat,&fcnn->Layer[i].NablaWbMat,RValue);
26          MatDelete(&TransM);
27          MatDelete(&ActiM);
28          MatDelete(&MulM);
29          MatDelete(&ProdM);
30          MatDelete(&TAM);
31          i:=i-1
32      };
33      return <==1 and RValue:=NULL;
34      skip
35      )
36  };
```

According to the design of the operation NNBackward in Fig. 7, The calculation for the output layer is different from that for other layers. We implement an auxiliary function NNOuputLayerBackward to realize the calculation for the output layer. It is invoked in Line 5 of Listing 3. The rest statements of the function NNBackward are direct realization of their counterparts in the design.

4.3   Construction of a BP Neural Network

Based on the implementation of data structures and operations, we formulate a detailed process for constructing a general BP neural network, until the network is well trained. The process is sketched in Fig. 8.

The process starts from collecting requirements from users through a group of parameters. These parameters involve the numbers of training and test samples, the number of hidden layers, the number of neurons and the activate function of each layer, and the choices of weight initialization and loss functions. They are organized as a temporary data structure Customization and input into the process. With these parameters, corresponding attributes of the data structures of the framework are assigned.

The second step is data set construction. In this step, batch-related parameters, such as the number of batches and the size of the last batch, are calculated, and referring to these parameters the required space is allocated. After that, the data set is imported into the DataSet structure.

The third step is neural network initialization. In this step, the space for all the parameters of the BP neural network is allocated, as well as auxiliary space for intermediate results of matrix operations. After that, the weights of the neural network are initialized.

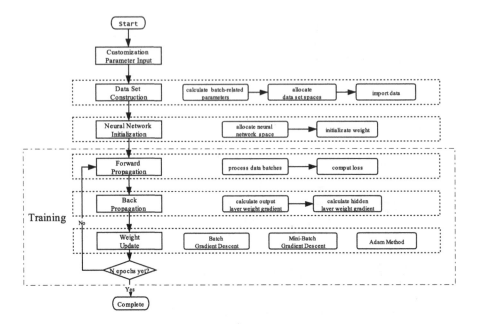

Fig. 8. Construction of a BP Neural Network

Then, the construction enters the training phase. In this phase, an iterative training epoch is performed for a specific number of N times. Each epoch is a sequential composition of a forward propagation to calculate the loss, a BP to calculate the gradients, and an updation of weights according to the gradients. Specifically, the forward propagation processes all the batches of the training data. Based on their outputs, the total loss is calculated by invoking the function LossFunction. The BP calculates the gradients of the loss in two stages: the calculation of the output layer, and then the calculation of hidden layers. Finally, all the weights are updated according to their corresponding gradients. For good training efficiency, the updation involves invoking certain optimization methods, such as BGD, MBGD and Adam. They have been implemented as MSVL functions.

5   Experiment

In this section, we carry out an experiment to test the performance of the modeling framework. Specifically, we use the framework to model instances of BP neural networks for the classification task of handwritten font recognition.

For training and testing the neural network, we adopt MNIST[1] which is a standard data set of handwritten digits. MNIST consists of a training data set of 60,000 images and a test data set of 10,000 images. Both of them are

---

[1] Data set acquisition address: http://yann.lecun.com/exdb/mnist/.

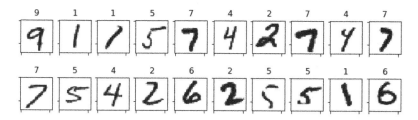

Fig. 9. MNIST data examples

randomly selected from a pool of images, and are thus considered to follow the same empirical distribution. As is shown in Fig. 9, an image looks like a one-digit number in terms of handwritten strokes, and the task is to classify any image into one of the ten categories: from 0 to 9. Specifically, each image has 784 (28×28) pixels, and each pixel takes a value between 0 and 255 to indicate the grayscale. Thus, an image can be represented as a vector of 784 features. In this experiment, the MNIST data set is reorganized into ".msd" files and then imported into the framework.

BP Neural Network Construction. For the classification task, we construct an instance of BP neural network with two hidden layers. The numbers of neurons of the input layer, the two hidden layers and the output layer are 784, 512, 256 and 10, respectively. As for the activation functions, both the hidden layers are activated by relu, but the output layer is activated by softmax. As for the loss function, we choose the cross entropy loss. As for the optimization of weight update, we choose the Adam method. Based on these requirements, the framework generates an MSVL function main for constructing, including training and testing, the instance, shown in Listing 4. In this experiment, variants of this instance, e.g. with different optimization strategies, are also constructed and their performances are measured.

Listing 4. Function main for Constructing an Instance

```
1    function main ( int  RValue )
2    {
3        frame(NueronNums,ActiFuncNums,user,data,nn,layer,adamPara,loss,losstest,N,i,j,acc) and (
4        Customization user and skip;
5        DataSet data and skip;
6        BPNN nn and skip;
7        FCLayer layer and skip;
8        AdamPara adamPara and skip;
9        int NueronNums[4]<=={784,512,256,10} and skip;
10       int ActiFuncNums[4]<=={0,3,3,5} and skip;
11       float   loss <==0.0 and skip;
12       float   losstest <==0.0 and skip;
13       float   acc<==0.0 and skip;
14       int  N<==1 and skip;
15       int  i<==0 and skip;
16       InitCustom(&user,RValue);
17       InitDataSet(&data,RValue);
18       InitFCNN(&nn,RValue);
19       InitFCLayer(&layer,RValue);
20       initAdam(nn,&adamPara);
21       MinstHWDataLoading();
22
23       user . CompleteSampleNum:=70000;
24       user . TrainSampleNum:=60000;
25       user . TestSampleNum:=10000;
```

```
26    user.SampleDimensionNum:=784;
27    user.HiddenLayerNum:=2;
28    user.ClassificationNum:=10;
29    user.LossFuncNum:=1;
30    user.WeightInitWayNum:=3;
31    user.BatchSize:=200;
32    user.NeuronNumArray:=NueronNums;
33    user.ActiFuncNumArray:=ActiFuncNums;
34    DumpCustom(user,RValue);
35    LoadParaFromCustom(user,&data,&nn);
36
37    DatasetConstruction(user,&data);
38    CreateNNSpaceAndLoadinPara2FCLayer(&nn,user,RValue);
39    NNWeightinit(&nn,RValue);
40
41    while( i<N )
42    {
43        int j<==0 and skip;
44        while( j<data.BatchNum )
45        {
46            NNforward(data.BatchTrainFeature[j],&nn);
47            loss:=Lossfunction(data.BatchTrainLabelOneHot[j],&nn, RValue);
48            NNBackward(&nn,RValue);
49            Adam(&nn,&adamPara);
50            j:=j+1
51        };
52        NNforward(data.TestFeature,&nn);
53        losstest :=Lossfunction(data.TestLabelOneHot,&nn, RValue);
54        acc:=testAcc(nn,data,RValue);
55        i:=i+1
56    }
57    )
58 };
```

In this function, Lines 3–20 are for variable declaration and initialization, as well as data import. Then, Lines 12–34 are for parameter customization, and Lines 36–38 for data set construction and neural network initialization. Finally, Lines 40–55 are for training and testing. The function can be complied and executed by the MSVL compiler MC.

Experimental Results. The experiment is performed on a 32-bit x86 win10 platform, with the CPU frequency 2.1 GHz. We conduct a series of experimental instances and test their performances concerning the standard metrics of neural networks: loss and accuracy. All the results are average values obtained from at least 3 instances.

We implement the same network structure using Python, and compare the loss and accuracy between the MSVL and Python implementations, both adopting the Adam optimization. The results are visualized in Fig. 10(a), where the dotted curves represent the loss and the full curves represent the accuracy. As the number of epochs increases, the two implementations achieve almost the same expectations of accuracy (0.98 above) and loss (nearly 0), indicating that the MSVL model is trained as effectively as the Python implementation. On the other hand, the performance of the MSVL model is more stable. By contrast, the accuracy and loss curves of the Python implementation have more serious jitters.

We also compare the loss and accuracy among the commonly used optimization methods of weight update: BGD, MBGD and Adam. The results of MSVL instances with these methods are visualized in Fig. 10(b), and the dotted and full curves respectively represent the loss and accuracy, too. As the number of epochs increases, the losses of the instances of MBGD and Adam converge quickly to achieve good accuracy, but the loss for the traditional BGD method fails to

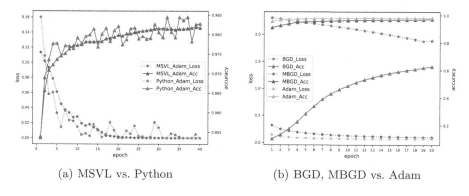

(a) MSVL vs. Python   (b) BGD, MBGD vs. Adam

Fig. 10. Results of loss and accuracy

approach 0. Among the three optimization methods, the performance of Adam
is the best.

6   Conclusions

In this work, we propose an MSVL-based framework for formal modeling of
BP neural networks. The framework is comprehensive, capable of modeling various aspects of a BP neural network concerning both the structure and the
behavior. Especially, the framework supports the construction and training of
a neural-network model according to user-customized parameters. Through an
experiment of handwritten font recognition, we show that the models generated
by the framework perform well under standard metrics of loss and accuracy.

For future work, we are going to develop methods for formal verification
of BP neural networks based on this framework. MSVL has provided a good
temporal-logic basis that supports model checking and theorem proving. The
main challenge lies in the exploration and formalization of meaningful properties
of these networks. In addition, it is meaningful to extend the framework to
various categories of neural networks, such as convolutional neural networks and
recurrent neural networks. In fact, the formalization of basic computing units
such as matrix and tensor enables further modeling of different layer structures.

References

1. Chen, Y., Chi, Y., Fan, J., Ma, C.: Gradient descent with random initialization:
   fast global convergence for nonconvex phase retrieval. Math. Program. **176**(1–2),
   5–37 (2019). https://doi.org/10.1007/s10107-019-01363-6
2. Clarke, E.M., Grumberg, O., Peled, D.A.: Model Checking. The MIT Press, Hoboken (2000)
3. Williams, R.J., Rumelhart, D.E., Hinton, G.E.: Learning representations by back-
   propagating errors. Nature **323**, 533–536 (1986)

4. Duan, Z.: Temporal Logic and Temporal Logic Programming. Science Press, Beijing (2006)
5. Duan, Z., Tian, C.: A unified model checking approach with projection temporal logic. In: Liu, S., Maibaum, T., Araki, K. (eds.) ICFEM 2008. LNCS, vol. 5256, pp. 167–186. Springer, Heidelberg (2008). https://doi.org/10.1007/978-3-540-88194-0_12
6. Duan, Z., Yang, X., Koutny, M.: Framed temporal logic programming. Sci. Comput. Program. **70**(1), 31–61 (2008)
7. Ghodsi, Z., Gu, T., Garg, S.: Safetynets: verifiable execution of deep neural networks on an untrusted cloud. In: NIPS, pp. 4672–4681 (2017)
8. Glorot, X., Bengio, Y.: Understanding the difficulty of training deep feedforward neural networks. In: Whye Teh, Y., Titterington, M. (eds.) Proceedings of the Thirteenth International Conference on Artificial Intelligence and Statistics, Proceedings of Machine Learning Research, Chia Laguna Resort, Sardinia, vol. 9, pp. 249–256. PMLR (2010)
9. He, K., Zhang, X., Ren, S., Sun, J.: Deep residual learning for image recognition. In: CVPR, pp. 770–778. IEEE Computer Society (2016)
10. Huang, X., Kwiatkowska, M., Wang, S., Wu, M.: Safety verification of deep neural networks. In: Majumdar, R., Kunčak, V. (eds.) CAV 2017. LNCS, vol. 10426, pp. 3–29. Springer, Cham (2017). https://doi.org/10.1007/978-3-319-63387-9_1
11. Kanso, K., Setzer, A.: A light-weight integration of automated and interactive theorem proving. Math. Struct. Comput. Sci. **26**(01), 129–153 (2016)
12. Katz, G., Barrett, C., Dill, D.L., Julian, K., Kochenderfer, M.J.: Reluplex: an efficient SMT solver for verifying deep neural networks. In: Majumdar, R., Kunčak, V. (eds.) CAV 2017. LNCS, vol. 10426, pp. 97–117. Springer, Cham (2017). https://doi.org/10.1007/978-3-319-63387-9_5
13. Khirirat, S., Feyzmahdavian, H.R., Johansson, M.: Mini-batch gradient descent: faster convergence under data sparsity. In: CDC, pp. 2880–2887. IEEE (2017)
14. Kingma, D.P., Adam, J.B.: A method for stochastic optimization. In: ICLR (Poster) (2015)
15. Pang, T., Xu, K., Dong, Y., Du, C., Chen, N., Zhu, J.: Rethinking softmax cross-entropy loss for adversarial robustness. CoRR, abs/1905.10626 (2019)
16. Singh, G., Gehr, T., Püschel, M., Vechev, M.: An abstract domain for certifying neural networks. In: Proceedings ACM Programming Language 3(POPL) (2019). Article 41
17. Tian, C., Duan, Z.: Expressiveness of propositional projection temporal logic with star. Theoretical Comput. Sci. **412**, 1729–1744 (2011)
18. Wang, X., Tian, C., Duan, Z., Zhao, L.: MSVL: a typed language for temporal logic programming. Front. Comput. Sci. **11**(5), 762–785 (2017). https://doi.org/10.1007/s11704-016-6059-4
19. Randall Wilson, D., Martinez, T.R.: The general inefficiency of batch training for gradient descent learning. Neural Networks **16**(10), 1429–1451 (2003)
20. Yang, K., Duan, Z., Tian, C., Zhang, N.: A compiler for MSVL and its applications. Theor. Comput. Sci. **749**, 2–16 (2018)
21. Zhang, H., Cheng, X., Zang, H., Park, D.H.: Compiler-level matrix multiplication optimization for deep learning. CoRR, abs/1909.10616 (2019)
22. Zhang, N., Duan, Z., Tian, C.: Model checking concurrent systems with MSVL. Sci. China Inf. Sci. **59**(11), 101–118 (2016). https://doi.org/10.1007/s11432-015-0882-6

A Case Study on Combining Agile Requirements Development and SOFL

Fumiko Nagoya(⊠)

College of Commerce, Nihon University, Tokyo, Japan
nagoya.fumiko@nihon-u.ac.jp

Abstract. This paper presents a requirement development process combined with agile software development and the Structured Object-Oriented Formal Language (SOFL) to produce reliable software. Agile methods have made outstanding contributions to handle changes by short iterative development, though the requirements are less rigorous for verification of the corresponding programs. SOFL supports defining, and modifying requirements, and verifying programs based on the specifications, as a result of unifying the power of structured methods and object-oriented methods. We conducted a case study to assess the combined requirement development process and observe reworks caused by requirement changes. The result shows that our proposed process is effective to define the data and constraints, though changes in domains' properties need continuous studies.

Keywords: SOFL · Agile · Requirements development

1 Introduction

Software requirements are properties of system behavior desired by various stakeholders such as paying customers, users, and developers. Software engineers gather users' needs and identify the priorities for solving some real-world problems, and they define goals, functions, external interfaces, quality attributes, and constraints placed on a software product or service. Many researchers and practitioners have developed diverse techniques, methods, and tools [1] for dealing well with requirements engineering activities. The requirements engineering activities can be roughly classified into two: requirements development and requirements management [2]. The requirements development includes elicitation, analysis, specification, validation of requirements [3]. The requirements management comprises identification, documentation, maintenance, communication, tracking & tracing requirements throughout the life cycle of a system, product, or service [4].

Zave [5] has mentioned that traditional requirements engineering studies focused on the requirements development activities by translations into formal specifications from informal observations of the real world. Formal methods, such as VDM [6], Z [7], and Alloy [8], contribute to specifying precise and unambiguous formal specifications, and such formal expressions permit verifying properties or models by supporting tools. In contrast, agile software development has

© Springer Nature Switzerland AG 2021
J. Xue et al. (Eds.): SOFL+MSVL 2020, LNCS 12723, pp. 23–33, 2021.
https://doi.org/10.1007/978-3-030-77474-5_2

been mainly driven by the software industry for dealing with frequent change requests from clients or business environments during a project. As the manifesto [9] talks of welcoming change, agile software development manages customer requirements flexibly by iterative and incremental development.

Some studies [10] propose a combination of formal methods and agile software development for producing reliable software. Most agile practitioners in the software industry do not use formal methods. Succeeding in the software business [11,12] has more to do with managing expectations and gaining consensus from their customers than developing secure and reliable products at first release. Agile philosophy has been critical of writing requirements documents and specifications at the beginning of a project as a waste of time and unrealistic. The reason is that the requirements will change over time. Meyer [13] argues against the criticism that writing a product requirements document provides a sound basis for discussion about the system's future functions. Especially, it is helpful to decide which function to remove.

To tackle the criticism of writing requirements documents and response demand of specifications, we propose to use SOFL [14]. First, SOFL aids to integrate *structured methods* and *object-oriented methods*. It uses Vienna Development Method Specification Language (VDM-SL) [6] as textual notations. VDM-SL gives precise definitions of data and operations by simple propositional logics, basic set theory, and predicates for describing formal specifications. Also, SOFL provides graphical notations by adopting Data Flow Diagram [15], and Petri Nets [16]. The graphical notations help inexperienced persons to give an understandable overall architecture, associations with functions, and a hierarchic structure of the system. Second, SOFL supports transforming into formal descriptions from informal descriptions by a phased approach. In general, formal specifications use formal descriptions based on set theory, logic, algebra. Whereas, user requirements in agile software development are written in natural language. The transformation into formal descriptions in SOFL is called the three-step specification approach and constructs informal, semi-formal, and formal specifications. In this approach, informal and semi-formal specifications keep a good balance between preciseness and readability for even an inexperienced person to formal descriptions. Third, SOFL can effectively facilitate the combination of prototyping development and formal specifications [17,18] in an iterative and incremental development manner. Rapid software prototyping is commonly used in agile software development as we will mention in the next section. Also, we conducted a case study to observe whether this combined process can handle changes caused by feedback from stakeholders. The result gives an interesting indication by revealing what kind of requirements and where changes occur during projects.

This paper is organized as follows. Section 2 introduces the background of our study on agile software development. Section 3 gives detailed instructions on our requirement development process with the informal and semi-formal specifications of SOFL. Section 4 explains the case study and discusses the results. Section 5 reviews related work. Finally, in Sect. 6 we conclude the paper and point out future research directions.

2   Background

Agile software development is not a single development methodology, but a superset of principles, practice, roles, and artifacts in each agile method such as Extreme Programming (XP) [19], Scrum [20], and Crystal [21]. For instance, Scrum takes in an iterative and incremental development manner for accepting changes at any time. In this section, we discuss the agile artifacts produced by typical agile requirements development to find a seamless transition process from informal descriptions written in natural language into formal descriptions. Prototypes, use cases and scenarios [22], and story cards [23] are commonly used in agile requirements development. These agile artifacts give more insight into designing a final product and improve communication between various stakeholders.

A prototype is a model of a product sketched ideas as depicted on the left-hand side of Fig. 1. It provides useful feedback from stakeholders in the initial stages of product development. Snyder [24] expresses that paper prototyping facilitates brainstorming, designing, creating, testing, and refining user interfaces. Nevertheless, these activities do not record automatically, nor we reproduce them. To overcome these challenges, numerous web designers use mock-up tools. A mock-up is also a model of a product illustrated by desktop, mobile, or online applications. And, the model seems the final product as if the functions provide. Especially, some online mock-up tools permit collaborative editing by a team; as a result, team members' feedback or questions save in the cloud, and the editor response anytime and anywhere. Despite these benefits, a paper prototype or mock-up is not a document written in any natural language, but a picture. Consequently, it would not by itself define what to be done by the system precisely.

A use case diagram represents a system behavior with labeled oval shapes and stick figures as shown in the middle of Fig. 1. Each ellipse has a name as a user goal, what we call "use case". A user case consists of scenarios, and a scenario is a sequence of actions and interactions that occur under certain conditions. A story card is a piece of paper used to write down a "user story" as illustrated on the right-hand side of Fig. 1. A user story describes a small unit of functionality that will be valuable to a user of the system.

Both use case and user story utilize the scenarios which indicate the properties of the system's functionality from the users' point of view. A scenario is merely one episode of user interaction. No matter how many episodes, a scenario is not itself a constituent behavior of the system. And above all, generating tests based on such episodes do not satisfy test case completeness. These reasons are these typical agile artifacts do not cause the actions of decomposition, composition, encapsulation, abstraction, and generalization, in comparison with *structured methods* and *object-oriented methods*. In summary, agile artifacts are insufficient for comprehensive analysis to produce reliable software.

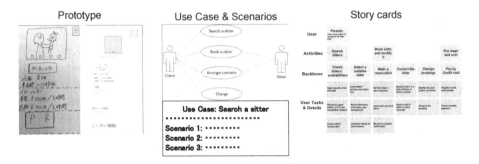

Fig. 1. Agile requirements development

3   Requirements Development Process

SOFL provides the three-step specification approach: informal, semi-formal, and formal specifications which enable to build formal specifications from informal descriptions written in a natural language step by step. Especially, informal and semi-formal specifications have an important role in functional decomposition and object composition. This section explains with an example of the development of informal and semi-formal specifications. Additionally, we propose an integrated requirement development process with the informal and semi-formal specifications of SOFL.

3.1   Informal Specification

The informal specification is a well-organized document written in a natural language as with scenarios described in use cases and user stories. However, SOFL makes a shift in perspective from user to system. Agile requirements development describes system functions from the user's perspective as mentioned above. In contrast, SOFL requires an informal specification to clearly define from the point of view of systems. The informal specification contains three items: functions to be implemented, data resources to be used, and necessary constraints on both functions and data resources. For example, an informal specification for developing a mobile application to find a babysitter is given as follows.

Functions

- Receive a request: This system receives the time, date, and location which a customer specifies to find an available babysitter.
- Display search results: The system shows the candidate babysitters that match the input data. When there is no available babysitter, the system shows the message that the customer needs to select a wider range area for search.
- Provide babysitters' profiles: The system gives a babysitter's profile depend on the customer's selection among the search results. A profile includes personal

data, hourly pay rate, available optional services, and reviews from other customers.

– Book babysitter: The system enables to book one babysitter with some optional services and asks to agree on pay rate and responsibility.
– Arrange contact: The system makes communication go smoothly with the customer and the babysitter by phone for an interview directly.
– Cancel or change booking: The system accepts a cancellation or changing request from the customer, though there's a cancellation charge under some conditions.
– Collect monthly services fees: The system calculates a monthly charge for babysitter service and collects the amount from each customer by credit card. On the other hand, the system calculates a monthly wage for each babysitter in consideration of babysitter service and sends the amount by bank transfer.

Data Resources

– sitter data: ID, password, name, email, phone number, address, bank account, profile data, hourly rate, customer reviews.
– customer data: ID, password, name, email, phone number, address, credit card number, child data.
– child data: age, gender, allergies, special supports.
– booking data: location, date, start time, end time, sitter data, client data, specified optional services.
– charge amount: hourly rate, total service time, additional fee for optional services.

Constraints

– A password consists of six or more character sets.
– The maximum number of browsing historical log data is 10
– All windows for showing search results are visible but not editable.
– This program prohibits multiple running

3.2 Semi-formal Specification

The semi-formal specification is described as a set of modules to encapsulate required functions, data resources, and constraints in a hierarchical fashion. A module is composed of a module name, constant declarations, type declarations, variable declarations, an invariant section, and a list of processes as illustrated in Fig. 2. The module name represents a relation between the high-level module and its decomposition module. The constant declarations, type declarations, and variable declarations support clarifying the data items defined in the formal specification. The invariant section defines the constraints which are applied to the whole specification. A process carries out an operation with process name, input and output ports, precondition, and postcondition. The precondition describes a constraint on the input data flows before the execution of the process, while the

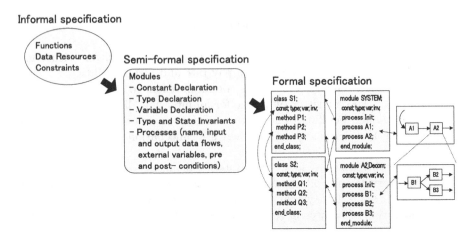

Fig. 2. The three-step specification approach

postcondition provides a constraint on the output data flows after the execution. The semi-formal specification obeys the syntax of VDM-SL, but the precondition and postcondition are written in a natural language.

Two graphs illustrated by the right-hand side in Fig. 2 represent system behavior of modules in the formal specification, respectively. Also, the graphs show a decomposition from the upper module into the lower module in the formal specification. Generally, visualizations of system behavior strongly support understanding the big picture and facilitating communications as with agile software development. SOFL does not restrict whether graphical notations should be used for expressing modules in semi-formal specifications instead of formal specifications. For this reason, we decide to draw roughly data flow diagrams to identify a hierarchical structure at the semi-formal specifications as we describe below in a combined requirement development process.

3.3   A Combined Requirement Development Process

We propose a requirement development process combined with agile software development and the SOFL informal and semi-formal specifications. It is possible to adapt frequent change requests from stakeholders and support constructing formal specifications. Figure 3 explains that *the combined requirement development process* has five steps: **prototype, use case & scenario, informal specification, Data Flow Diagram**, and **semi-formal specification**. The **prototypes** represent ideas for user interfaces of final products, and include not only paper prototypes but also mock-ups. In **use cases & scenarios,** a system designer describes episodes from a viewpoint of product users by diagrams and/or documents. However, the system designer changes the perspective from the beneficiary receiver of the product into the system supplier after **informal specification**. As we explained above, the designer needs to refine informal descriptions to formal specifications with the aid of **Data Flow Diagram**, and **semi-formal specification** step by step. In *the combined requirement development process,* each artifact is refined by stakeholder feedback during a short-cycled iteration just as "sprint" in Scrum [20]. SOFL serves as a bridge to ensure a smooth transition from the agile artifacts into formal specifications.

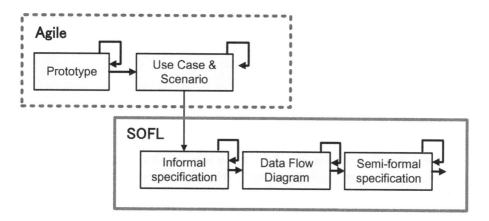

Fig. 3. The combined requirements development process

4   Case Study

We conducted a case study to evaluate the combined requirement development process for inexperienced undergraduate students in formal descriptions. Twelve undergraduate students who major in business participated in this experiment as project managers. One professor who has experience in developing software and knowledge of formal methods took on the facilitator. Each project consisted of four to eight team members, one project manager, and one facilitator. The manager was in charge of one mobile application development project, respectively. And each target domain for the project was based on social experiences through part-time jobs or internships. After they got six months of training in agile software development and SOFL, they decided on target domains. The target domains were finding a babysitter, employee shift planning, umbrella rental service, and bus routing guide. And then, they carried out brainstorming, designing, creating, and modifying the artifacts: **prototypes, use case & scenario, informal specification, Data Flow Diagram**, and **semi-formal specification**.

Table 1. The result of case study

	Prototype	Use case & scenario	Informal specification	Data Flow Diagram	Semi-formal specification
interface	3	0	0	0	0
domain	2	1	2	1	3
functions	2	3	1	0	1
data	0	1	1	8	0
constrains	0	2	3	0	1
total	8	7	7	9	5

4.1 Results

The manager kept a record of when and what items he or she revised based on feedback from other team members. Each step of *the combined requirement development process* generally took two or three iterations, and each iteration was carried out during the two-week sprint duration. The total time for the experiment took almost six months. The periods were from November 2017 to June 2018, and from November 2018 to June 2019.

The facilitator analyzed feedback and reactions, and categorized requirement changes into five parts: interface, domain, functions, data, and constraints. Table 1 shows that each column represents the feedback point, and it arranges according to the timeline. The rows mean the category of reactions. We can find two features from the Table 1.

First, **informal specification, Data Flow Diagram**, and **semi-formal specification** steps support discovering data and constraints. Second, requests for changing the domain continue from the beginning to the end of *the combined requirement development process*. The problem of the change needs more discussion for handling development if we apply the combined requirement development process in practice. We mention project managers' actions during reworking requirement changes in the next part.

4.2 Findings

During the case study, the facilitator realized some project managers were forgetting the most important services to provide the system. The missing core services occurred when the managers focused on the feedback from other team members too much. Additionally, some projects returned the previous step for changing problem domains, for instance, adding a new target user. The reworks occurred during **informal specification, Data Flow Diagram**, and **semi-formal specification.**

To address the former case, the facilitator decided iteration goals and a set of acceptance criteria in advance. The iteration goals clearly define what the team accomplish. The acceptance criteria help to judge disagreement or agreement of stakeholders' feedback. The latter case expresses that our proposed process is not easy to adapt to the changes in domains' properties without repeating the activities from the previous step to the current step.

5   Related Work

Some studies focus on the changes in domain properties and for managing continuous changes. Zave and Jackson [25] have emphasized that it is important to distinguish the machine and problem domains carefully. Because, the machine behavior is to be created by programming, whereas the problem domains have given properties and behaviors. The domains' properties and behaviors might be given, in actuality, they are influenced by environmental conditions. Also, Jackson [26] has mentioned that *pre-formal work* creates a bridge from the stakeholders' purposes and desires, leading to a detailed software specification. He has explained his proposed "Problem Frames approach" [27] applied for cyber-physical systems as *pre-formal work*.

Ghezzi [28] addresses the problem of environmental change and shows a model for cyber-physical systems. The model makes it possible to achieve self-adaptation software to changes in the environment. He shows how to incorporate formal modeling and verification iteratively and incrementally of agile software development. However, he suggests further research is needed to adapt modeling and verification.

We use SOFL as *pre-formal work* to ensure a smooth transition from the agile artifacts into formal specifications. However, it is not limited to apply for cyber-physical systems, we need more studies on the changes in domains' properties for the sake of the development of an integrated tool to manage our proposed requirement development process.

6   Conclusions

This paper describes the combined requirement development process with agile requirements development and the SOFL informal and semi-formal specifications. The proposed process aims both to adapt frequent change requests from stakeholders and develop secure and reliable products, simultaneously. The case study shows that the proposed process contributes to discovering the data and constraints at the latter steps. In contrast, the requests for changing the domain exist at every step of the proposed process. It means that the proposed process is successful to supply agile development with structured methods and object-oriented methods. On the other hand, it is not enough to prevent returning the previous step for adapting after changes in domains' properties. We need more studies for the changes in domains' properties and behaviors and examine the associations with self-adaptation software for managing continuous changes in our future research.

Acknowledgment. We would like to thank Kaede HOSHINO for developing GUI models, including writing the SOFL specifications for a mobile application to find a babysitter.

References

1. Nuseibeh, B., Easterbrook, S.: Requirements engineering: a roadmap. In: Proceedings of the Conference on The Future of Software Engineering. ICSE 2000, New York, pp. 35–46. Association for Computing Machinery (2000)
2. Wiegers, K.E., Beatty, J.: Software Requirements 3. Microsoft Press, Redmond (2013)
3. Bourque, P., Fairley, R.E. (eds.): SWEBOK: Guide to the Software Engineering Body of Knowledge. Version 3.0 edn. IEEE Computer Society, Los Alamitos, CA (2014)
4. ISO/IEC/IEEE: International standard - systems and software engineering - life cycle processes - requirements engineering. ISO/IEC/IEEE 29148(E), 1–104 (2018)
5. Zave, P.: Classification of research efforts in requirements engineering. ACM Comput. Surv. **29**, 315–321 (1997)
6. Jones, C.B.: Systematic Software Development Using VDM. Prentice Hall International Ltd., Hoboken (1986)
7. Woodcock, J., Davies, J.: Using Z: Specification, Refinement, and Proof. Prentice-Hall Inc., Hoboken (1996)
8. Jackson, D.: Alloy: a lightweight object modelling notation. ACM Trans. Softw. Eng. Methodol. **11**, 256–290 (2002)
9. Beck, K., et al.: Manifesto for agile software development (2001). http://www.agilemanifesto.org/
10. Black, S., Boca, P.P., Bowen, J.P., Gorman, J., Hinchey, M.: Formal versus agile: survival of the fittest. Computer **42**, 37–45 (2009)
11. Bernstein, D.: Beyond Legacy Code: Nine Practices to Extend the Life (and Value) of Your Software. Pragmatic Bookshelf, Pragmatic programmers (2015)
12. McConnell, S.: More Effective Agile: A Roadmap for Software Leaders. Construx Press, Bellevue (2019)
13. Meyer, B.: Agile!: The Good, the Hype and the Ugly. Springer Publishing Company, Incorporated, New York (2014). https://doi.org/10.1007/978-3-319-05155-0_11
14. Liu, S.: Formal Engineering for Industrial Software Development. Springer Verlag, Heidelberg (2004). https://doi.org/10.1007/978-3-540-30482-1_4
15. DeMarco, T.: Structured Analysis and System Specification. Prentice Hall PTR, Upper Saddle River (1979)
16. Reisig, W.: Petri Nets: An Introduction. Springer-Verlag, New York (1985). https://doi.org/10.1007/978-3-642-69968-9
17. Nagoya, F., Liu, S.: Development of a web dictionary system using SOFL. Wirel. Pers. Commun. **94**(2), 253–266 (2016). https://doi.org/10.1007/s11277-016-3291-z
18. Nagoya, F., Liu, S.: A case study of a GUI-aided approach to constructing formal specifications. In: Liu, S., Duan, Z., Tian, C., Nagoya, F. (eds.) SOFL+MSVL 2016. LNCS, vol. 10189, pp. 74–84. Springer, Cham (2017). https://doi.org/10.1007/978-3-319-57708-1_5
19. Beck, K., Andres, C.: Extreme Programming Explained: Embrace Change, 2nd edn. Addison-Wesley Professional, Boston (2004)

20. Schwaber, K., Beedle, M.: Agile Software Development with Scrum, 1st edn. Prentice Hall PTR, Hoboken (2001)
21. Cockburn, A.: Crystal Clear a Human-Powered Methodology for Small Teams, 1st edn. Addison-Wesley Professional, Boston (2004)
22. Cockburn, A.: Writing Effective Use Cases, 1st edn. Addison-Wesley Longman Publishing Co. Inc., Boston (2000)
23. Cohn, M.: User Stories Applied: For Agile Software Development. Addison Wesley Longman Publishing Co. Inc., Hoboken (2004)
24. Snyder, C.: Paper Prototyping: The Fast and Easy Way to Design and Refine User Interfaces. Morgan Kaufmann Publishers Inc., San Francisco (2004)
25. Zave, P., Jackson, M.: Four dark corners of requirements engineering. ACM Trans. Softw. Eng. Methodol. **6**, 1–30 (1997)
26. Jackson, M.: Behaviours as design components of cyber-physical systems. In: Meyer, B., Nordio, M. (eds.) LASER 2014. LNCS, vol. 8987, pp. 43–62. Springer, Cham (2015). https://doi.org/10.1007/978-3-319-28406-4_2
27. Jackson, M.: Problem Frames: Analyzing and Structuring Software Development Problems. Addison-Wesley Longman Publishing Co. Inc., Hoboken (2000)
28. Ghezzi, C.: Formal Methods and Agile Development: Towards a Happy Marriage. In: Gruhn, V., Striemer, R. (eds.) The Essence of Software Engineering, pp. 25–36. Springer, Cham (2018). https://doi.org/10.1007/978-3-319-73897-0_2

Formal Modeling and Verification
of Microservice-Based Cyber-Physical System

Jingzi Wang, Hongyan Mao[✉], and Ningkang Jiang[✉]

Shanghai Key Laboratory of Trustworthy Computing, East China Normal University, Shanghai, China
{hymao,nkjiang}@sei.ecnu.edu.cn

Abstract. Cyber-Physical System (CPS) has attracted extensive attention in diverse application fields. However, the modeling and verification of CPS is a great challenge because of its complexity and the changing interactive environments. Hence, how to simplify the complicated system design, improve the flexibility and correctness is a concerned research issue. Therefore, we provide a microservice-based framework of CPS application, named MSBF. The MSBF uses a level structure to explicit the interface and communication, and adopts the microservice architecture to guarantee the flexibility. To prove the correctness and reliability of MSBF, the formal method Communication Sequential Processes (CSP) is adopted to model and verify the MSBF. A method is proposed for transforming the main component of MSBF to CSP. Moreover, a case study of smart museum system is given, which has several requirements to be satisfied. The system is built by MSBF, and transformed to CSP. The modeling of the system includes the modules and interactive communications, and that illustrates the feasibility and sustainability of the framework. The Process Analysis Toolkit (PAT) is used to verify the properties of the constructed model. The verification results show that the deadlock does not exist and the requirements are satisfied.

Keywords: Cyber-Physical System · Formal modeling · Microservice-based framework · CSP · Smart museum system

1 Introduction

With the development of communication technology, intelligent control technology and smart sensing technology, the traditional embedded systems can be interconnected and composed to a complex system, named Cyber-Physical Systems (CPS) [1]. CPSs integrate the network and physical environment, and augment entity devices on dynamic sensing and interaction control. Accordingly, it has a great application prospect in intelligent systems, such as smart building and intelligent manufacturing in IoT [2].

Because environments and the requirements for the control of CPSs are changed frequently, CPSs should guarantee the specification even in complicated conditions and ease to update for functional changes. To satisfy the requirements, the architecture of CPSs must adapt to situations when the environment or function changing, and ease to maintain.

© Springer Nature Switzerland AG 2021
J. Xue et al. (Eds.): SOFL+MSVL 2020, LNCS 12723, pp. 34–53, 2021.
https://doi.org/10.1007/978-3-030-77474-5_3

The perfect CPS is hard to build due to the complexity and unpredictable changes, which is a challenge to system designers [3].

To solve the problems, other development and design technologies can be used. One is Web Service [4], which provides service composition and decomposition for a comprehensive interactive system, extensively used in application development. Some work has been done to increase the flexibility and reliability based on SOA in [18, 19]. Recently, microservice is an evolution of the SOA. It focuses on decoupling and decomposition services as individual modules, which is suited for building at the cloud side [20]. Microservice can be combined with the traditional layer-based architecture, a microservice-based framework enables system reliability, compositionality, and maintainability.

To guarantee services running correctness when the environment and function changes, hence it's necessary to verify the function specification of the CPS. Formal method is a reliable approach to ensure the system effectiveness. Communication Sequential Process (CSP) [6, 7] is a powerful tool on formal method for modeling and verifying complex concurrent systems. By represent entity devices and services as processes, CSP can describe the communication and interaction of microservice-based CPS. It also can be implemented in Process Analysis Toolkit (PAT) [8, 9], which is a verification tool covering all possible conditions of the built model.

The main contributions of this paper are embodied in the following aspects.

- A microservice-based framework, named MSBF, is proposed to facilitate the design of CPS. The framework includes the traditional layer-based framework and microservice, and enables CPS reliable and flexible.
- We propose an approach to transform MSBF to CSP model, which is a formal modeling ease to ensure its reliability. It can be easy to construct and verify.
- A smart museum system is constructed using our framework, and PAT is applied to verify and ensure the reliability and flexibility of the system.

The rest of this paper is organized as follows. Section 2 discusses the related work. Section 3 demonstrates the microservice-based framework of CPS. Section 4 is a brief introduction to CSP syntax. Section 5 proposes a method for transforming the MSBF to CSP. Section 6 supplies a smart museum system architecture and introduces its requirements. Section 7 presents the modeling of the museum system and the formal description using CSP. Section 8 shows the verification of the specification and robustness of the model. Section 9 concludes the work.

2 Related Work

The design challenges of CPS are shown to integrate the network and the entity, security, flexibility, device-independent and so forth, when facing varied requirements and environment. To solve these problems, some methodologies and frameworks are proposed.

Layer-based methodology is an important technology which divides the whole systems into hierarchical layers. Every layer uses the interface of lower layers to implement functions, and provides interface to upper layers. An approach for layer-based methodology is proposed in [10], which discuss the definition of CPS, and proposes a 5-level architecture for design. It defines the attributes and functions of each level. Another approach for layer-based framework is proposed [11], which separates CPS into three layers: computational layer, physical layer, and communication layer, and the model-centric method issued to design CPS.

Simple layer-based methodologies just define a specification for relationship and functions of layers, not a framework in detail. In the further works, Service-oriented architectures (SOA) and multi-agent systems (MAS) are two important software technologies which can be adopted in CPS. They are applied in many fields of complex systems like energy management [12] and data analytics [13] because of its advantages.

Multi-agent-based framework divided CPS into agents, and the functions of CPS is implemented by interactive and cooperation of the agents. An agent-based approach is proposed in [14], which is exploited the model-driven agent-based CPS. The approach combines the model-driven principle and metamodel in order to facilitate CPS development for reconfigurability and resilience. Another agent-based approach is proposed in [15], which has effort on temporal-spatial traits and interaction with physical environment. It uses a five-tuple to formulate the CPS-agent, and gives classic CPS architecture decryptions by five-tuple. Moreover, an agent-oriented modeling using Petri nets is proposed in [16], which synthesizes individual models to obtain a complete system model. [17] proposes an agent-based control centric methodology. In this work, a four-phase method is proposed for analysis and design of CPS, which helps avoiding common pitfalls of multithreaded programming. A model transformation method to construct a representative MAS design model for CPS and IoT systems is presented in [22], which uses a source model that describes components and labeled relations between these components. Although multi-agent-based frameworks have advantages of distributed, autonomous and modularity, the large-scaled agents often is difficult to maintain and change functions.

Compare to agent-based methodologies, service-based architecture is more suited for interoperability and flexibility. SOA is a software technology in the field of Web Service, which proposes a loosely coupled group of services and use services composition to implement complex system. A service-based approach is proposed in [18], which provides a separation between domain modeling, planning execution, monitoring and actuation service. It has several benefits such as reusability and flexibility. Another service-based approach is proposed in [19], which uses SOA to solve the problem of autonomic computing. A case of application on CPS using SOA is proposed in [20], which presents a Cyber Physical Systems oriented e-business platform using SOA.

Microservice is an evolution of SOA, which enables independent development and loose coupling. Our work takes advantages of microservice, and provides a flexible framework for complicated system.

3 Microservice-Based CPS Framework

In this section, a microservice-based CPS framework MSBF is proposed. The MSBF adopts tradition layer-based framework and microservice technology by explicating the relationship between layers and modules in microservice. And more, an approach of service description is proposed for service modeling of CPS (Fig. 1).

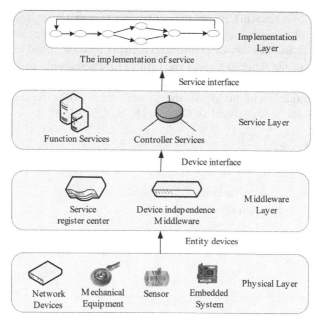

Fig. 1. The structure of the MSBF

The MSBF consists of four layers, and which is physical layer, middleware layer, service layer and implementation layer. The framework is showed in Fig. 2.

Implementation Layer. The implementation of services is responsible for realize the system function, including the specific input/output processing, command choosing, another service calling and so forth. By leaving the interface unchanged, implementation can be changeable for the new specification of system or new environment, and the rest of CPS can be maintained.

Service Layer. As its name implies, there are services in this layer. Two types of service are proposed, function services and controller services. Function services are responsible for the main function of CPS, which handle the data from device, and conclude the return command to device. And controller functions tackle the relationship between services such as synchronization, for the composition of services. Every service should satisfy the single responsibility principle and the interface segregation principle to keep flexibility. The service layer provides the interface of communication between devices and services, including the interface of calling and return. The service layer can be built on the cloud.

Middleware Layer. This layer mainly solves two problems. One is device independence. There are different kinds of component in physical layer, and they should use a same method to discover and communicate with services. Middleware layer should have the function to guarantee that the service interface is not relay on device.

To utilize the flexibility of microservice architecture, a middleware between service and device should be proposed for loosing coupled. If service is changed, the change can be registered on the middleware, which can avoid mainly modifying about the system.

Physical Layer. Machines in CPS and their components in this layer. There are sensors, mechanical control systems and embedded programs. This layer provides the function of data acquiring, basic mechanical control and network module to find services. For the varied environment and functions, just basic control function should be implemented in this layer.

After the introduction of the MSBF, the services are specified formally below. The transition system service is defined as $TS = (s_0, S, E, V, T)$:

- s_0 is the initial state;
- S is a set of states;
- E is a set of events;
- $V = v_1, v_2 \ldots v_n$ is a set of variables;
- $T = S \times E \times V$ indicates a set of transitions.

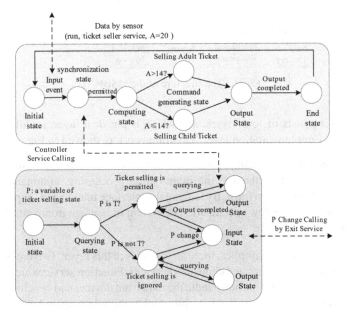

Fig. 2. The state transition of ticket seller service

The set of states S often includes initial state, input state, synchronization state, computing state, output state and end state. The initial state and end state represent the beginning and ending of the service. The input state and output state represent that the service is tackling the input and output, and they will be transformed to other states when the input/output event occurs. The synchronization state represents the service is communicating to other service for synchronization. The computing state represents the service is running for computing which command will be sent to entity devices.

And an interface of communication between service and device is a tuple (R, B, P)

- R is a set of devices/services;
- B is a set of command for device/services;
- P is a set of parameters of commands

The definition of interface refers to the resource-behavior methodology. All devices/services are seen as resource, which have a set of semantic well-defined behavior. The functions of resource which have semantic similarity can be combined to one behavior. The resource-behavior methodology in favor of the device independence, and the specific parameter should be appointed for devices have large different.

In order to describe the frame work and service, an example of the ticket seller service is proposed in Fig. 2. There is a ticket seller system for a museum, which should sell tickets to customers. Moreover, to avoid the museum crowded, selling should stop when too many tickets are sold. When the museum is not crowded, if the customer is a child (age below 14), the ticket seller will sell the child ticket, otherwise sell the adult ticket. When a call information comes, service will tackle the input, and query the state of selling tickets on the synchronization state. The synchronization is implemented by a controller service, which works like a simple state machine. The independent controller service help maintain CPS when the requirement of synchronization changes. And the exit service will change the state to permitted when the customers exit and the museum is not crowded. If the query is permitted, the service will compute what command it should send, and output the command to entity device. The device will be controlled correctly by command.

4 CSP

CSP a is a process-algebraic formal method for modeling concurrent processes with communication. Hence its powerful expression for the complex concurrent system, CSP is widely applied for structure modeling and specification verifying. Modeling in CSP, we can abstract each base service unit as a process.

A brief introduction about CSP syntax of the language is: P and Q are two processes. a and b are two actions. And c is a channel.

P, Q := Skip | Stop | a → P | c?x → P | c!v → Q | x := e | P;Q | P||Q | P|||Q | if b then P else Q | [cond]a->P

Skip denotes that a process does nothing but terminates successfully.

Stop denotes that the process is in the state of deadlock and does nothing.

a → P represents that the process first engages inaction a, then the subsequent behavior is like P.

c?x → P receives a message through the channel c and assigns it to a variable x, then behaves like P.

c!v → Q sends a message v using the channel c, then the behavior is like Q.

x := e assigns value e to x.

P; Q performs P and Q sequentially.

P‖Q denotes that P runs in parallel with Q.

P‖‖Q indicates that P interleaves Q which means P and Q run concurrently and randomly.

if b then P else Q denotes the conditional choice. If the value of b is true then it behaves like P else like Q.

[cond]a->P denotes if cond is satisfied, engages inaction a, then the subsequent behavior is like P; if cond not be satisfied, the process will wait for cond. Check cond and do a is an atomic behavior.

5   The Transformation Between MSBF and CSP

In this section, the methodology for transforming two typical modules (entity devices and services) to CSP is proposed. The modeling of entity devices is similar by CSP, and so the modeling of service is. Therefore, the similar modules should be modeled in the same way.

A. The Model of Entity Devices

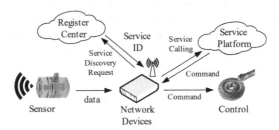

Fig. 3. The typical process of entity devices

A typical entity device is showed in Fig. 3. First, the device acquires data by sensor. After a simple data processing, the request for service discovery is sent to the register center, and the register center will answer by service ID. Then the device generates the service calling using the data from sensor, ands send the calling to the service platform. When the device receives the command from the service platform, the mechanical part of the device will be controlled by the command.

As above mentioned, a typical entity device has two sessions of communication: to register center and service platform. Four channels in CSP can represent the communication: register center request channel, service discovery channel, service calling channel, and command receiving channel. Moreover, the data sensor also can be represented by a channel, named sensor channel. And the mechanical control can be represented by a process.

A typical model of the entity device is like:

Sensor_channel?data->register_center_request_channel!deviceID->
Service_discovery_channel?serviceID->
service_calling_channel! behavior.serviceID.parameter ->
command_receiving_channel? command->DeviceControl(command,parameter)

B. The Model of Services

A typical function service is showed in Fig. 4. First, the function service should interpret the input. Then, if the service is limited by a request of synchronization, it should query the controller service. If necessary, the service should send a change request to the controller service to change the state of synchronization. The function service computes and generate the command when the it receive the permission from the controller service. Finally, the service sends the output to the entity device and transforms to the input state. The synchronization state could be multiple depending on the situation of synchronization.

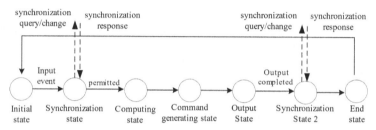

Fig. 4. The typical process of function services

The function service can be modeled by the states. Every state is represented by a process in CSP. The input state and output state should tackle the input/output, two channel, service input channel and service output channel, should be used in the two state. The synchronization state has a communication to a controller service, and two channels, service synchronization request channel and service synchronization response channel, should be used for the communication of synchronization. If the response is permitted, the service can be transformed to the computing state. Otherwise, service should be transformed to the input state. The computing state is the main part of the service, and it should be implemented differently because of the function.

A typical model of the function service is like:

ServiceInitState = service_run_event-> ServiceInputState
ServiceInputState = service_input_channel?input->input_tackling_event->
ServiceSynchronizationState
ServiceSynchronizationState = service_synchronization_request_channel!request->
service_synchronization_response_channel?response
->ServiceSynchronizationCheck(response)
ServiceSynchronizationCheck (response) = resopose_is_permitted-> ServiceCom-
putingState |
      resopose_is_not_permitted-> ServiceInputState
ServiceComputingState = computing_event-> ServiceOutputState
ServiceOutputState = service_output_channel!output-> ServiceInputState

The controller service like a simple state machine, and it also can be modeled by the state. Every state is represented by a process in CSP. A state includes two parts for the state querying and the state changing. In the state querying part, the controller service just receives request by the service synchronization request channel, and sends output the result of permission, depending on which state the service on. In the state changing part, the controller service receives the change request and computes which state should be transformed or not.

A typical model of the controller service is like:

ControllerServiceState1 = service_synchronization_request_channel?request->
    ControllerServiceStateComputing(request)
ControllerServiceStateComputing(request) = request_is_querying->
service_synchronization_repsonse_channel!the_response_of_this_state |
request_is_changing_->
(the_state_should_be_transformed-> ControllerServiceState2 |
    he_state_should_not_be_transformed-> ControllerServiceState1)

6 The Museum System Architecture

There are increasing application demands based on CPS technology, such as intelligent industrial production systems and smart home systems. With the growth of cities, there are lots of diverse museums. To ensure the security and decrease the waiting time, the automatic and intelligent application system is constructed. We construct a CPS application about the museum system, which could consist of multiple services conveniently to extend. It could have tickets selling, tickets checking and crowd controlling services, etc. The architecture of the museum system is shown in Fig. 5.

Customers visiting the museum should follow the path of Entrance, the Ticket Office, the Exhibition Area, finally exit the museum. Ticket Office sells tickets to the museum. Exhibition Areas are the major parts of the exhibition of the museum, and customers watch exhibits in there.

In fact, to protect the exhibits and guarantee the proper operation of the museum, the museum system has some running constraints. The realistic requirements are listed as follow:

- *Requirement 1: Exhibition Area cannot contain too many (above 3) people at the same time*

Requirement 1 is for the order of the exhibition. If too many customers enter the Exhibition Areas, they will have a bad experience. Requirement 1 could be violated when some customers enter the Exhibition Area at the same time. The problem could be solved by three methods: making visitors buy tickets one by one, triggering the lock of ticket sell service when a visitor buys tickets and using an atomic operation consisted of buying and decreasing the rest of tickets.

- *Requirement 2: Exhibition Area only allows the customer with tickets.*

Requirement 2 prevents people from having no tickets from entering the exhibition. The requirement may be violated when irrelevant people are in the wrong place.

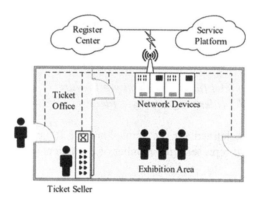

Fig. 5. The museum architecture

To avoid violating Requirement 2 and Requirement 3, a valid identity verification procedure is necessary to design.

- *Requirement 3: If the Exhibition Areas are full, no ticket can be sold.*

Requirement 3 is a method for crowd control. If the Exhibition Areas are full, for the feeling of customers and the order of the museum, no tickets should be sold. Requirement the could be violated when the customer buys a ticket at the moment of Exhibition Areas getting a full load.

7   Museum System Modeling

In this section, the museum system is modelled by CSP. All components are seen as processes in CSP. To model the museum system by the MSBF, particularly the behavior of customers, the CPS is divided into four kinds of processes: entity devices, microservices on the cloud, the register center, and behaviors of people. The sets and channels in CSP model are listed, and the four kinds of processes are described below, then the museum system is modeled in CSP.

A. Channels and Sets

In the museum, customers can go through apart of rooms. Depends on their identity, customers have two states: having a ticket or no ticket. The set Identity is defined, which contains all people who can enter this museum. The set State is defined, which contains the conditions mentioned. The definition of set Visitor:

State=def {ticket, no_ticket}
Visitor=def {identity, state | identity ∈ Identity, state ∈ State}

In this model, for representing the behavior of customers, who is in the room should be modeled. Otherwise, the action of customers, such as buying tickets and go to another room, cannot be described. For the reason, the customers of these rooms can't be ignored. A set *Room* is defined there, and it contains sets of people in a specific room. The set *Exhibition_Area_People* is for people in Exhibition Area, *Ticket_Office_People* is for people in Ticket Office.

Exhibition_Area_People=def {identity | identity ∈ Identity}
Ticket_Office_People=def {identity | identity ∈ Identity}

The set *Variable* is defined for the semaphore for Requirement 3. The variable *exexhibition_area_count* represents the number of customers in Exhibition Area.

Variable=def {exhibition_area_count}

The set *DeviceName* and *ServiceId* is defined for service discovery. The content of *DeviceName* is the identity of all entity devices, and *ServiceId* is the identity of all services.

DeviceName=def {ticket_door,ticket_seller,exhibition_area_door,exit_door}
ServiceId=def {door_service,ticket_seller_service,exhibition_door_service,
ticket_sell_controller_service}

As shown in Fig. 6, the communication may occur between the register center and entity devices, or services and entity device. Moreover, the service composition also needs some method to exchange messages. These communications should be represented by channels. Referring to Fig. 6, a device has three channels, including sensor (for getting data from the sensor), discovery (for service discovery), command (for getting command from service). And the register center and the service platform need a channel to communicate with devices. Moreover, every service should have a channel for receiving input, and a channel for receiving synchronization message. To illustrate the channel clearly, the name of channels is like this: a sensor channel of the door of ticket office to the corridor is *ticket_door_sensor*. These channels are declared:

Channels { ticket_door_sensor, ticket_door_discovery, ticket_door_command, ticket_seller_sensor, ticket_seller_discovery, ticket_seller_command, exhibition_area_sensor, exhibition_area_discovery, exhibition_area_command, exit_sensor, exit_ discovery, exit_command, register_in, service_platform_in, door_service_input, ticket_seller_service_input, exhibition_area_controller_service_input, exhibition_area_door_service_input, exhibition_area_door_service_synchronization, ticket_seller_service_synchronization }

B. The Model of Entity Devices

In the MSBF, most of logic parts are implemented in service, which means entity devices are easy to be described by CSP. Entity devices which has similar behaviors, and they can be modeled as the similar form.

The Door of Ticket Office. The Door of Ticket Office is a typical entity device. Its sensor acquires the message of people who want to enter the ticket office, visits the register center to service discovery, sends message to the service platform, and gets command it should do. If the door opens and a customer enter into the ticket office, the set *Ticket_Office_People* should change to represent the behavior of customer. By the way, a series of set operation is defined there:

- *delete (id, set)* delete id from the set.
- *contain (id, set)* query if set contains id.
- *update (id, set)* update id to set and save the ticket state of id.

And two operation for the set Identity is defined there:

- *getstate(id)* query the ticket state of id.
- *changestate(id,state)* change the ticket state of id,

The typical entity device is modeled by two processes, communicate part and control part. The definition of the door of ticket office are:

TicketDoor =$_{def}$ ticket_door_sensor?id.state->
register_in!ticket_door->
ticket_door_discovery?service_id->
service_platform_in! ticket_door.service_id.id.state ->
ticket_door_command?command->TicketDoorControl(id,state,command)
TicketDoorControl(id,state,command)=$_{def}$
If command==open
*   update(ticket_office,id,state)->TicketDoor()*
}
else
*   TicketDoor*

Other Devices. Except the door of ticket office, there are the door of exhibition area, the door of exit and the ticket seller. They are similar with the door of ticket office, and can be described as same form. Therefore, just the definition of ticket seller is proposed here:

TicketSeller =$_{def}$ ticket_seller_sensor?id.state.index->
register_in!ticket_seller->ticket_seller_discovery?service_id->
service_platform_in!ticket_seller.service_id.id.state->
ticket_selerl_command?command->TicketSellerControl(id,command)
TicketSellerControl(id,command)=
If command==open
*   changestate(id)*
else
*   TicketSeller*

C. The Model of Register Center

The register center is a middleware for service discovery. It can be implemented as a key-value cache so that an if-else model is proposed here. The definition of the register center is:

RegisterCenter = register_in?device_name->ServiceDiscovery(device_name);
ServiceDiscovery(device_name)=
If device_name==ticker_door
*   ticket_door_discovery!door_service->RegisterCenter*
else if device_name==ticket_seller
*   ticket_sell_discovery!ticker_seller_service->RegisterCenter*
else if device_name==exhibition_area_door
*   exhibition_area_discovery!exhibition_area_door_service->RegisterCenter*

D. The Model of Customer

The model in this part is not for the MSBF. In order to the verification work, the customers in the museum and their behaviors should be described, for the sensor acquiring data and the CPS running. Two models for the people should be defined here.

The Entering. The entering just simulate that customers enter the museum and start the CPS. If the behavior of entering is lost, the verification is hard to run. The definition of the behavior of entering is:

$Entering=def$
$||| i \in Visitor\ (ticket\_door\_sensor!i.no\_ticket->Skip)$

Customers in Room. The museum has two rooms, the ticket office and the exhibition area. In different places, the behavior customers can do is different. In the ticket office, customers can buy tickets and go to exhibition area. And in exhibition area, the customers just can leave. In this model, customers are described as a choice of behavior. For example, the customers in the ticket office is:

$$PeopleInTicketOffice =_{def} GoToExhibitionArea1\ \square BuyTickets$$
$$GoToExhibitionArea1 =_{def}$$
$$exhibition\_area\_1\_sensor!\ i_{\in Ticket\_Office\_People} .getstate(i)->$$
$$PeopleInTicketOffice$$
$$BuyTickets =_{def}$$
$$ticket\_seller\_sensor!\ !\ i_{\in Ticket\_Office\_People} .getstate(i)->$$
$$PeopleInTicketOffice$$

E. The Model of Services

The models of services are proposed in this part. The service platform has three modules, including a request dispatcher (for interpreting request and calling correct service), a command sender (for sending command to correct device), and services. The request dispatcher and command sender can be described as a key-value structure, like the register center. But for the service composition and reuse, the command may send to another service, and the key-value of *service id – service synchronization channel* should also in the command sender. The definition of the request dispatcher and command sender are:

ServicePlatform =$_{def}$ service_platform_in?device_name.service_id.id.state
->ServiceRun(device_name,service_id,id,state)
ServiceRun(device_name,service_id,id,state)=$_{def}$
If service_id==door_service
  door_service_input!device_name.person.id->ServicePlatform
else if service_id==ticket_seller_service
  ticket_sell_service_input!device_name.person.id->ServicePlatform
else if service_id==exhibition_area_service
  exhibition_area_door_service_input!device_name.person.id->ServicePlatform
CommandSender(device_name,command)=$_{def}$
if evice_name==ticket_door
  ticket_door_command!command->RegisterCenter
else if device_name==ticket_seller
  ticket_sell_command!command->RegisterCenter
else if device_name==exhibition_area_door
  exhibition_area_command!command->RegisterCenter
else if device_name==exhibition_area_service

  exhibition_area_synchronization!command-> RegisterCenter
else if device_name==ticket_seller_service
  ticket_seller_service_synchronization!command-> RegisterCenter
else if device_name== exhibition_area_controller_service
  exhibition_area_controller_service_input! device_name.command
  ->RegisterCenter

The Service of Doors. The door of the ticket office has no extra requirement, the service can be reused. And it is just needed for opening when someone wants to enter the room. The definition of door services is:

DoorService=$_{def}$ door_service_input?device_name.id.state->
CommandSend(device_name,open);DoorService;

The Service of The Exhibition Area's Door. A little more complicated service is proposed in this part. In Sect. 5, the typical model of services is proposed. The service of the exhibition area's door and the exit follow the typical model, so only the model of the exhibition area's door is proposed here. To satisfy the requirement 3, the exhibition area's door and the exit door need communication to count the customers in the exhibition area. And the state of the exhibition area should be provided for the service of ticket seller to control the seller. Therefore, a controller service for the state of exhibition area is needed. For the requirement 3, the controller service is implemented as a state machine. The full state means the exhibition area is full, and the not full state is contrary. The definition of the controller service is:

ExhibitionAreaController =$_{def}$ ExhibitionAreaNotFull
ExhibitionAreaNotFull =$_{def}$
exhibition_area_controller_service_input?service_id.parameter->
if parameter == plus && exhibition_area_count == 2
  {exhibition_area_count=exhibition_area_count+1}
  -> ExhibitionAreaFull
else if parameter == minus
  {exhibition_area_count=exhibition_area_count-1}
  -> ExhibitionAreaNotFull
else if parameter == query
  CommandSend(service_id,open)
ExhibitionAreaFull =$_{def}$
exhibition_area_controller_service_input?service_id.parameter->
if parameter == minus
  {exhibition_area_count=exhibition_area_count-1}
  -> ExhibitionAreaNotFull
else if parameter == query
  CommandSend(service_id,close)

The Service of The Exhibition Area's Door is described by the state. As shown in Fig. 3, a typical service has four state: initial state, synchronization state, computing state and command generating state. Initial state is the state of beginning. The synchronization state is the state of calling controller service for the synchronization message. For the exhibition area door service, the service should communicate with controller service for open permission. If the exhibition area is not full, the service of the exhibition area's door will receive the permission. Which command generating state should be arrived is judged in computing state, then the correct command is generated and sent.

Not only the service of the exhibition area's door, the exit door and the ticket seller are also modeled in this form. Therefore, just the definition of the service of the exhibition area's door is proposed:

ExhibitionAreaDoorServiceInit $=_{def}$
exhibition_area_door_service_input?device_name.id.state
->ExhibitionAreaDoorServiceSynchronization (device_name,id,state)
ExhibitionAreaDoorServiceSynchronization (device_name,id,state)$=_{def}$
-> exhibition_area_controller_service_input! exhibition_area_door_service.query
->exhibition_area_service_synchronization?command ->
if command == open
    ExhibitionAreaDoorComputing(device_name,id,state)
else
    ExhibitionArea1DoorFailed(device_name,id,state)
ExhibitionAreaDoorComputing$=_{def}$
if state== ticket
    ExhibitionAreaDoorSuccess(device_name,id,state)
else
    ExhibitionAreaDoorFailed(device_name,id,state)
ExhibitionAreaDoorSuccess(device_name,person,id)$=_{def}$
CommandSend(device_name,open);
CommandSend(exhibition_area_controller_service,plus);
ExhibitionAreaDoorServiceInit
ExhibitionAreaDoorFailed(device_name,person,id)$=_{def}$
CommandSend(device_name,close);ExhibitionAreaDoorServiceInit

Finally, the definition of the whole museum system is as follow:

Service$=_{def}$
ServicePlatform||DoorService||TicketSellServiceInit||ExhibitionAreaDoorServiceInit||
ExhibitionAreaController||ExitServiceInit
People$=_{def}$ *PeopleInTicketOffice||PeopleInExhibitionArea*
Museum$=_{def}$ *Entering||TicketDoor||TicketSeller||ExhibitionAreaDoor||ExitDoor*
System$=_{def}$ *Service||People||Museum||RegisterCenter*

8   The Verification of Museum System Model

The CSP model of the museum system is translated to PAT, and the requirements are verified. A part of codes of the model is shown in Fig. 6.

In the model, deadlock may occur when the Ticket Office has an unpredicted situation of synchronization. The deadlock means some people cannot enter the room they are able to get into. In PAT, the statements are used to check this:

#assert System () deadlockfree;

To check whether the behaviors are consistent with the requirements, the definitions of unexpected state would be verified. Three wrong conditions are set for the requirement, if the condition is reached (it means the verification result is valid in PAT), the requirement will not be satisfied. In this part, two new variables are listed there. The variable *temp_entering_id* is the customer who entering the exhibition area lately. The variable *sellsign* represents the behavior of ticket selling. And the variable *exhibition_area_count*

```
/ESP museum_changed.csp
58        TicketDoor()
59    };
60
61    PeopleInTicketOffice()=GoToExhibitionArea1()[]BuyTickets();
62    GoToExhibitionArea1()=
63    if(ticket_office_index>0)
64    {
65        exhibition_area_1_sensor!ticket_office_people[ticket_office_index-1].ticket_office_id[ticket_office_index-1]
66        ->{ticket_office_index=ticket_office_index-1;}->PeopleInTicketOffice()
67    }
68    else
69    {
70        PeopleInTicketOffice()
71    };
72
73    BuyTickets()=
74    if(ticket_office_index>0)
75    {
76        ticket_sell_sensor!ticket_office_people[ticket_office_index-1].ticket_office_id[ticket_office_index-1].ticket_office_index-1
77        ->PeopleInTicketOffice()
78    }
79    else
80    {
81        PeopleInTicketOffice()
82    };
83
84    TicketSellMachine()=ticket_sell_sensor?person.id.index->register_in!TICKET_SELL
85    ->ticket_sell_discovery?service_id->service_platform_in!TICKET_SELL.service_id.person.id
86    ->ticket_sell_command?command->TicketSellControl(command,index);
87
88    TicketSellControl(command,index)=
89    if(command==OPEN)
90    {
91        {ticket_office_id[index]=TICKET;sellsign=1;sellsign=0;}->TicketSellMachine()
92    }
93    else
```

Fig. 6. The PAT code of museum model

is mentioned in Sect. 7, for the count of customers in the exhibition area. The definitions of the opposition state are:

#define wrongcontain (exhibition_area_count > 3);

#define noticket (temp_entering_id_ ==noticket);

#define wrongsold (exhibition_area_count >=3&&sellsign ==1);

Wrongcontain means too many customers in Exhibition Area.

Noticket means a visitor enters the Exhibition Area without a ticket.

Wrongsold means a ticket is sold when Exhibition Area is full.

In PAT, the statements are used to check them:

#assert System() reaches wrongcontain;

#assert System() reaches noticket;

#assert System() reaches wrongsold;

The verification result is shown in Fig. 7. According to the conclusion, we know the deadlock-free is valid, and the rest of the asserts is not valid, which means our model satisfying the requirements.

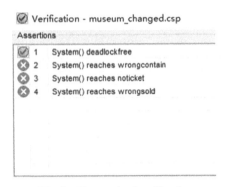

Fig. 7. The result of verification

9   Conclusion

In this paper, we present a microservice-based framework MSBF for CPS design. The MSBF adopts the layer-based methodology for separating the components and functions of CPS, and it is based on microservice architecture to guarantee the flexibility. Moreover, a CSP model is constructed for a smart museum system. The specific model is built based on three requirements about museum service, and the model are verified. By the museum case, the method for transforming the MSBF to CSP is proposed. The typical modules of CPS are modeled in the museum system, including services, entity devices and register center. The verification result shows our model satisfies the system requirements, and it means the microservice-based framework is reliable for CPS design. In future work, we plan to find a general way to resolve the gap between CPS and modeling and use the framework modeling other realistic CPS applications.

Acknowledgment. This work was supported financially by the National Natural Science Foundation of China ((No. 61572195, 61872145), the Open Project of Shanghai Key Laboratory of Trustworthy Computing (No. 07dz22304201603).

References

1. Rajkumar, R., Lee, I., Sha, L., Stankovic, J.: Cyber-physical systems: the next computing revolution. In: Design Automation Conference. IEEE (2010)
2. Sha, L., Gopalakrishnan, S., Liu, X., Wang, Q.: Cyber-physical systems: a new frontier. In: 2008 IEEE International Conference on Sensor Networks, Ubiquitous, and Trustworthy Computing (SUTC 2008), Taichung. IEEE (2008)
3. Lee, E.: Cyber physical systems: design challenges. In: IEEE Symposium on Object Oriented Real-time Distributed Computing. IEEE Computer Society (2008)
4. Paik, H.-y., Lemos, A.L., Barukh, M.C., Benatallah, B., Natarajan, A.: Web service composition: overview. In: Paik, H. (ed.) Web Service Implementation and Composition Techniques, pp. 149–158. Springer, Cham (2017). https://doi.org/10.1007/978-3-319-55542-3_5
5. Hasselbring, W., Steinacker, G.: Microservice Architectures for Scalability, Agility and Reliability in E-Commerce, pp. 243–246 (2017)

6. Hoare, C.A.R.: Communicating Sequential Processes. Prentice Hall International in Computer Science, Boston (1985)
7. Brookes, S.D., Hoare, C.A.R., Roscoe, A.W.: A theory of communicating sequential processes. J. ACM **31**(3), 560–599 (1984)
8. PAT: Process Analysis Toolkit. http://pat.comp.nus.edu.sg/
9. Sun, J., Liu, Y., Dong, J.S.: Model checking CSP revisited: introducing a process analysis toolkit. In: Margaria, T., Steffen, B. (eds.) ISoLA 2008. CCIS, vol. 17, pp. 307–322. Springer, Heidelberg (2008). https://doi.org/10.1007/978-3-540-88479-8_22
10. Lee, J., Bagheri, B., Kao, H.A.: A cyber-physical systems architecture for Industry 4.0-based manufacturing systems. Manuf. Lett. **3**, 18–23 (2015)
11. Masin, M., et al.: Cross-layer design of reconfigurable cyber-physical systems. In: 2017 Design, Automation and Test in Europe Conference and Exhibition (DATE). IEEE (2017)
12. Hong, Y., et al.: A novel multi-agent model-free control for state-of-charge balancing between distributed battery energy storage systems. IEEE Trans. Emerg. Top. Comput. Intell. **99**, 1–10 (2020)
13. Barik, R.K., Dubey, H., Mankodiya, K.: SoA-Fog: secure service-oriented edge computing architecture for smart health big data analytics. In: 2017 IEEE Global Conference on Signal and Information Processing (GlobalSIP). IEEE (2018)
14. Batchkova, I., Ivanova, T.: Model-driven development of agent-based cyber-physical systems. IFAC-Papers OnLine **52**(25), 258–263 (2019)
15. Hu, Y., Zhou, X.: CPS-Agent oriented construction and implementation for cyber physical systems. IEEE Access 1 (2018)
16. He, X., et al.: A framework for developing cyber physical systems. In: The 29th International Conference on Software Engineering and Knowledge Engineering (2017)
17. Cicirelli, F., et al.: Model continuity in cyber-physical systems: a control-centered methodology based on agents. Simul. Model. Pract. Theory Int. J. Feder. Eur. Simul. Soc. **83**, 93 (2018)
18. Feljan, A.V., et al.: SOA-PE: a service-oriented architecture for planning and execution in cyber-physical systems. In: International Conference on Smart Sensors and Systems. IEEE (2017)
19. Mohalik, S.K., et al.: Adaptive service-oriented architectures for cyber physical systems. In: 2017 IEEE Symposium on Service-Oriented System Engineering (SOSE). IEEE (2017)
20. Bigheti, J.A., Fernandes, M.M., Godoy, E.D.P.: Control as a service: a microservice approach to Industry 4.0. In: IEEE International Workshop on Metrology for Industry 4.0 and Internet of Things National Service of Industrial Training (Senai), Lençóis Paulista, São Paulo State University (Unesp) (2019)
21. Pop, E., Gifu, D.: A cyber-physical systems oriented platform using web services. In: 2019 22nd International Conference on Control Systems and Computer Science (CSCS) (2019)
22. Nakagawa, H., et al.: A model transformation approach to constructing agent-oriented design models for CPS/IoT systems. In: SAC 2020: The 35th ACM/SIGAPP Symposium on Applied Computing. ACM (2020)

Design and Implementation of Virtual Reality Geometric Modeling in Apla^{+VR}

Jiewen Huang[1,2], Jinyun Xue[1(✉)], Zhen You[1], and Zhehong Zhou[1,2]

[1] National-Level International S & T Cooperation Base of Networked Supporting Software, Nanchang, China
jinyun@vip.sina.com
[2] School of Computer Information Engineering, Jiangxi Normal University, Nanchang 330022, Jiangxi, China

Abstract. The geometric modeling languages for virtual reality could be classified into graphical modeling languages and script modeling languages. The graphical modeling languages are easier to use, but difficult to ensure the precision of 3D models. While the script modeling languages are so complex that harder to be coded by programmers. In order to address the above problems, this paper proposes a novel virtual reality modeling language Apla^{+VR}, which not only combines into our original abstract modeling language Apla, but also extends a new function of constructing 3D models of virtual reality systems conveniently and abstractly. Meanwhile, the correctness of Apla^{+VR} programs also be ensured by using PAR method and theory of FMDE (Formal Model-Driven Engineering). Furthermore, a code generator called Apla^{+VR} → MAXscript, could translate abstract Apla^{+VR} programs into MAXscript scripts, which can be complied in 3DSMax engine, and then be created into 3D models effectively. Finally, it is proved that Apla^{+VR} and its tools can increase the efficiency and reliablility of developing 3D models through a case study of the minimum sum problem virtual reality system.

Keywords: Virtual reality · Geometric modeling · Apla^{+VR} · MAXscript

1 Introduction

Virtual Reality (VR) technology refers to a human-computer interaction technology that combines computers, sensors, artificial intelligence, 5G, and other technologies. Through the existing information technology, a digital environment similar to the real world is generated in terms of sight, hearing, touch, smell, etc., and the interaction between the users and objects in the virtual environment is realized through virtual reality equipment, so that people can get an immersive feeling [1, 2]. The three-dimensional model is an important part of building a virtual reality system, and its authenticity will affect the immersion of the virtual reality system [3]. There are various geometric modeling languages, and they are applied in different fields (such as VTK [4] and MAXScript [5]). The geometric modeling languages in the virtual reality field still have some challenging problems: (1) The language is complex and tedious, and the degree of abstraction is not

J. Xue et al. (Eds.): SOFL+MSVL 2020, LNCS 12723, pp. 54–65, 2021.
https://doi.org/10.1007/978-3-030-77474-5_4

high; (2) The development efficiency and reliability of the modeling program are difficult to be ensured.

3DSMax [6] software is one of the most widely used 3D design software in the world. It provides an integrated development environment. Users can use the mouse for graphical modeling or create models through MAXScript scripts. It provides a rich and flexible tool combination and computational rendering engine, which can easily simulate the real scenes. This makes it very suitable for the development of virtual reality 3D models. The 3D models in recent applications [7] have attracted the attention of users. 3DSMax can also batch process models by using a scripting language to speed up manual steps.

With the guidance of Formal Model-Driven Engineering (FMDE), we develop abstract programs for 3D models by using our proposed Apla^{+VR} language in this paper. And then the Apla^{+VR} programs could be automatically generated into Maxscript codes with the help of our supporting tool Apla$^{+VR} \rightarrow$ MAXscript. The target MAXscript could be compiled in the 3DSMax framework to create the 3D models required by virtual reality systems. Model designers and interactive developers who use the Apla^{+VR} language can jointly build a model resource library to facilitate the development of virtual reality systems. The main contribution of our paper is that a novel virtual reality geometric modeling language Apla^{+VR} is designed. Compared with MAXScript code, the Apla^{+VR} program is more generic and abstract. Therefore, it could efficiently relieve the burden of programmers, who don't pay more attention to the complex syntax details. Another advantage of abstraction is that it would be easier to formally verify the correctness of Apla^{+VR} program. A case study, which is developed by using generator Apla^{+VR} $\rightarrow$ MAXScript, demonstrates the expression ability, effectiveness and dependence of Apla^{+VR} language.

2 Related Work

2.1 Virtual Reality Geometric Modeling

Classification of Geometric Modeling. The current virtual reality geometric modeling mainly includes three-dimensional software graphical modeling (3DSMax [5], ZBrush [8], etc.), scanning modeling (Z+F IMAGER [9], EXAscan [10], etc.), script modeling (VTK [4], VRML [11], etc.).

- Graphical modeling can intuitively generate 3D models by dragging through the real-time visual interface, and the effect is intuitive. Graphical modeling is one of the most common modeling methods used by model designers.
- Instrument and equipment generate 3D models by scanning the physical surface. Its portability and easy-to-operate characteristics give it unique advantages in archaeology, medicine and other fields. [10] use 3D scanning to build digital cultural relics archives.
- Script modeling generates models by compiling codes, which can accurately represent the model. VTK and ITK [12] are more inclined to medical image processing, corresponding to visualization display and underlying image processing algorithms respectively. VRML [9] is a graphic description language for Web-oriented 3D modeling and rendering, but its ability to manage large scenes is poor and outdated.

Each of the three modeling methods have its advantages and disadvantages. script modeling can simulate behavior through algorithms or dynamic particle effects when it needs to simulate a real dynamic scene, and the effect is more realistic.

2.2 MAXScript Geometric Modeling Language and 3DSMax Framework

MAXScript Geometric Modeling Language. 3DSMax provides two geometric modeling methods (MAXScript script geometric modeling and graphical modeling), as shown in Fig. 1. From the functional perspective, MAXScript script geometric modeling and graphical modeling are equivalent, script modeling can achieve all the functions of graphical modeling, and vice versa. The monitoring and plug-in functions provided by MAXScript are a supplement to 3DSMax's graphical geometric modeling. MAXScript can also implement high-precision control and batch operations that are difficult to achieve with graphical geometric modeling.

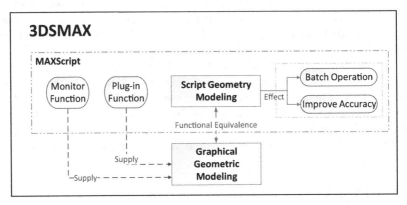

Fig. 1. The relationship between script modeling and graphical modeling in 3dsmax

Virtual reality itself is a product of multi-domain integration. Indoor architecture [13] can be used as exhibition, and the game field [14] can bring new interactive experiences. The MAXScript scripting language can meet the needs of multi-domain modeling and development. In addition, MAXScript can develop high-precision models. Therefore, MAXScript is also the target language of Apla^{+VR}.

3DSMax Framework. The 3DSMax framework is mainly composed of three parts, including standard primitives, modifiers and other operations. The 3DSMax framework components correspond to the specific development steps of MAXScript.

Standard Primitives. Primitives are the basis of geometric modeling. The geometric primitives in the real world exist in the form of basketball, water pipe, etc. In the framework, it is a sphere, tube, pyramid, etc. Geometric modeling usually selects a primitive which is close to the appearance of the 3D model. The closer the primitive is to the structure of the original design model, the more time required for modeling can be saved.

Modifiers. Modifiers can quickly change the appearance of primitives. A variety of modifiers in the framework, such as free deformation FFD_3 $\times$ 3 $\times$ 3 modifier, edit polygon modifier and so on. By using different modifiers, users can simplify the modeling process and create complex and sophisticated models.

Other Operations. The operations of the first two parts can create a mesh description model, but the 3D model at this time has no surface details. To make the model more realistic, it is also necessary to add operations such as materials and textures. These operations can determine the material state and visual appearance of the mesh surface of the model, bringing an intuitive sense of three-dimensional space. Finally, render or export.

2.3 PAR Platform

Partition and Recurrence (PAR) method [15, 16] is a formal development method based on model-driven, which is a development method for solving the problem of developing high-reliability and high-confidence software design. PAR proposed custom generic algorithm design language and its generation rules, abstract programming language and a series of executable language generation system. PAR has successfully solved a large number of classical algorithm problems. Among them, the graph planarity algorithm [17] proposed by Turing Award winners Hopcroft and Tarjan has been improved, implemented in the PAR platform and shown the results to himself.

The PAR method uses advanced development techniques such as MMD's formal development methods and software automation. The entire development process can be embodied in the following five models, as shown in Fig. 2. (1) Requirement model—Structured Natural Language (SNL) describes the requirement of the problem to be solved. (2) Specification model—the formal specification for describing problems in Radl language, which can be automatically converted from SNL to Radl specification. (3) Algorithm model—By using the Radl language to express the algorithm for solving the problem, it can be semi-automatically converted from the Radl specification to the Radl algorithm. (4) Abstract program model—Apla language [18] develops abstract program, which can be automatically converted from Radl algorithm to Apla program. (5) Executable program model—executable programming language represents specific programs, which can be automatically converted from Apla programs to executable programs (such as C++ [19], C# [20], JAVA [21], etc.).

Apla language [22] defines an abstract programming language with generic mechanism in order to realize the PAR method of formal development of algorithm programs. The language mechanism of function abstraction and data abstraction reduces the complexity of describing the problem, and makes the composed program very concise and easy to understand. Apla language provides standard data types, custom simple types, predefined abstract data types and custom abstract data types. The complete type system simplifies the programming process. The rich reusable component library can greatly improve the efficiency of software development, and a large number of program modules can be reused through the same component library. It also supports formal deduction to ensure the correctness of the program.

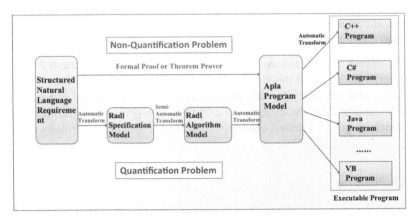

Fig. 2. PAR platform architecture

3 Apla^{+VR} Language Design and Code Generator Development

With extending basic data type with modeling, data structure and geometry data type, we design Apla^{+VR}, which is not only combined with our original Apla language, but also implement the virtual reality geometric modeling. Meanwhile, a generator called Apla$^{+VR} \to$ MAXScript is developed, and it would be used to generate MAXScript destination program from Apla^{+VR} source program.

3.1 Apla^{+VR} Syntax

Apla^{+VR} program consists of two parts: program header and program body. The program header contains language components such as custom functions and abstract data types. The program body is mainly composed of simple program statements and control structures to realize its specific program functions. The code in Sect. 4.1 is a virtual reality geometric modeling program written according to Apla^{+VR} syntax specifications.

An important feature of Apla^{+VR} is that it has a rich data type system (predefined ADT: tree, graph, sequence, etc.), but it still cannot meet the needs of virtual reality modeling. In order to facilitate the development of Apla^{+VR} modeling, six standard data types related to graphic design have been added, which are point3, point2, color, angleaxis, eulerangle and matrix3. Taking point3 as an example, it can locate the three-dimensional model in space, and accurately describe the directions of the three coordinate axes of x-axis, y-axis, and z-axis, which are defined as follows:

```
var <name>: point3;
<name>:= [<int_or_real>,<int_or_real>,<int_or_real>];
```

Apla^{+VR} pioneered the addition of geometric data types, including box, cone, sphere, cylinder, torus and plane. Geometry types are abstracted from analysis the modeling framework 3DSMax and the interaction framework Unity, which facilitates the expansion of virtual reality interactive functions while achieving geometric modeling.

When modifying the appearance of the model, modifiers are provided as type operations to the geometry type. Type operations are implemented through Apla^{+VR} component library, see Sect. 3.2 for details. Geometric data types not only ensure the simplicity of the language, but also use the language features of the original Apla^{+VR}'s predefined ADT, and users can use them like basic data types. Taking the sphere geometry type as an example, some of its definitions and operations are as follows:

```
type sphere = record
                rad : real;
                segs : integer;
                smooth : boolean;
                hemisphere : real;
                center:point3;
                ...
        end.
specify ADT sphere()
  var s1,s2 :sphere;
  s1.rad = <real>;
  s2.segs = <integer>;

  s1 ∩ s2 ;
  s1.mirror(axisName_string)
  s1.addModifier(modifier_name);
  s1.moveFace(array_faces, point3, axis_point3);
  s1.noisem(integer_seed,point3_strength,real_scale);
  ...
endspec.
```

3.2 Code Generator

The code generator converts the modeling program described by Apla^{+VR} into an executable MAXScript script. The code generator is composed of analysis module, generation module, and component library, as shown in Fig. 3. The generated MAXScript script contains all the codes needed for the primitives, modifiers, materials and textures that make up the appearance of the 3D model.

Analysis Module. The analysis module is mainly composed of lexical analysis, Syntax and semantic analysis and error handling. Lexical analysis scans and decomposes the characters that make up the program, and outputs the corresponding token sequence. Syntax and semantic analysis recognizes and processes various grammatical components from the results of lexical analysis markers according to related grammars and reviews them, and uses top-down recursive descent method to judge and match tokens one by one, and transfers to the corresponding branch. If spelling, structural errors, semantic mismatch and other errors are detected, then transferred to the corresponding error handling module to handle the errors. If the variable p is of type point3, in the assignment operation, the system will first read the characters in sequence and determine whether they are identifiers, numbers or other characters, and then check whether the two sides of the equation are of the same type according to the grammatical requirements, and output an error prompt when an error occurs.

Generation Module. The generation module is the core module of the code generator, which contains a generation rule library that satisfies the virtual reality modeling mechanism. During the code generation period, the program generation rules are used to generate the target program based on the semantic information. Program generation rules include type definition generation, function definition generation, expression generation, and program body generation, etc.

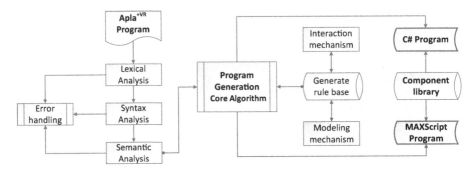

Fig. 3. Code generator architecture

Component Library. Geometric data types have been added to Apla^{+VR}. Most of the operations of these types are encapsulated in the component library and called when needed. There are three kinds of compound operations ($\cap$, $\cup$, $-$), seven basic operations (move, rotate, scale, copy, mirror, select, delete), and a variety of complex operations (bevelFace, extrudeFace, exportAll, etc.). The realization component can be realized in two ways: One is to use monitoring function of MAXScript to convert operations into macro records for encapsulation. The other is to use the API of the 3DSMax framework. Directly calling the API can reduce repetitive work and facilitate modification and expansion. Completing data type operations in the form of components can facilitate the migration of script modeling platforms.

3.3　Development Steps of Virtual Reality Models Based on PAR Method

Apla^{+VR} modeling based on the PAR method can simplify the steps of traditional script modeling and save modeling time. Specific steps are as follows:

(1) The user firstly uses the Apla^{+VR} language to specify the geometric data type that approximates the appearance of the real object, and the operations required to modify the geometric type corresponding to the appearance of the three-dimensional model.

(2) The code generator converts Apla^{+VR} program into the corresponding MAXScript script.

(3) Then add MAXScript scripts to the 3DSMax framework, and create the required 3D model after compilation.

4   A Case Study

The problem of the minimum sum of the array segments refers to: Given an integer array a[0:n−1], the minimum sum of adjacent elements in a is calculated. Virtual reality technology can intuitively describe abstract algorithm problems in the form of three-dimensional graphics, and the solution steps can be intuitively expressed in the minimum sum problem. First of all, the n numbers in the array need to be materialized, that is, geometric modeling. Figure 4 shows the steps method for generating the digital model.

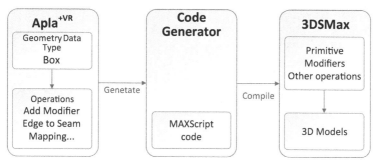

Fig. 4. Steps of 3D model generation

4.1   Apla^{+VR} Implementation of 3D Model

In order to visually indicate the numerical value of the case, the box geometry type is selected to simulate, and different lengths are used to distinguish values of different sizes. Due to the elements in the integer array are positive and negative, they can be identified by texture.

According to the Apla^{+VR} Syntax rules, the program code to pre-implement the model case is as follows:

In this case, we generate a cuboid of equal proportional length, and the length of the 3D model can also be modified by precise numerical values. The specific value should be changed with the value of array a[0: n−1] in the minimum sum virtual reality system. Using Apla^{+VR} can reduce the length of the code. Functions that originally required more than a dozen lines of code to implement only need to call a few lines of encapsulated type operations, which ensures code readability. At the same time, one-time batch generation of models can save development time and improve development efficiency.

```
program createNumModel;
var nm : box; I : integer;
function numModel(size : integer, pos : point3);
begin
  nm.len, nm.wid, nm.hei, nm.pos := size,5,5,pos;
  nm.name:= "nunModel" + size;
  nm.addModifier(UVWUnwrap);
  nm.setEdgeToSeam(1,5,7,10,18,26,34,42,44,46,66) ;
  ... // Omit some operations
end.
begin
  i := 0;
  do ( i < 5) → size, pos := 4 * (i +1), [0,30 * i,0];
  numModel(size, pos);
  i := i + 1;
  od;
  map(all,D:\numModel\positive.jpg ,1,70,33,0.6);
  export(all," D:\\numModel","num",1);
end.
```

4.2 Generation

Next, the code generator will convert the Apla^{+VR} program into MAXScript script code. After the generated code file is imported into the 3dsmax framework, the required model can be obtained after compilation. The specific 3D model used in the minimal sum virtual reality system is shown in Fig. 5 below.

Fig. 5. Application of digital models in virtual reality system

In architecture Fig. 3, there is the generation of C# scripts to realize the interaction and environment management in the virtual reality system. This is one of our main tasks in the later period. The virtual reality case of minimum sum is written with interactive code through C#.

4.3 Formal Verification

For the above core code, The new definition of the loop invariant method and the new development strategy in the PAR can be used to derive the loop invariant, and the Dijkstra's weakest predicate method [23] can be used to verify the formal correctness of the Apla^{+VR} program.

Pre-condition: $\{Q: i=0 \land size = 4 \land pos = [0, 0, 0]\}$
Post-condition: $\{R: i=5 \land size = 20 \land pos = [0, 120, 0]\}$
Loop invariant: $\{\rho : 0 \leq i < 5 \land size = 4 * (i + 1) \land pos = [0, 30*i, 0]\}$
Limit function: $\tau = 5 - i$

The verification process is as follows:

(1) Prove $Q \Rightarrow \rho$
∵ $\rho \equiv \{size=4*(i+1) \land pos = [0,30*i,0]\}_0^i$
    $\equiv \{size = 4 \land pos = [0,0,0]\}$
    $\{Q: i = 0 \land size = 4 \land pos = [0,0,0]\}$
∴ $Q \Rightarrow \rho$ is valid
(2) Prove $\rho \land C \Rightarrow wp("s", \rho)$
∵ $wp("s", \rho) \equiv wp("size, pos, i := 4*(i+1), [0,30*i,0], i + 1",$
          $size=4*(i+1) \land pos = [0,30*i,0])$

     $\equiv \{size=4*(i+1) \land pos = [0,30*i,0]\}_{4*(i+1)}^{size} {}_{[0,30*i,0]}^{pos} {}_{i+1}^{i}$

     $\equiv True$
∴ $\rho \land C \Rightarrow wp("s", \rho)$ is valid
(3) Prove $\rho \land \neg Guard \Rightarrow R$
∵ $\rho \land \neg Guard \equiv 0 \leq i < 5 \land size = 4 * (i + 1) \land pos = [0,30*i,0] \land i \geq 5$
          $\equiv False$
∴ $\rho \land \neg Guard \Rightarrow R$ is valid
(4) Prove $\rho \land Guard \Rightarrow \tau > 0$
∵ $\rho \land Guard \equiv 0 \leq i < 5 \land size = 4 * (i + 1) \land pos = [0,30*i,0] \land i < 5$
          $\equiv 0 \leq i < 5 \land size = 4 * (i + 1) \land pos = [0,30*i,0]$
  $\tau > 0 \equiv 5 - i > 0 \equiv i < 5$
∴ $\rho \land Guard \Rightarrow \tau > 0$ is valid
(5) Prove $\rho \land C \Rightarrow wp("\tau_1 := \tau; s", \tau < \tau_1)$
     ∵ $\rho \land C \equiv 0 \leq i < 5 \land size = 4 * (i + 1) \land pos = [0,30*i,0] \land i < 5$
          $\equiv 0 \leq i < 5 \land size = 4 * (i + 1) \land pos = [0,30*i,0]$
     $wp("\tau_1 := \tau; s", \tau < \tau_1) \equiv wp("\tau_1 := 5 - i; size, pos, i := 5 * (i + 1),$
          $[0,30*i,0], i + 1", 5 - i < \tau_1)$

     $\equiv \left[(5 - i < \tau_1)_{i+1}^i {}_{4*(i+1)}^{size} {}_{[0,30*i,0]}^{pos} \right]_{5-i}^{\tau_1}$

     $\equiv 4 - i < 5 - i$
∴ $\rho \land C \Rightarrow wp("\tau_1 := \tau; s", \tau < \tau_1)$ is valid

According to (1)(2)(3)(4)(5), it is proved that the Apla^{+VR} program in this case is completely correct. On the premise that the code generator is reliable, the correctness of the generated MAXScript program can also be guaranteed.

5 Conclusions

The Apla^{+VR} language is simple and highly abstract, which overcomes the weakness of low-efficiency and lacking-verification of reliability by using the geometric modeling language. It can quickly create and generate Three-dimensional model scripts in virtual reality systems. The complication of the generated MAXScript codes would be processed by 3DSMax. Hence, it is not only useful to lighten our work of developing platform, but also easier to realize platform independence and facilitates transplantation.

Apla^{+VR} helps to strengthen the connection between model designers and interactive developers. Developers can create 3D models well without learning graphic modeling technology.

In future work, Apla^{+VR} should continue to be improved in some details. Meanwhile, the PAR method could be extended to virtual reality interaction and environment management, in order to achieve complete automation of virtual reality system development.

References

1. Zhao, Q.P.: Overview of virtual reality. Sci. China (Series F: Inf. Sci.) **39**(1), 2–46 (2009)
2. Boas, Y.: Overview of virtual reality technologies. Interact. Multimedia Conf. **13**(1), 48–69 (2013)
3. Xue, J.Y., Huang, J.W., You, Z.: Research on virtual reality modeling mechanism based on apla language[J/OL]. J. Huazhong Univ. Sci. Technol. (Nat. Sci. Ed.) 1–7 (2020). https://doi.org/10.13245/j.hust.210209
4. Pavao, A.C., Pouzada, E.V.S., Mathias, M.A.: Electromagnetic field visualization through VTK software. In: Proceedings of the 2001 SBMO/IEEE MTT-S International Microwave and Optoelectronics Conference. Belem: IEEE, pp. 21–24 (2001)
5. Hua, W.: 3ds MAXScript Scripting Language Complete Learning Manual. Ordnance Industry Press, Tianjin (2006)
6. 3ds Max HELP GUIDES. [EB/OL] (2020) https://help.autodesk.com/view/3DSMAX/2021/ENU/.Autodesk
7. Digital protection of Nefertari's tomb. [EB/OL]. https://www.nefertaritomb.com/vr-nowadays
8. Scott, S.: ZBrush Character Creation: Advanced Digital Sculpting, 2nd edn. Sybex Inc, U.S (2011)
9. Zhang, J.H., et al.: Research on the 3D digital protection of ancient buildings and cultural relics based on 3D laser scanning—taking the Dacheng hall of Confucian temple in Leshan, Sichuan as an example. Mapp. Spatial Geographic Inf. **39**(07), 42–44 (2016)
10. Li, Q., Cheng, X.J.: Accuracy test and analysis of self-positioning handheld 3D laser scanner. Bull. Surveying Mapping, (10), 65–68+96 (2016)
11. Ames, A.L., Nadeau, D.R., Moreland, J.L.: VRML2.0 SourceBook. Wiley, New York (1997)
12. Pieper, S., et al.: The NA-MIC Kit: ITK, VTK, pipelines, grids and 3D slicer as an open platform for the medical image computing community. In: 3rd IEEE International Symposium on Biomedical Imaging: Nano to Macro, pp. 698–701 (2006)
13. Li, J.J.: Realization of 3D modeling and interactive system for indoor architecture based on Unity3D. China University of Mining and Technology (2014)
14. Blaha, J., Gupta, M.: Diplopia: a virtual reality game designed to help amblyopics. IEEE Virtual Reality (VR) **2014**, 163–164 (2014)

15. Xue, J.Y.: PAR method and its supporting platform. In: Prof of the 1st International Workshop on Asian Working Conference on Verified Software. [s.n.], pp. 159–169 (2006)
16. Xue, J.Y.: Formal derivation of graph algorithmic programs using partition-and-recur. J. Comput. Sci. Technol. **13**(6), 553–561 (1998). https://doi.org/10.1007/BF02946498
17. Gries, D., Xue, J.Y.: The Hopcroft-Tarjan planarity algorithm, presentation and improvements. Technical Report, 88–906, Computer Science Department, Cornell University (1988)
18. Xie, W.P.: Radl→Apla Program Generation System and its Reliability Research. Jiangxi Normal University Library, Nanchang (2009)
19. Yong, L.: Development of Apla to C++ Automatic Program Conversion System. Jiangxi Normal University Library, Nanchang (2002)
20. Zuo, Z.K.: Design and Implementation of Apla→C# Automatic Program Conversion System. Jiangxi Normal University Library, Nanchang (2004)
21. Shi, H.H.: Apla-Java Automatic Program Conversion System Supporting Generic Programming. Jiangxi Normal University Library, Nanchang (2004)
22. Xue, J., Zheng, Y., Qimin, H., You, Z., Xie, W., Cheng, Z.: PAR: a practicable formal method and its supporting platform. In: Sun, J., Sun, M. (eds.) Formal Methods and Software Engineering: 20th International Conference on Formal Engineering Methods, ICFEM 2018, Gold Coast, QLD, Australia, 12−16 November 2018, Proceedings, pp. 70–86. Springer International Publishing, Cham (2018). https://doi.org/10.1007/978-3-030-02450-5_5
23. Dijkstra, E.W.: A Discipline of programming. Prentice Hall, New Jersey (1976)

Model Checking

An Unified Model Checking Approach of APTL

Haiyang Wang[✉]

Xi'an University of Technology, Xi'an, China
hywang@xaut.edu.cn

Abstract. This paper investigates an unified model checking procedure for Alternating Projection Temporal Logic (APTL) based on automaton. The method for transforming an APTL formula to an alternating Büchi automaton over Concurrent Game structure (BCG) has been illustrated. The algorithm for the product of two BCGs is presented in this paper. In addition, the APTL model checking algorithm for open system is given and examples are also presented to illustrate how the procedure works.

Keywords: Model checking · APTL · BCG · Open system

1 Introduction

Model checking [1,2] is an automatic technique for verifying the properties of concurrent systems, where the formalized representation of systems is specified by temporal logic formulas, and the process of model checking depends on efficient and flexible algorithms of reachability problem based on graph theory. Model checking technique has attracted great attention from universal scholars and has got a rapid development. Model checking has been widely used in various fields of society, such as circuit design and protocol verification, etc. [3–6].

The properties of system are formally described by temporal logic formulas, so temporal logic plays a vital role in model checking. Alternating temporal logic (ATL) [7] is a temporal logic, which is proposed by Alur and he used it to verify the properties of reactive systems, as well as it regards the interactive process of a reactive system as a game process between an open system and its environment. Proposition projection temporal logic (PPTL) [8] can conveniently describe the properties of finite and infinite state paths. PPTL formulas are simple and intuitive, and can express completely regular properties; PPTL plays an important role in the field of model checking. Alternating projection temporal logic (APTL) [9,10] is an extended logic of PPTL, it is able to not only express properties specified in classical temporal logic LTL, but also express interval related sequential and periodical properties, as well as express game related properties of open systems and multi-agent systems.

This research is supported by the NSFC Grant No. 413619001.

J. Xue et al. (Eds.): SOFL+MSVL 2020, LNCS 12723, pp. 69–78, 2021.
https://doi.org/10.1007/978-3-030-77474-5_5

With the motivation that to complete the APTL model checking fully automatically. We have illustrated the logic laws of APTL and the algorithms of transforming APTL formula to a BCG [11]. Also, an improved method for checking the satisfiability of APTL formulas has been presented [12]. The symbolic model checking of APTL has been designed [10]. In this paper, the algorithm for the product method of two BCG is presented and an unified model checking approach of APTL based on BCGs is also illustrated. Finally, a case study is presented to illustrate how the procedure works.

The next section introduces some fundamental essentials. Section 3, the approach of product construction of BCGs is given, furthermore, the algorithm for the APTL model checking is also presented. A case study is presented in Sect. 3.2. Finally, conclusions are drawn in Sect. 4.

2 Preliminaries

In order to express my scientific research work explicitly, in this section the primary issues are expound clearly.

2.1 Alternating Projection Temporal Logic

APTL Syntax. The temporal logic alternating interval based temporal logics are defined with respect to a finite set $\mathcal{P}$ of atomic propositions and a finite set $\mathcal{A}$ of agents. The formula of PPTL is given by the following grammar:

$$P ::= p \mid \neg P \mid P \vee Q \mid \bigcirc_{\ll A\gg} P \mid (P_1, \cdots, P_m)prj_{\ll A\gg}Q$$

where $p \in \mathcal{P}$, $P_1, \ldots, P_m$, P and Q are all well-formed APTL formulas. The operator $\ll\gg$ is a path quantifier, and $\bigcirc_{\ll A\gg}$ (next) and $prj_{\ll A\gg}$ (projection) [8–10] are basic temporal operators with path quantifier, that the path quantifiers are parameterized by set of agents.

APTL Semantics. The notation of Concurrent Game Structures (CGS) for using interval based temporal logics. A Concurrent Game Structure (CGS) is defined by $C = (\mathcal{P}, \mathcal{A}, S, s_0, l, \Delta, \tau)$, the detail issues are represented in paper [7,11]. Following the definition of CGSs, we define a state s over $\mathcal{P}$ to be a mapping from $\mathcal{P}$ to $B = \{true, false\}$, $s : \mathcal{P} \rightarrow B$. A computation $\lambda(s)$ starting from a state s in a concurrent game structure satisfies the APTL formula P, denoted by $\lambda(s) \models P$.

A computation $\lambda = s_0, s_1, \ldots$ is a non-empty sequence of states, which can be finite or infinite. The length, $|\lambda|$, of λ is ω if λ is infinite, and the number of states minus 1 if λ is finite. To have a uniform notation for both finite and infinite intervals, we will use extended integers as indices. That is, we consider the set N_0 of non-negative integers and ω, $N_\omega = N_0 \cup \omega$, and extend the comparison operators, $=$, $<$, $\leq$, to N_ω by considering $\omega = \omega$, and for all $i \in N_0$, $i < \omega$. Moreover, we define $\preceq$ as $\leq -\{(\omega, \omega)\}$. Let Γ denotes the set of all computations.

For any computation $\lambda \in \Gamma$ and indexes $0 \leq i \leq j \preceq |\lambda|$ we use $\lambda[i]$, $\lambda[0, i]$, $\lambda[i, |\lambda|]$, and $\lambda[i, j]$ to denote the i-th state in λ, the finite prefix $s_0, s_1, \ldots, s_i$ of λ, the suffix $s_i, s_{i+1}, \ldots$ of λ, and an interval $s_i, \ldots, s_j$ of λ respectively.

Let $\lambda = s_0, s_1, \ldots$ be a computation, and $r_1, \ldots, r_k$ be integers ($h \geq 1$) such that $0 = r \leq \ldots \leq r_h \preceq |\lambda|$. The projection of λ onto $r_1, \ldots, r_h$ is the computation, $\lambda \downarrow (r_1, \ldots, r_h) = s_{t_1}, s_{t_2}, \ldots, s_{t_l}$ where $t_1, \ldots, t_l$ are obtained from $r_1, \ldots, r_h$ by deleting all duplicates. That is, $t_1, \ldots, t_l$ is the longest strictly increasing subsequence of $r_1, \ldots, r_h$. For example, $s_0, s_1, s_2, s_3, s_4 \downarrow (0, 0, 2, 2, 2, 3) = s_0, s_2, s_3$.

The satisfaction relation ($\models$) is inductively defined as follows:

- $\lambda(s) \models p$ for propositions $p \in \mathcal{P}$, iff $p \in l(s)$.
- $\lambda(s) \models \neg P$, iff $\lambda(s) \not\models P$.
- $\lambda(s) \models P \vee Q$, iff $\lambda(s) \models P$ or $\lambda(s) \models Q$.
- $\lambda(s) \models \bigcirc_{\ll A \gg} P$ iff $|\lambda(s)| \geq 2$, and there exists a strategy f_A for the agents in A, such that $\lambda(s) \in out(s, f_A)$, and $\lambda(s)[1, |\lambda|] \models P$.
- $\lambda(s) \models (P_1, \ldots, P_m) prj_{\ll A \gg} Q$ iff there exists a strategy f_A for the agents in A, and $\lambda(s) \in out(s, f_A)$, and integers $0 = r_0 \leq r_1 \leq \ldots \leq r_m \leq |\lambda(s)|$ such that $\lambda(s)[r_{i-1}, r_i] \models P_i$, $0 < i \leq m$ and $\lambda \models Q$ for one of the following λ:
  (a) $r_m < |\lambda(s)|$ and $\lambda = \lambda(s) \downarrow (r_0, \ldots, r_m) \cdot \lambda(s)[r_m + 1, \ldots, |\lambda(s)|]$ or
  (b) $r_m = |\lambda(s)|$ and $\lambda = \lambda(s) \downarrow (r_0, \ldots, r_m)$ for some $0 \leq h \leq m$.

Note that these path quantifiers. As special cases, $\ll A \gg$ and $\ll \phi \gg$ corresponds to existential $\exists$ and universal $\forall$ path quantification, respectively. When $\mathcal{A} = \phi$, the APTL formulas are in fct PPTL formulas. As the dual of $\ll \gg$, we use $[[]]$, defined by $[[A]] \overset{\text{def}}{=} \ll \mathcal{A} \backslash A \gg$.

2.2 From APTL Formulas to BCGs

An APTL formula can be transformed into a BCG [9,12]. The details of the procedure is shown in Fig. 1. Firstly, lexical analysis of APTL formula ϕ, and then construct the syntax tree. Secondly, we make preprocess to eliminate all implications, equivalence, double negations, skip, len(n), $\Diamond$ in formula ϕ. Thirdly, we construct labeled normal form graph (LNFG) according to the normal form of formula ϕ, then transform the LNFG to a generalized alternating Büchi automaton over concurrent game structure (GBCG). Finally, the BCG is developed from the obtained GBCG.

3 Model Checking for APTL

3.1 Model Checking Algorithm for APTL

In the following, we provide an unified model checking algorithm for APTL formulas. The algorithm used for checking whether an APTL formula P is satisfied by a CGS s. The method is relies on a reduction procedure that a certain product construction of the BCG for the system s with the BCG for the APTL formula P.

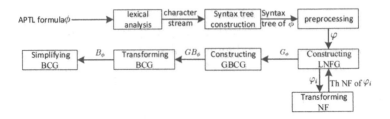

Fig. 1. The transformation process of an APTL formula to BCG.

Definition 1. *Product of the system automata BCG and the property automata BCG. For the system automata BCG $B_1 = (\mathcal{P}, \mathcal{A}, Q_1, Q_{01}, \delta_1, F_1)$ and the BCG for the complement property is $B_2 = (\mathcal{P}, \mathcal{A}, Q_2, Q_{02}, \delta_2, F_2)$, the product automata $B = B_1 \otimes B_2 = (\mathcal{P}, \mathcal{A}, Q_1 \times Q_2, Q_{01} \times Q_{02}, \delta, F)$ where δ is*

$$\frac{q_1 \xrightarrow[\ll A_1 \gg]{P_1}{}_{\delta_1} q_1' \wedge q_2 \xrightarrow[\ll A_2 \gg]{P_2}{}_{\delta_2} q_2'}{(q_1, q_2) \xrightarrow[(\ll A_1 \gg, \ll A_2 \gg)]{(P_1, P_2)}{}_{\delta} (q_1', q_2')}$$

where $P_1 \wedge P_2 \neq false$ and $F = \{f_i | f_i = (q_{1i}, q_{2i}), q_{1i} \in F_1$ and $A_1 \wedge A_2 \neq \phi$ or $q_{1i} \in F_1 \wedge q_{2i} \in F_2\}$.

It follows that if the product automata B is empty then the system automata B_1 satisfy the formula P, where B_2 is the automata of the complement to formula P. That is to say the system satisfy formula P.

As a result, the skeleton in Algorithm 1 can be used to check whether the CGS S satisfies the APTL formula P.

3.2 A Case Study

Security protocols are excellent case studies for the techniques we have illustrated the model checking techniques. We considering the two-party contract signing scenario, the ASW (Asokan-Shoup-Waidner) [13–15] protocol as the verifying system.

In two-party contract signing, both players have initially agreed on some contract text. A valid contract consists of nonrepudiation tokens on the contract text by each player. A fair contract signing protocol must ensure that either both players end up with contracts or neither does. The contract signing procedure is shown as the Fig. 2.

Algorithm 1. Model-checking algorithm for APTL formula

Input: an CGS S and an APTL formula P

Output: true if the product automata of the system automata and the property
automata is empty. Otherwise false plus a counterexample for P.

$B_1 =$ BCG(S); /*construct the BCG of system S*/
$N =$ NF(P); /*transform P to its normal form*/
$CN =$ CONF(N); /*rewrite N as complete normal form*/
$NN =$ NEG(CN); /*obtain the negation formula's normal form*/
$G =$ LNFG(NN); /*construct the LNFG of the negation formula*/
$GB =$ GBCG(G); /*obtain the GBCG of the negation formula*/
$B'_2 =$ GBTB(GB); /*transform the GBCG to BCG*/
$B_2 =$ SIMPLIFY(B_2);/*simplify the BCG*/
if B_2 is not empty **then**
    $B = B_1 \otimes B_2$;
else return *true*;
$B' =$ SIMPLIFY(B); /*simplify the product BCG*/
if B' is *empty* **then**
    return *true*;
else return *false* and a counterpath.

We model the ASW protocol as bellow. The set of agents is $P = \{A, B, T, C\}$, A is the Originator, B is the Recipient, T is the third party and C is the channel. Now we introduce the atomic propositions, X_m_i: agent X has obtained message m_i; A_a_1: agent A has generate the abort message a_1; B_{quit}: B decides to give up, then the protocol run terminates simply; $C/T\_A.a_1$: agent C or T has received the abort request; A/B_r_1: agent A or B has generates the resolve message, in order to send the resolve request to the agent T; $C/T\_A/B.r_1$: agent C or T has received the resolve request that send by agent A or B; $X\_TY.aborted$: agent X has obtained the aborted message that the abort request is raised by the agent Y; $X\_TY.resolved$: agent X has obtained the resolved message that the resolve request is raised by the agent Y; $A\_contract$: agent A has received the valid contract; $B\_contract$: agent B has received the valid contract; *aborted*: the contract signing procedure has been aborted; *resolved*: the agent A or B has obtained the valid contract via sends the resolve request to the agent T.

The model of the ASW protocol is shown as Fig. 3. Now we verify two properties of the ASW protocol. A fair contract signing protocol must ensure that either both players end up with valid contracts or neither does. We verify whether the model contains the situation that agent B obtained valid contract but agent A does not obtained finally. The property is formally as an APTL formula: $\neg\Diamond_{<B,C,T>}(B\_contract \wedge \neg\Diamond_{\ll A\gg}A\_contract)$. The BCG of the APTL formula is shown as Fig. 4.

Main protocol:

$$\begin{array}{lll}
 & A \qquad\qquad\qquad\qquad\qquad\qquad B & \\
\text{M1} & \xrightarrow{\ m_1 = Sig_A(A,B,T,t,h(N_A))\ } give\ up?\ quit & \text{M1} \\
\text{M2 } give\ up?\ Abort & \xleftarrow{\ m_2 = Sig_B(h(m_1),\ h(N_B))\ } & \text{M2} \\
\text{M3} & \xrightarrow{\quad m_3 = N_A \quad} \qquad give\ up?\ Resolve & \text{M3} \\
\text{M4 } give\ up?\ Resolve & \xleftarrow{\quad m_4 = N_B \quad} & \text{M4}
\end{array}$$

Abort protocol:

$$\begin{array}{ll}
\quad A \qquad\qquad\qquad\qquad\qquad T & \\
\text{A1} \qquad \xrightarrow{\ a_1 = Sig_A(abort,\ m_1)\ } & if\ resolved(m_1) \\
 & then\ a_2 := Sig_T(m_1,\ m_2) \\
 & else\ aborted(m_1) := T \\
 & \qquad a_2 := Sig_T(aborted,\ a_1) \\
\text{A2} \qquad\qquad\qquad \xleftarrow{\quad a_2 \quad} &
\end{array}$$

Resolve protocol:

$$\begin{array}{ll}
\quad A\ or\ B \qquad\qquad\qquad\qquad T & \\
\text{R1} \qquad \xrightarrow{\ r_1 = (m_1, m_2)\ } & if\ aborted(m_1) \\
 & then\ r_2 := Sig_T(aborted,\ a_1) \\
 & else\ resolved(m_1) := T \\
 & \qquad r_2 := Sig_T(m_1,\ m_2) \\
\text{R2} \qquad\qquad\qquad \xleftarrow{\quad r_2 \quad} &
\end{array}$$

Fig. 2. ASW protocol

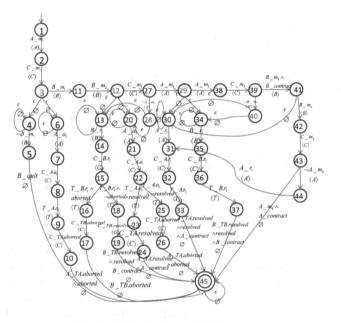

Fig. 3. BCG S of the ASW protocol

Then we calculate the product of the system model and the property BCG as the Definition 1 illustrated. The product BCG of the ASW protocol BCG S and the property BCG G_1 is show in Fig. 5. Then we simplifying the BCG G_1' as the algorithm SIMPLIFY illustrated. We obtained the conclusion that

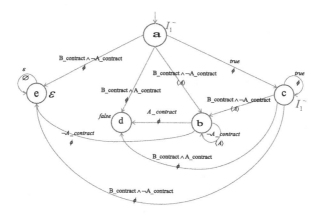

Fig. 4. The BCG G_1 of $\diamond_{<B,C,T>}(B\_contract \wedge \neg \diamond_{\ll A \gg} A\_contract)$, the node a denote the APTL formula $true;_{<B,C,T>} (B\_contract \wedge \neg \diamond_{\ll A \gg} A\_contract)$, b denote $\neg(true;_{\ll A \gg} A\_contract)$, c denote $true;_{<B,C,T>} (B\_contract \wedge \neg \diamond_{\ll A \gg} A\_contract)$, d denote $false$, e denote ε, the accepting set is $F = \{b, e\}$

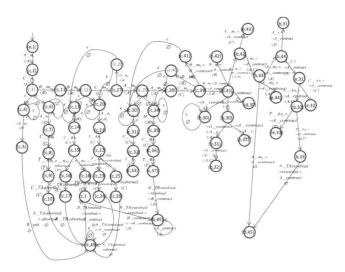

Fig. 5. The BCG G_1 of $S \times G_1$

the product BCG is *empty*, viz, the ASW protocol satisfy the APTL formula $\neg\diamond_{<B,C,T>}(B\_contract \wedge \neg\diamond_{\ll A \gg}A\_contract)$. The other property is formally expressed by APTL formula as $\neg\diamond_{<B,C,T>}(B\_contract \wedge \diamond_{\ll A \gg}A\_contract)$. The BCG G_2 of the formula is shown in Fig. 6. The product BCG G'_2 is calculated as the Definition 1 shows and illustrated in Fig. 7. Then we simplifying the BCG G'_2 as the algorithm SIMPLIFY illustrated. After simplify the G'_2 we obtained the BCG as the Fig. 8 shows. Obviously, the product BCG is not empty, i.e., the ASW protocol is not satisfy the APTL formula

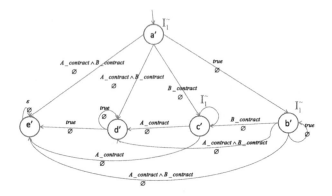

Fig. 6. The BCG G_2 of $\Diamond_{<B,C,T>}(B\_contract \wedge \Diamond_{\ll A\gg}A\_contract)$, the node a' denote the APTL formula $true;_{<B,C,T>}(B\_contract \wedge \Diamond_{\ll A\gg}A\_contract)$, b' denote $true;_{<B,C,T>}(B\_contract \wedge \Diamond_{\ll A\gg}A\_contract)$, c' denote $true;_{\ll A\gg}A\_contract$, d' denote $true$ and e' denote ε. The accepting set $F = \{d', e'\}$

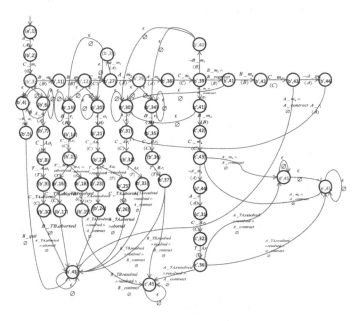

Fig. 7. The product BCG G_2' of $S \times G_2$

$\neg\Diamond_{<B,C,T>}(B\_contract \wedge \Diamond_{\ll A\gg}A\_contract)$. From the above two example, we illustrated the APTL formula model checking procedure perfectly. By our experience, the decision procedures given in this paper are indispensable for complete the model checking procedure automatically.

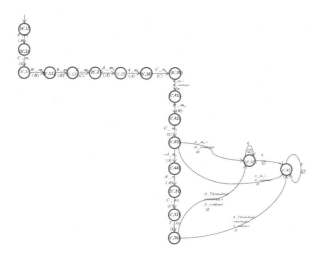

Fig. 8. The simplifying BCG, $F = \{[d', 45], [e', 45]\}$

4   Conclusion

To specify and verify open systems, we provide the unified APTL model checking algorithm based on BCGs. And a case study is also presented to illustrate the whole process. In the future, we will further investigate and improve the method.

References

1. Baier, C., Katoen, J.-P.: Principles of Model Checking. MIT Press, Cambridge (2008)
2. Burch, J.R., Clarke, E.M., McMillan, K.L., Dill, D.L., Hwang, L.-J.: Symbolic model checking: 1020 states and beyond. Inf. Comput. **98**(2), 142–170 (1992)
3. Cui, J., Duan, Z., Tian, C., Hongwei, D.: A novel approach to modeling and verifying real-time systems for high reliability. IEEE Trans. Reliab. **67**(2), 481–493 (2018)
4. Yu, B., Duan, Z., Tian, C., Zhang, N.: Verifying temporal properties of programs: a parallel approach. J. Parallel Distrib. Comput. **118**, 89–99 (2018)
5. Albert, E., Gmez-Zamalloa, M., Isabel, M., Rubio, A., Sammartino, M., Silva, A.: Actor-based model checking for Software-Defined Networks. J. Log. Algebraic Methods Program. **118**, 100617 (2021)
6. Yu, C.-M., Tala't, M., Shen, L.-H., Feng, K.-T.: A multi-objective model checking for transmission policy optimization in hybrid powered small cell networks. IEEE Access **8**, 71339–71352 (2020)
7. Alur, R., Henzinger, T.A., Kupferman, O.: Alternating-time temporal logic. J. ACM **49**(5), 672–713 (2002)
8. Duan, Z., Tian, C., Zhang, N.: A canonical form based decision procedure and model checking approach for propositional projection temporal logic. Theor. Comput. Sci. **609**, 544560 (2016)

9. Tian, C., Duan, Z.: Model checking open systems with alternating projection temporal logic. Theor. Comput. Sci. **774**, 65–81 (2019)
10. Wang, H., Duan, Z., Tian, C.: Model checking multi-agent systems with APTL. Ad Hoc Sens. Wirel. Networks **37**(1–4), 35–52 (2017)
11. Tian, C., Duan, Z.: Alternating interval based temporal logics. In: Dong, J.S., Zhu, H. (eds.) ICFEM 2010. LNCS, vol. 6447, pp. 694–709. Springer, Heidelberg (2010). https://doi.org/10.1007/978-3-642-16901-4_45
12. Wang, H.Y., Duan, Z.H., Tian, C.: Tool for checking satisfiability of APTL formulas. Ruan Jian Xue Bao/J. Softw. **29**(6), 1635–1646 (2018). (in Chinese)
13. Kremer, S., Raskin, J.-F.: Game analysis of abuse-free contract signing. In: 15th IEEE Computer Security Foundations Workshop. Proceedings. IEEE (2002)
14. Asokan, N., Shoup, V., Waidner, M.: Asynchronous protocols for optimistic fair exchange. In: 1998 IEEE Symposium on Security and Privacy. Proceedings. IEEE (1998)
15. Slanina, M., Sipma, H.B., Manna, Z.: Deductive verification of alternating systems. Formal Aspects Comput. **20**(4–5), 507–560 (2008)

Model Checking Multi-interruption Concurrent Programs with TMSVL

Jin Cui and Lianxiang Zhu[✉]

Xi'an Shiyou University, 710071 Xi'an, People's Republic of China

Abstract. Concurrent programs are commonly used in real-time system software. Verifying the correctness of concurrent programs is an important job to ensure the reliability of real-time system software. The causes of concurrency in a real-time system program include task scheduling and interrupt mechanism, where multi-interruption is an effective means of real-time response to asynchronous events. This paper studies the modeling approach for multi-interruption concurrent programs based on TMSVL (Timed Modeling, Simulation and Verification Language), so as to verify temporal properties of multi-interruption concurrent programs, such as safety and liveness properties. The formal syntax and semantics of multi-interruption concurrent programs is established based on TMSVL, and the correctness and practicability of our approach is demonstrated with a case study.

Keywords: Model checking · Concurrent programs · Multi-interruption · Formal verification

1 Introduction

Real-time system software is widely used in safety-critical systems such as unmanned vehicle, aerospace, nuclear industry and so on. It is significant to ensure the reliability of real-time system software. Interrupt is an effective means for real-time systems to respond to asynchronous events timely, and it is one of the major factors causing concurrent execution of programs. The causes of concurrency also include multitasking (threads) scheduling, thread blocking, etc. Since interrupt events can occur at any time and preempt the executing program, it will lead to a large number of concurrent interleaving execution traces of programs, thus causing unpredictable system error behaviors [1]. It is a challenge task to ensure the correctness of multi-interruption concurrent programs (namely the programs that contain responses to interrupt events).

Formal verification uses strict mathematical methods to prove whether a system satisfies desired properties and find errors, especially potential hazards that cannot be found by testing [2]. Theorem proving and model checking are

This research is supported by Shaanxi provincial key research and development program No. 2020GY-038.

J. Xue et al. (Eds.): SOFL+MSVL 2020, LNCS 12723, pp. 79–87, 2021.
https://doi.org/10.1007/978-3-030-77474-5_6

two important methods in formal verification. Model checking [3] proposed by Clarke et al., winner of the Turing Award, verifies whether the system satisfies the desired property by traversing the state space of the model and searching counter-example, which can be carried out automatically without manual intervention.

In recent years, there have been some researches on modeling and verification of multi-interruption concurrent systems. In literature [4], a framework based on the theorem proving tool Coq for verifying the preemptive operating system kernel with multi-interruption was designed. The framework is applied to the functional correctness verification of key modules of the μC/OS-II scheduler, interrupt handler, message queue, mutex semaphores and so on. Based on the compositional framework, literature [5] introduces device drivers and interruptions into the kernel layer to verify the functional correctness of the operating system kernel. Literature [6] models interrupt-driven systems with timed Petri net. By transforming the timed Petri net model into timed automata, the invariant properties are verified by symbolic coding and SMT solver based bounded model checking approach. Literature [7] defines the formal language iDola for modeling multi-interruption mechanisms in embedded systems. With the language iDola, the interrupt driven systems are modeled in a declaration manner, and the temporal properties of LTL (Linear Temporal Logic) and CTL (Computation Tree Logic) are verified using timed automata based approach. Literature [8] defines the formal semantics for multi-interruption programs with a new modeling language. The modeling language can model the main program and interrupt handlers, it describes the time information by means of predicate function. The modeling language provides an effective method for modeling the interrupt behavior of multi-interruption systems and for making time analysis. Literature [9] generates a formal model for interrupt processing systems using fixed-length bit vectors, and proposes a SMT-based bounded model checking approach for interrupt processing systems. Literature [10] proposes interrupt sequence diagram (ISD) to model interrupt systems. ISD is extended from UML sequence diagram by designing special interaction segments for priority-based preemptable interrupt handlers. For the verification purpose, the authors defines the ISD semantics based on automata, thus using reachability analysis of hybrid automata theory for ISD model checking.

To verify the interruption concurrent systems, the theorem proof approach mainly focuses on the functional correctness, but rarely verifies the temporal properties, while the model checking approach is effective in verifying temporal properties described by LTL and CTL. However, LTL and CTL are difficult to describe periodicity and interval related properties [11–13]. This paper studies the modeling approach of multi-interruption concurrent programs based on TMSVL (Timed Modeling, Simulation and Verification Language) [14], so as to verify the safety, liveness, timeliness, and other temporal properties of multi-interruption concurrent programs with unified model checking approach based on TMSVL [15]. The verification approach in this paper uses the property formula [16] to describe the desired property, which has full regular expressiveness and can describe the interval-related properties and periodic properties.

The remainder of the paper is organized as follows. The next section gives an introduction to our model checking approach. In Sect. 3, we show the modeling approach for multi-interruption concurrent programs with TMSVL. In Sect. 4, a case study is presented to illustrate the application of our approach to modeling and verifying of multi-interruption concurrent programs. Finally, conclusions and future work are drawn in Sect. 5.

2   Model Checking Approach

With our verification approach, the system to be verified is modeled by the TMSVL program M, and the desired property is specified with formula ϕ. Both of them are defined based on TPTL (Timed Projection Temporal Logic), and their definitions can be seen in [14]. The model checking approach is shown in Fig. 1. In the verification process, we need to transform M into its normal form, then construct normal form graph (NFG) for M. The definitions of normal form for TMSVL program M is shown in Definition 1.

Definition 1 (Normal form). *A TMSVL program M is in its normal form if it is of the following form:*

$$M \equiv \bigvee_{i=1}^{l_1} M_{ei} \wedge empty \vee \bigvee_{j=1}^{l_2} M_{cj} \wedge \bigcirc M_{fj}$$

where $l_1 + l_2 \geq 1$ and the following hold:
1) M_{fj} is a TMSVL program.
2) Each of M_{ei} and M_{cj} is either true or a state formula of the form $w_1 \wedge \ldots \wedge w_m$ ($m \geq 1$) such that $w_1, \ldots, w_m$ are either $v = e$, or p_v, or $\neg p_v$ (v is a variable, e denotes the value of v, and p_v is an atomic proposition).

The normal form graph describes the state space of the system M and presents the model satisfying the program M. For M, its NFG is a directed graph G, $G = (CL, EL)$, where CL represents a set of nodes and EL represents a set of edges. In CL, each node is represented by a TMSVL program, while in EL, each edge is a triplet (q, pe, r) from node q to node r and marked with the state formula pe.

In the verification process, we make state reduction for TMSVL program M, mainly by transforming M to the normal form, transform the negative of the property ϕ, namely $\neg \phi$ to normal form, and construct NFG for $M \wedge \neg \phi$. In the process of constructing NFG for $M \wedge \neg \phi$, we need to judge whether there exists an acceptable path. If there is no acceptable path, it indicates that M satisfies ϕ; otherwise M violates ϕ, and a counterexample path is found.

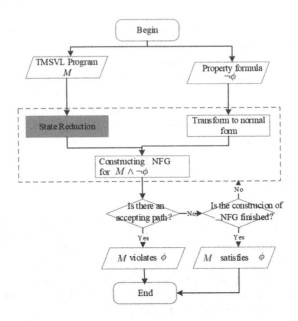

Fig. 1. Model checking approach for multi-interruption concurrent programs

3 Modeling Concurrent Programs with Interruption Using TMSVL

3.1 Modeling Single-Interruption Concurrent Programs

To facilitate establishing the formal model and semantics of interrupt concurrency, we analyze the behavior of single-interruption concurrent programs with an example. Figure 2 shows an execution scenario for a single-interruption program. The dark blue rectangle indicates that the main program is executing, and the light blue rectangle indicates that the interrupt handler $isrA$ is executing. We can see that during the execution of the main program, the interrupt handler may be preempted by $isrA$ in response to an external event. While $isrA$ is not preempted during execution, actually $isrA$ always executes sequentially.

Fig. 2. An execution scenario of single-interruption

In TMSVL, the statement Q when (b, r) do H denoted as N_1 is used to model the single-interruption concurrent program. In N_1, Q stands for the main program, b is a boolean variable recording whether to respond to an interrupt request or not, r is a propositional argument indicating whether the main program has finished execution, and H is an interrupt handler. In [14], the single interrupt semantics based on TPTL is proposed and is defined as follows:

$$Q \; when(b, r) \; do \; H \stackrel{\mathrm{def}}{=}$$
$$(((if(b)then\{H\}else \; skip \;)^{\circledast}, r \wedge \varepsilon) \; \mathsf{prj} \; (Q; r \wedge \varepsilon)) \wedge halt(r)$$

Its semantics are mainly defined by the projection operator (prj). Its semantics can be described by the semantic graph as shown in Fig. 3.

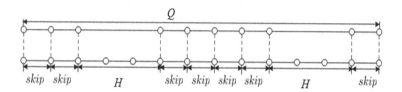

Fig. 3. The interval graph of $Q \; when(b, r) \; do \; H$

3.2 Modeling Multi-interruption Concurrent Programs

To model concurrent programs with multi-interruption, we take a concurrent system with two interruptions as an example, the execution scenario is shown in Fig. 4. The two interrupt handlers are $isr A$ and $isr B$, $isr A$ has a lower priority, while $isr B$ has a higher priority. In Fig. 4, during the execution of the main program, the cases where nested execution of interruption, single-interruption sequential execution and multi-interruption sequential execution are included. We define N_n for multi-interruption concurrent programs by extending the single-interruption model N_1. N_n can effectively describe various possible concurrent situations of multi-interrupt concurrent programs, including nested execution of interruptions, sequential executions of single-interruption and multi-interruption, thus automatically verify temporal properties of multi-interruption concurrent programs (such as safety, liveness, timeliness, etc.).

The syntax of N_n is $Q \; when(b[0]or...Orb[n-1], r)do \; R(rq, b, H, p, n)$, where Q is the main program; b is a boolean array, $b[i]$ indicates whether to respond to interrupt requests i, if $b[i]$ is $true$, the interrupt request i can be responded, otherwise, it will not be responded; r is a propositional variable; $H[i]$ is the interrupt handler for interrupt request i: p is a boolean array, and $p[i]$ stands for whether the execution of interrupt handler $H[i]$ terminates. $R(rq, b, H, p, n)$ (R for short) describes the preemption of the main program by the n interrupt

■ Interrupt handler *isr A* is executing
■ Interrupt handler *isr B* is executing
■ The main program *Main* is executing

Nested execution of   a sequential execution   sequential executions
multi-interrupt   of a single interrupt   of multi-interrupt

Main

isr A   *iret A*   *isr B*   *iret B*   *isr B*   *iret A*

isr B   *iret B*   *isr B* ends, *isr A* starts

Fig. 4. An execution scenario of multi-interruption concurrency

requests. Actually, N_n is equivalent to the TPTL formula $(((if\,(b[0] \vee b[1] \vee \ldots \vee b[n-1])\ then\ \{R\}\ else\ \{skip\})^*, r)\ prj\ (Q; r)) \wedge halt(r)$.

The semantics of N_n can be described by the interval graph shown in Fig. 5. The interval graph is a projection structure with the top and the bottom intervals ending simultaneously. Each sub-interval in Q (constituted by two consecutive states of Q) corresponds to *skip* or R in N_n on the bottom interval. If it corresponds to *skip*, it means that the two states in Q have not been interrupted and there is no concurrency between them. Otherwise the two states are interrupted by interrupt handlers, and there are start and end states of interrupt handlers between them, which constitutes the concurrent executions of the system.

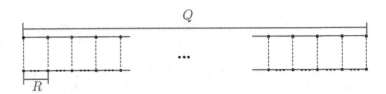

Fig. 5. The semantics diagram of N_n

Since there is preemption during the execution of the interrupt handler, there is still concurrency caused by interrupt sequential execution and interrupt nested execution in R. We need to recursively use the N_n structure to model the concurrency among interrupt handlers. Assume that the interrupt requests are $rq[0], \ldots, rq[n-1]$ and their priorities decrease in turn, then $R(rq, b, H, p, n)$ can be defined by the TMSVL program below:

$if\ (\neg rq[0] \wedge \ldots \wedge \neg rq[n-2] \wedge rq[n-1])\ then$
$H[n-1]\ when(p[n-1], b[0] \vee \ldots \vee b[n-2])\ do\ R(rq, b, H, p, n-1) \wedge$

$if\ (\neg rq[0] \wedge \ldots \wedge \neg rq[n-3] \wedge rq[n-2])\ then$
$H[n-2]\ when(p[n-2], b[0] \vee \ldots \vee b[n-3])\ do\ R(rq, b, H, p, n-2) \wedge$

$\ldots \wedge$
$if\ (rq[0])\ then\ H[0]$

4 A Case Study

Figure 6 shows an example program composed of the function main(), interrupt handlers ISR1() and ISR2(). The main function performs the division operation only when x is strictly less than y. ISR1() increases x by 1 and ISR2() decreases y by 1. Assume ISR1() is triggered by external event a_0, ISR2() is triggered by external event a_1, and a_0 has a higher priority than a_1. As a case study, we verify the safety property that the divisor in main() never equals to 0. Thus, we can use the multi-interruption structure N_n and TMSVL language to model the above instance, property formula to describe the desired property. Further, we utilize the TMSVL interpreter to verify whether the property is valid or not automatically.

The global variables and main function	The interrupt handlers

int x=0,y=1000,z;	void ISR1(){
	x++;
	return;
	}

void main(){
  while(x<y){
  z=1/(x-y);
  }
}
	void ISR2(){
	y--;
	return;
	}

Fig. 6. A design instance of the multi-interruption program

To model the above instance, let the TMSVL model of the design instance be M, the main function be Q, ISR1 be $H[0]$ and ISR2 be $H[1]$. Additionally, we use Dc to denote the global variable definition module, boolean variables $rq[0]$ and $rq[1]$ denote whether interrupt events a_0 and a_1 occur or not, respectively. Thus, M can be defined in TMSVL as follows:

Dc	Q

frame(x,y,z,iEv) and
int x<==0 and
int y<== 1000 and
int iEv[2], z and
skip
	while(x<y)
	{ if(iEv[0]=0 and iEv[1]=0)
	then{z=1/(x-y);}
	else{skip}
	}

H[0]	**H[1]**
x:=x+1; iEv[0]:=0 and skip	y:=y-1 ; iEv[1]:=0 and skip

Fig. 7. The TMSVL programs of the modules $Dc, Q, H[0]$ and $H[1]$

$$M \stackrel{\text{def}}{=} Dc; Q \ when(b[0] \ or \ b[1], r)do \ R(rq, b, H, p, 2)$$

$$R(rq, b, H, p, 2) \stackrel{\text{def}}{=} if \ \neg re[0] \wedge re[1] \ then \ H[1] \ when(b[0], p[1])do \ R(rq, b, H, p, 1) \ and$$
$$if \ re[0] \ then \ H[0] \ and$$
$$if \ \neg re[0] \wedge \neg re[1] \ then \ skip$$

$$R(rq, b, H, p, 1) \stackrel{\text{def}}{=} if \ b[0] \ then \ H[0] \ else \ skip$$

where Dc, Q, $H[0]$, and $H[1]$ are defined in Fig. 7, respectively. Specifically, the global variables in M consists of program variables x, y, z as well as the introduced variables iEv, a boolean arrays of size 2. iEv represents that whether interrupt events a_0 and a_1 occur, when the execution of interrupt handlers completes, the corresponding element in iEv is set to 0.

The desired property can be expressed by the property formula $\Box(x \neq y)$. The property is violated when main() is executed into the while loop, the statement $z = 1/(x - y)$ is about to be executed, while the interrupt handler makes $x = y$.

5 Conclusion

In this paper, the single-interruption structure of TMSVL is extended to model multi-interruption concurrent programs, so that we can model multi-interruption concurrent programs using the extended TMSVL, and temporal properties of multi-interruption concurrent programs, such as safety and liveness can be verified by the unified model checking approach. In the future, we will study the application of the approach in modeling and verification of real-time operating systems on the one hand; we will also study how to mitigate the state space explosion that occurs during the verification of multi-interrupt concurrent programs on the other hand.

References

1. Wu, X., Chen, L., et al.: Numerical static analysis of interrupt-driven programs via sequentialization. In: 2015 International Conference on Embedded Software (EMSOFT), pp. 55–64 (2015)
2. Wing, J.M.: A specifier's introduction to formal methods. Computer **23**(9), 8–22 (1990)
3. Graf, S.: Design and synthesis of synchronization skeletons using branching time logic (1984)
4. Xu, F., Fu, M., Feng, X., Zhang, X., Zhang, H., Li, Z.: A practical verification framework for Preemptive OS kernels. In: Chaudhuri, S., Farzan, A. (eds.) CAV 2016. LNCS, vol. 9780, pp. 59–79. Springer, Cham (2016). https://doi.org/10.1007/978-3-319-41540-6_4
5. Hao, C., Wu, N., et al.: Toward compositional verification of interruptible OS kernels and device drivers. J. Autom. Reasoning **51**(6), 1–49 (2017)
6. Hou, G., Zhou, K., et al.: Interrupt modeling and verification for embedded systems based on time petri nets. Comput. Sci. **8299**(66), 62–76 (2014)
7. Liu, H., Zhang, H., et al.: IDola: bridge modeling to verification and implementation of interrupt-driven systems. In: Theoretical Aspects of Software Engineering Conference (2014)
8. Huang, Y., He, J., Zhu, H., Zhao, Y., Shi, J., Qin, S.: Semantic theories of programs with nested interrupts. Front. Comput. Sci. **9**(3), 331–345 (2015). https://doi.org/10.1007/s11704-015-3251-x
9. Uemura, K., Yamane, S.: SMT-based bounded model checking of embedded assembly program with interruptions. In: 2019 IEEE International Conference on Dependable, Autonomic and Secure Computing, International Conference on Pervasive Intelligence and Computing, International Conference on Cloud and Big Data Computing, International Conference on Cyber Science and Technology Congress (DASC/PiCom/CBDCom/CyberSciTech), pp. 633–639 (2019)
10. Pan, M., Chen, S., et al.: Easy modelling and verification of unpredictable and preemptive interrupt-driven systems. In: Proceedings of the 41st International Conference on Software Engineering, pp. 212–222. IEEE Press (2019)
11. Yu, B., Duan, Z., et al.: Verifying temporal properties of programs: a parallel approach. J. Parallel Distrib. Comput. **118**, 89–99 (2018)
12. Wang, M., Tian, C., et al.: Verifying full regular temporal properties of programs via dynamic program execution. IEEE Trans. Reliab. **68**, 1101–1116 (2018)
13. Wang, H., Duan, Z., Tian, C.: APTL model checker for verifying multi-agent systems. Ruan Jian Xue Bao/J. Softw. **30**(2), 231–243 (2019)
14. Cui, J., Duan, Z., et al.: A novel approach to modeling and verifying real-time systems for high reliability. IEEE Trans. Reliab. **PP**(99), 1–13 (2018)
15. Duan, Z., Tian, C.: A unified model checking approach with projection temporal logic. In: Liu, S., Maibaum, T., Araki, K. (eds.) ICFEM 2008. LNCS, vol. 5256, pp. 167–186. Springer, Heidelberg (2008). https://doi.org/10.1007/978-3-540-88194-0_12
16. Cui, J., Cong, T., et al.: Verifying schedulability of tasks in ROS-based systems. J. Comb. Optim. **37**, 901–920 (2018)

An MSVL Based Model Checking Method for Multi-threaded C Programs

Xinfeng Shu[1], Zhenyu Wang[1], Weiran Gao[1(✉)], Xiaobing Wang[2(✉)], and Liang Zhao[2(✉)]

[1] School of Computer Science and Technology, Xi'an University of Posts and Telecommunications, Xi'an 710061, China
shuxf@xupt.edu.cn
[2] Institute of Computing Theory and Technology, Xidian University, Xi'an 710071, China
xbwang@mail.xidian.edu.cn, lzhao@xidian.edu.cn

Abstract. To solve the problem that software testing is unable to meet the verification needs of multi-threaded C programs, a novel verification approach with Modeling, Simulation and Validation Language (MSVL) is proposed. To this end, the rules for describing the parallel execution semantics of multi-threaded C program with MSVL are defined, , and a specific tool is developed for automatically translating a multi-threaded C program into its equivalent MSVL program. In addition, an example is given to illustrate how the approach works. The approach fully utilizes the powerful expressiveness of MSVL to verify the multi-threaded C programs in a direct way, and helps to improve the quality of the software system.

Keywords: Multi-threaded program · MSVL · Formal method · Program verification · Model checking

1 Introduction

With the rapid development and popularization of Internet technology, network software has become the dominant software form. C language, as a kind of classical programming language, is featured by simple grammar, strong expression ability and high operation efficiency. Its multi-threaded technique has been widely used in the development of various network software. However, the uncertain operation results ascribed to the concurrent execution of multi-threaded programs makes traditional testing methods hardly ensure the correctness of test conclusions when testing network software [1], causing hidden dangers for the safe and reliable operation of network software.

This research is supported by the Key Research and Development Projects of Shaanxi Province (No. 2020GY-210), and The Equipment Pre-research Key Laboratory Foundation (No. JZX7Y202001SY000901), and the NSFC (Grant Nos. 61672403, 61972301, 61572386).

J. Xue et al. (Eds.): SOFL+MSVL 2020, LNCS 12723, pp. 88–101, 2021.
https://doi.org/10.1007/978-3-030-77474-5_7

To solve the problem above, some scholars have introduced the model checking method [2] into the verification of multi-threaded programs. Paper [8] verifies POSIX multi-threaded C program by bounded model checking approach, which defines the rules to transform the multi-threaded programs into nondeterministic sequential programs and then uses CBMC, a bounded model checking tool, to verify the safety property of the program . In paper [6], Fehnker et al. employs Goanna static analysis tool [7] to transform C/C++ program model into NuSMV model and checks the defects of malloc and free operations. However, the method above, which mainly focuses on the safety of the program, can be hardly used to verify the program properties of liveness as well as fairness.

MSVL (Modeling, Simulation and Verification Language) [5], a logical programming language defined with Project Temporal Logic (PTL) [4], provides a rich set of data types [14] (e.g., char, int, float, pointer, structure, semaphore, etc.) and data structures (e.g., set, list, array, etc.), as well as powerful statements (e.g., sequence, selection, loop, concurrency, etc.). Besides, MSVL supports the function mechanisms [17] to model the complex system. Further, Propositional Projection Temporal Logic (PPTL), the propositional subset of PTL, has the expressiveness power of the full regular expressions [12], which enable us to model, simulate and verify the concurrent and reactive systems within a same logical system[3]. MSVL has a dedicated verification tool MSV [15], which has been successfully used in the validation of typical concurrent and distributed systems [9,13].

To solve problem of formal verifying multi-threaded C programs, we are motivated to extend the MSVL-based model checking approach of C programs[16] to multi-threaded programs. To this end, the rules for describing the parallel execution semantics of multi-threaded C programs with MSVL are defined, and the techniques for automatically rewriting a multi-threaded program into its equivalent MSVL program are formalized. Thus, the multi-threaded C program can be indirectly verified by model checking the corresponding MSVL program with the specific model checking tool MSV.

The rest of the paper is organized as follows. In the next section, MSVL and its semaphore technique are briefly introduced. In Sect. 3, the rules for converting multi-threaded programs to MSVL programs are defined and the related techniques are introduced. In Sect. 4, an example is given to illustrate how the method works in verifying multi-threaded programs. Finally, the conclusion is given in Sect. 5.

2   Preliminaries

2.1   Introduction of MSVL

Modeling, Simulation and Verification Language (MSVL) is an executable subset of Projection Temporal Logic (PTL) [4] with frame and used to model, simulate and verify concurrent systems. With MSVL, expressions can be regarded as the PTL terms and statements as treated as the PTL formulas. In the following, we briefly introduce the kernel of MSVL. For more deals, please refer to literatures [5].

Data Type. MSVL provides a rich set of data types [14]. The fundamental types include unsigned character (char), unsigned integer (int) and floating point number (float). Besides, there is a hierarchy of derived data types built with the fundamental types, including string (string), list (list), pointer (pointer), array (array), structure (struct) and union (union).

Expression. The arithmetic expressions e and boolean expressions b of MSVL are inductively defined as follows:

$$e ::= n \mid x \mid \bigcirc x \mid \ominus e \mid e_0 ope_1 (op ::= + \mid - \mid * \mid / \mid \%)$$
$$b ::= true \mid false \mid e_0 = e_1 \mid e_0 < e_1 \mid \neg b \mid b_0 \wedge b_1$$

where n is an integer and x is a variable. The elementary statements in MSVL are defined as follows:

(1) Immediate Assign $x \Leftarrow e \stackrel{def}{=} x = e \wedge p_x$

(2) Unit Assignment $x := e \stackrel{def}{=} \bigcirc x = e \wedge \bigcirc p_x \wedge skip$

(3) Conjunction S_1 and $S_2 \stackrel{def}{=} S_1 \wedge S_2$

(4) Selection S_1 or $S_2 \stackrel{def}{=} S_1 \vee S_2$

(5) Next $next\ S \stackrel{def}{=} \bigcirc S$

(6) Always $always\ S \stackrel{def}{=} \square S$

(7) Termination $empty \stackrel{def}{=} \neg \bigcirc true$

(8) Skip $skip \stackrel{def}{=} \bigcirc \varepsilon$

(9) Sequential $S_1; S_2 \stackrel{def}{=} (S_1, S_2) prj\varepsilon$

(10) Local $exist\ x : S \stackrel{def}{=} \exists x : S$

(11) State Frame $lbf(x) \stackrel{def}{=} \neg af(x) \rightarrow \exists b:(\ominus x = b \wedge x = b)$

(12) Interval Frame $frame(x) \stackrel{def}{=} \square(\bar{\varepsilon} \rightarrow \bigcirc(lbf(x)))$

(13) Projection $(S_1, \ldots, S_m) prj\ S$

(14) Condition $if\ b\ then\ S_1\ else\ S_2 \stackrel{def}{=} (b \rightarrow S_1) \wedge (\neg b \rightarrow S_2)$

(15) While $while\ b\ do\ S \stackrel{def}{=} (b \wedge S)^\star \wedge \square(\varepsilon \rightarrow \neg b)$

(16) Await $await(b) \stackrel{def}{=} \bigwedge_{x \in V_b} frame(x) \wedge \square(\varepsilon \leftrightarrow b)$

(17) Parallel $S_1 \| S_2 \stackrel{def}{=} ((S_1; true) \wedge S_2) \vee (S_1 \wedge (S_2; true))$
$\vee (S_1 \wedge S_2)$

where x is a variable, e is an arbitrary expression, b is a boolean expression, and $S_1, \ldots, S_m, S$ are all MSVL statements. The immediate assignment $x \Leftarrow e$, unit assignment $x := e$, $empty$, $lbf(x)$ and $frame(x)$ are basic statements, and the left composite ones.

For convenience of modeling complex software and hardware systems, MSVL takes the divide-and-conquer strategy and employees functions as the basic components like C programming language does. The general grammar of MSVL function is as follows [17]:

$function$ funcName(in_type_1 x$_1$, ..., in_type_m x$_m$,

   out_type_1 y$_1$, ..., out_type_n y$_m$, $return\_type$ RValue)

{ S }   //Function body

The grammar of function call is $funcName(v_1, \ldots, v_n)$. Parameter passing in MSVL is similar to that in C, i.e. all function arguments are passed by values (call-by-value). With call-by-value, the actual argument expression is evaluated, and the resulting value is bound to the corresponding formal parameter in the function. Even if the function may assign new values to its formal parameters, only its local copy is assigned and anything passed into a function call is unchanged in the caller's scope when the function returns. Furthermore, the pointer type is also supported by MSVL, which allows both caller and callee will be able to access and modify a same variable.

2.2   Introduction of MSVL Semaphore

To solve the synchronization and mutual exclusion between concurrent processes (threads), MSVL also provides a mechanism of semaphore [10] like operation system does. Semaphore in MSVL is a parameterized type $semaphore(n)$, where n is the maximum number of processes (threads) accessing the critical resource denoted by the semaphore variable. Besides, the following 3 MSVL functions are defined to initialize a semaphore variable, acquire a resource and release a resource respectively:

- function sem_init(semaphore(n)* sem, int value, int procNum): used to initialize semaphore. The parameter sem is the semaphore representing the critical resource, and $value$ is the initial number of critical resources, and $procNum$ is the maximum number of processes (threads) using the resource.
- function $sem\_acquire$(semaphore(n)* sem, int id): used to apply for a critical resource for the processes (threads). The parameter sem is the semaphore to apply for resource, and id is the identification of processes (threads) to apply for resource.
- function $sem\_release$(semaphore(n)* sem, int id): used to release a resource occupied by the process (thread) release. The parameter sem is the semaphore to release resource, and id is the identification of process (thread) to release resource.

3   Model Checking Mutli-threaded C Program

The research object of this paper is the multi-threaded C program based on POSIX multi-threaded library (Pthread library). The basic strategy of model checking multi-threaded C programs is to transform the program into its equivalent MSVL program and in turn, verify the MSVL program model indirectly to check whether the original multi-threaded C program satisfies the desired property.

3.1   Transforming C Program into MSVL Program

In this subsection, we first introduce the rules for transforming the basic C programs into MSVL[16], and then extend the method to multi-thread area.

Transformation of Basic C Programs. The rewriting rules from basic data types and expressions of C language into MSVL are shown in Table 1 and Table 2 respectively. The data type provided by MSVL is almost consistent with that provided by C language, except for the following two aspects. First, as a logical programming language, MSVL does not further divide integers into long, int and short types. Second, structure members are connected by operator *and*. To facilitate descriptions, *c_type* (including the form with subscript) refers to any C language data type in Table 1 and below, whereas *m_type* (including the form with subscript) is the corresponding MSVL type. The arithmetic operation and relational operation expressions of MSVL are defined in the same way with C language, except for replacing the operators && and || of C language with *and* and *or* respectively.

Table 1. Transforming rules of data types

Index	C Data Type	MSVL Data type
1	char	Char
2	long, int, short	int
3	float, double	float
4	[ ]	[ ]
5	c_type *	m_type *

6	struct sname{
	   ctype_1 mem_1;
	   ...
	   ctype_n mem_n;
	 };
		struct sname{
		   mtype_1 mem_1 and
		   ... and
		   mtype_n mem_n
		 }

The transforming rules of basic statements from C language to MSVL are shown in Table 3. For the variable declaration statement of C Language *c_type x*, the corresponding variable *m_type x* should be defined in MSVL and frame technology should be used to remain the value of x in the scope of variable x. As for the assignment statement $x = e$ of C language, a specific function E2MSVL is employed to transform the expression e to an MSVL expression according to the transformation rules in Table 2 and then assign the result to variable x. Moreover, MSVL still supports the sequence, selection and loop statements like C language does, besides, we need employ the functions E2MSVL and S2MSVL to recursively transform the sub-boolean expression b and sub-statement S (S1/S2)contained in C language into the corresponding MSVL

Table 2. Transforming rules of expressions

Index	C expression	MSVL expression
1	x [+|-| * | / | % | != | == | > | >= | < | <=] y	x [+ | - | * | / | % | != | = | > | >= | < | <=] y
2	b1 & & b2	b1 and b2
3	b1 || b2	b1 or b2
4	!b	!b

expressions and statements according to the transformation rules in Table 2 and Table 3 respectively.

Table 3. Transforming rules of basic statements

Index	C Statement	MSVL Statement
1	c_type x ;	frame(x) and m_type x and (......)
2	$x = e$	x := E2MSVL(e)
3	$S1$; $S2$;	S2MSVL($S1$) ; S2MSVL($S2$)
4	if (b)	if (E2MSVL(b)) then
	{ $S1$; }	{ S2MSVL($S1$) }
	else	else
	{ $S2$; }	{ S2MSVL($S2$) }
5	while(b)	while(E2MSVL(b))
	{ S; }	{ S2MSVL(S) }

The rules for transforming a C function is as follows:

- The function name and parameters' name remain unchanged, and the type $c\_type_i(1 \leq i \leq n)$ of each formal parameter is transformed to m_type_i corresponding to Table 1;
- The function body statement S is transformed to the statement of MSVL according to Table 3;
- If the function has returned value of type c_type, a new formal parameter $RValue$ with type m_type corresponding to c_type is added at the end of the formal parameter of MSVL function;
- For the returned statement $return\ e$ in the C function, replace it with MSVL statement $RValue$:=E2MSVL(e).

C language starts with the function $main$ by default. Accordingly, a function call statement $main()$ to call MSVL function main is added to the end of the transformed MSVL program, so that the MSVL program also starts from the function main.

Transforming Multi-threaded C Programs. Pthread library follows POSIX standard and defines the functions to manipulates concurrent threads, among which *pthread_create* and *pthread_join* are two commonly used functions to create and synchronize threads. The interfaces of the two functions are defined as follows:

- int pthread_create(pthread_t *tidp, const pthread_attr_t *attr, (void*) (*start), void *arg)
- int pthread_join(pthread_t tid, void **thread_return)

In function pthread_create, parameter *tidp* is a pointer to the thread identifier; parameter *attr* is used to set thread property; parameter *start_rtn* is the address of the thread entry function; *arg* is the parameter pointer passed into the function *start_rtn*. In function pthread_join, parameter *tid* is the identifier of the waiting thread; *thread_return* is the secondary pointer to the value returned by the waiting thread. For simplicity, we only consider the case of thread_return being NULL.

The execution process of multi-threaded C program can be depicted in Fig. 1. Once the main thread creates the sub-thread successfully through calling the function *pthread_create*, the remaining program segment S2 of the main thread and the program segment S3 in the entry function of sub-thread will execute concurrently. When the main thread executes the call statement of function *pthread_join*, it will suspend and wait for the sub-thread to finish executing segment S3. If *pthread_join* function is not used in the main thread, the main thread will forcibly terminate the sub-thread after it finishes executing S2. In such case, if the sub-thread has not finished executing S3, it may cause the loss of data processed by S3.

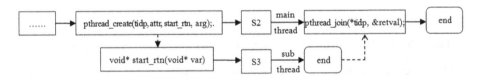

Fig. 1. Schematic diagram of executing of a multi-threaded C program

In this paper, we only consider multi-threaded C program with *pthread_create* and *pthread_join* functions, and limits the number of creation threads to a finite number. The rules for rewriting multi-thread related statements of C programs into MSVL are defined as below:

R1. Define a specific new global boolean variable *_Exit* at the beginning of the MSVL program with initial value *false*, and then transforms the main function *void main(){S}* of C program into MSVL function *main(){S2MSVL(S)*; *_Exit := true}*, i.e., in addition to transforming the statement S of the C program main function into an MSVL statement, add an assignment statement *_Exit := true* at the end to identify the completion of the entire program.

$R2$. Convert the thread identifier type $pthread\_t$ in C program to the integer type int of MSVL.

$R3$. Transform the definition statements of thread entry function in C programs, i.e., $void * fun(void * par)\{\ldots (ctype\_1*) par;\ldots; return\ e;\ldots\}$ into MSVL function $function\ fun(int *tid, mtype\_1 *par, mtype\_2\ RValue)\{\ldots par; \ldots; RValue := E2MSVL(e)\ ;\ldots; *tid := 0\}$.

In $R3$, a new parameter tid is added to the MSVL function to keep the pointer of thread identifier variable; the type $mtype\_1$ of second parameter par is the correspond MSVL type of c_type which is used to access the value of parameter par; the type $mtype\_2$ of third parameter $RValue$ is identified by checking the type of expression e; at the end of the function body, a new assignment statement $*tid := 0$ is appended to indicate the end of thread execution.

$R4$. For thread creation statement $pthread\_create(tidp,\ attr,\ start, arg);\ S$, replace it with MSVL statement $(tidp <== TID\_NUM)\ and\ start(tidp,\ arg, retval)\ ||\ S2MSVL(S)$, where TID_NUM is an integer constant as the unique identifier allocated for each thread.

In C language, each new thread identifier is automatically assigned by Pthread library when calling $pthread\_create$ function, but similar support is unavailable in MSVL. Therefore, in $R4$, a dedicated threads counter TID_NUM with the initial value of 1 is introduce to store the thread identifier. While creating a new thread, the value of the counter is assigned to the thread and then is added by 1. Further, once the new thread is successfully created, it will concurrently execute function $start$ with the remaining statement S of the main thread, so it is transformed into the concurrently calling of the $start$ function with executing the corresponding MSVL statements of S, i.e., $S2MSVL(S)$. In addition, the second parameter $attr$ of the statement, i.e., thread property, is not considered in the transformation process.

$R5$. Transform the statement $pthread\_join(TID, NULL)$ in the C program into the MSVL statement $await(tid = 0)$ to wait for the thread to terminate execution.

The statement $await(tid = 0)$ in $R5$ is used to coordinate with the statement $*tid := 0$ at the end of thread body in $R3$, so that the main thread must keep waiting until the sub-thread tid completes.

Transforming Semaphore. While developing a multi-threaded C program, semaphore mechanism is usually used for the synchronization and mutual exclusion among concurrent threads. The rules for transforming semaphore between C language and MSVL are defined as follows:

$R6$. Transform the semaphore type sem_t of C program into that of MSVL $semaphore(Num)$, where Num is the maximum number of threads accessing the semaphore in the C program.

$R7$. Semaphore initialization statement $sem\_init(\&sem, pshared, value)$ in C program is transformed into $sem\_init(\&SEM, value, MaxNum)$ of MSVL, where, MaxNum is the maximum number of threads using critical resource sem. The parameter $pshared$ indicates whether the semaphore type is shared between threads within a process (value 0) or between processes (value 1) and it is not considered in course of transformation.

In $R6$ and $R7$, the maximum number of threads using critical resources is obtained by counting the number of created threads in a multi-threaded C program in course of transformation.

$R8$. Replace the semaphore operation statements $sem\_wait(\&sem)$ and $sem\_post(\&sem)$ of C program with that of MSVL $sem\_acquire(\&sem, tid)$ and $sem\_release(\&sem, tid)$ respectively to allocate or release a critical resource respectively, where tid is the identifier of the thread that contains MSVL semaphore operation statement.

3.2   Validation Procedures

With the transformation rules above, we have developed a tool for model checking POSIX multi-threaded C program, of which the validation process is given in Fig. 2. The tool consists of four parts, i.e., pretreatment module, C program converter, code builder and MSV validator. The pretreatment module firstly makes static analysis on multi-threaded C program through lexical analysis tool "lex" and grammar analysis tool "yacc", and then constructs a Hierarchical Syntax Chart (HSC) for the program [11]. The C program converter uses the algorithm to dynamically traverse the HSC of C program, and generates the corresponding HSC of MSVL program with the previous transformation rules, and counts the number of created threads (the specific algorithm is omitted). The code builder traverses the HSC of MSVL program and transforms it into an MSVL program, which the relevant algorithms can be found in paper[11]. Finally, we input the MSVL program obtained and the expected properties expressed by positional Projection Temporal Logic (PPTL) [12] into the MSV validator to indirectly check whether original multi-threaded C program meets the desired property.

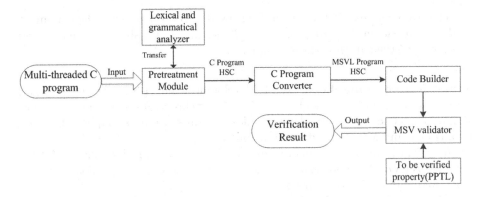

Fig. 2. Validation procedure.

4   Case Study

In this section, we give an example of multi-threaded C program for producer-consumer problem to show how the proposed method works.

4.1   Problem Description

The producer-consumer problem is a classic inter-process synchronization problem. In such a problem, the producer process repeatedly produces goods and puts them into the warehouse (shared buffer space), and if warehouse is not empty, the consume process continuously takes the goods away from the warehouse for consumption. For ease of description, we assume the problem to be single producer, single consumer, and single buffer zone. The POSIX multi-threaded C program of the problem is given in Table 4, where, semaphore variables $semSpace$, $semProd$ and $semBuf$ represent the critical resources buffer space, product and buffer zone, and their initial values are $1, 0, 1$ respectively. Moreover, the activities of both the producer and the consumer are abstracted as two threads with the entry functions $Producer$ and $Consumer$ respectively. Furthermore, the global variable $flag$ represents which thread is currently accessing the buffer zone, and it takes the value 1 denoting the producer is in the buffer zone, otherwise, it takes the value 2.

Table 4. Multi-threaded C program for producer consumer problem.

1 #include <pthread.h>	17 sem_wait(&semBuf);
2 sem_t semSpace, semProd;	18 flag=2;
3 sem_t semBuf;	19 sem_post(&semBuf);
4 int flag;	20 sem_post(&semSpace);
5 void* Producer(){	21 }
6 while(1){	22 }
7 sem_wait(&semSpace);	23 void main (void){
8 sem_wait(&semBuf);	24 pthread_t proid, conid;
9 flag=1;	25 sem_init (&semSpace, 0, 1);
10 sem_post(&semBuf);	26 sem_init (&semProd, 0, 0);
11 sem_post(&semProd);	27 sem_init (&semBuf, 0, 1);
12 }	28 pthread_create(&proid,NULL,Producer, NULL);
13 }	29 pthread_create(&conid,NULL,Consumer,NULL);
14 void* Consumer(){	30 pthread_join(pid, NULL);
15 while(1){	31 pthread_join(cid, NULL);
16 sem_wait(&semProd);	32 }

The HSC of the C program for producer-consumer problem is shown on the left side of Fig. 3. For the function $main$ in the C program, a special compound statement is created in the HSC, whose name node (node <1>) is constructed according to the function declaration of function *main* (Line 23 of the program), and whose content nodes (nodes <2>–<6>) are defined sequentially according to statements (Line 24–31 of the program) contained in the function *main*. Since body of the function *main* is a sequential program, all the nodes in the HSC of the function *main* are common nodes.

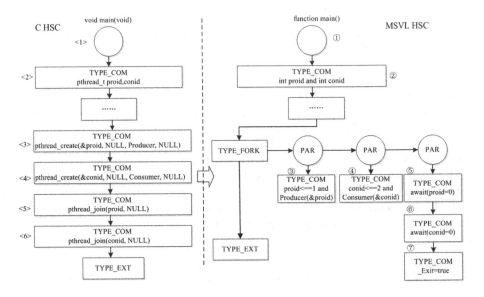

Fig. 3. The Transformation from C HSC to MSVL HSC.

Then, we transform the HSC of C program into the HSC of the corresponding MSVL program according to the transformation rules given in the previous section, and the result obtained is shown on the right side of Fig. 3. In the following, we only give some interpretation to the transformation of key nodes.

– Node <1> is a function declaration statement *void main(void)*, according to the transformation rule of ordinary function, it is transformed into the MSVL function declaration statement *main()*, see node ①.
– Node <2> refers to the definition of thread identifier *pthread_t proid, conid*, according to rule *R2*, it is transformed into the MSVL statement *int proid and int conid*, see node ②.
– Node <3> is a thread creation statement *pthread_create(&proid, NULL, Producer, NULL)*. This is the first thread whose identifier number is 1. According to rule *R3*, the thread is transformed to the MSVL statement *proid <== 1 and Producer(&proid)* (node ③), and a TYPE_FORK node is also created to describe the concurrent execution structure between threads, and the thread forms the first PAR branch of the concurrent structure. Similarly, node <4> is transformed to the second PAR branch of the concurrent structure (see node ④), and its thread identifier is 2.

- Node <5> and <6> are the remaining statements *pthread_join(proid, NULL)* and *pthread_join(conid, NULL)* of of the main thread. According to rule R5, the two nodes are transformed into the MSVL statements *await(proid = 0)* and *await(conid = 0)* respectively, which forms the third PAR branch of the concurrent structure (see ⑤ and ⑥).
- According to rule R1, at the end of the main function, statement _Exit = true is inserted, which corresponds to the node ⑦ at the third PAR branch of the concurrent structure.

Subsequently, we employ the algorithm *HSC2MSVL* [11] to traverse the HSC of MSVL and generate the corresponding MSVL program. The result MSVL program for producer consumer-problem is shown in Table 5.

Table 5. MSVL program for producer-consumer problem

frame(semProd,semBuf,semSpace,flag,	sem_acquire(&semProd,*tid);
_Exit)and(semaphore(2) semProd and	sem_acquire(&semBuf,*tid);
semaphore(2) semBuf and	flag:=2;
semaphore(2) semSpace and int flag and	sem_acquire(&semBuf,*tid);
bool _Exit<==false and skip;	sem_acquire(&semSpace,*tid)
function Producer(int *tid){	});
termi(_Exit) and (	*tid:=0
while(true){	};
sem_acquire(&semSpace, *tid);	function main(){
sem_acquire(&semBuf, *tid);	frame(proid,conid) and (
flag:=1;	int proid and int conid and skip
sem_release(&semBuf, *tid);	sem_init(&semSpace,1,2);
sem_release(&semProd, *tid);	sem_init(&semProd,0,2);
}	sem_init(&semBuf,1,2);
);*tid :=0	(proid<==1 and Producer(&proid))
};	||(conid<==2 and Consumer(&conid))
function Consumer(int *tid){	||(await(proid=0) and await(conid=0))
termi(_Exit) and (	)};
while(true){	main())

Finally, we verify a liveness property of the program, that is, after the producer puts a product into the buffer zone (i.e., *flag* = 1) at some time point, the consumer will definitely take the product from the buffer zone for consumption in the future (i.e., *flag* = 2). The property described by PTL formula is $\Diamond(flag = 1); \Diamond(flag = 2)$. We also need rewrite the formula into a PPTL formula for further model checking. Let atomic proposition p denote $flag = 1$ and q be $flag = 2$, thus the liveness property in PPTL formula is $\Diamond p; \Diamond q$.

We input both the MSVL program and the liveness property in PPTL into the MSV tool, select the verification model to do model checking. The verification results is shown in Fig. 4, there does not exist any counter-example path, which indicates that the MSVL program satisfys the liveness property, and thus the conclusion also holds for the original multi-threaded C program.

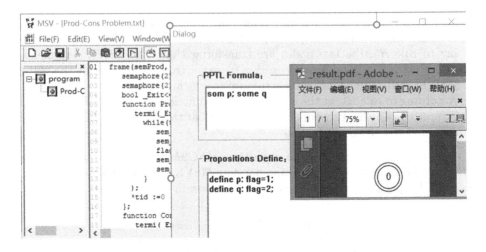

Fig. 4. Verification result.

5   Conclusion

In this paper, we present a MSVL based model checking approach to verify POSIX multi-threaded C program, and a validation tool for POSIX multi-threaded C program is development. The tool can automatically transform the multi-threaded C program into an equivalent MSVL program, and employs the rich expressive power of PPTL to validate the liveness, fairness and other complex properties. However, this paper only focus on the multi-threaded C program that uses thread function *pthread_create* and *pthread_join*. In the near future, we will extend the work to the program that contains more thread functions in Pthread library (e.g., *pthread_exit*, *pthread_cancel*, etc.), and apply the method to verify some practical network softwares.

References

1. Bianchi, F.A., Margara, A., Pezzè, M.: A survey of recent trends in testing concurrent software systems. IEEE Trans. Softw. Eng. **44**(8), 747–783 (2018). https://doi.org/10.1109/TSE.2017.2707089
2. Clarke, E.M.: The birth of model checking. In: Grumberg, O., Veith, H. (eds.) 25 Years of Model Checking. LNCS, vol. 5000, pp. 1–26. Springer, Heidelberg (2008). https://doi.org/10.1007/978-3-540-69850-0_1
3. Duan, Z., Tian, C.: A unified model checking approach with projection temporal logic. In: Liu, S., Maibaum, T., Araki, K. (eds.) ICFEM 2008. LNCS, vol. 5256, pp. 167–186. Springer, Heidelberg (2008). https://doi.org/10.1007/978-3-540-88194-0_12
4. Duan, Z., Tian, C., Zhang, N.: A canonical form based decision procedure and model checking approach for propositional projection temporal logic. Theor. Comput. Sci. **609**, 544–560 (2016). https://doi.org/10.1016/j.tcs.2015.08.039

5. Duan, Z., Yang, X., Koutny, M.: Framed temporal logic programming. Sci. Comput. Program. **70**(1), 31–61 (2008). https://doi.org/10.1016/j.scico.2007.09.001
6. Fehnker, A., Huuck, R.: Model checking driven static analysis for the real world: designing and tuning large scale bug detection. Innov. Syst. Softw. Eng. **9**(1), 45–56 (2013)
7. Fehnker, A., Huuck, R., Jayet, P., Lussenburg, M., Rauch, F.: Goanna—a static model checker. In: Brim, L., Haverkort, B., Leucker, M., van de Pol, J. (eds.) FMICS 2006. LNCS, vol. 4346, pp. 297–300. Springer, Heidelberg (2007). https://doi.org/10.1007/978-3-540-70952-7_20
8. Inverso, O., Tomasco, E., Fischer, B., La Torre, S., Parlato, G.: Bounded model checking of multi-threaded C programs via lazy sequentialization. In: Biere, A., Bloem, R. (eds.) CAV 2014. LNCS, vol. 8559, pp. 585–602. Springer, Cham (2014). https://doi.org/10.1007/978-3-319-08867-9_39
9. Ma, Q., Duan, Z.H.: Automatic theorem proving technique for MSVL. J. Xidian Univ. **43**(01), 75–81 (2016). https://doi.org/10.3969/j.issn.1001-2400,2016.01.014
10. Shu, X., Duan, Z.: Extending MSVL with semaphore. In: Dinh, T.N., Thai, M.T. (eds.) COCOON 2016. LNCS, vol. 9797, pp. 599–610. Springer, Cham (2016). https://doi.org/10.1007/978-3-319-42634-1_48
11. Shu, X., Li, C., Liu, C.: A visual modeling language for MSVL. In: Liu, S., Duan, Z., Tian, C., Nagoya, F. (eds.) SOFL+MSVL 2016. LNCS, vol. 10189, pp. 220–237. Springer, Cham (2017). https://doi.org/10.1007/978-3-319-57708-1_13
12. Tian, C., Duan, Z.: Expressiveness of propositional projection temporal logic with star. Theor. Comput. Sci. **412**(18), 1729–1744 (2011). https://doi.org/10.1016/j.tcs.2010.12.047
13. Wang, X.B., Guo, W.X., Duan, Z.H.: Communication mechanism and its implementation for msvl based on message pass. J. Softw. **29**(6), 1607–1621 (2018). https://doi.org/10.13328/j.cnki.jos.005471
14. Wang, X., Tian, C., Duan, Z., Zhao, L.: MSVL: a typed language for temporal logic programming. Front. Comput. Sci. **11**(5), 762–785 (2017). https://doi.org/10.1007/s11704-016-6059-4
15. Yang, K., Duan, Z., Tian, C., Zhang, N.: A compiler for MSVL and its applications. Theor. Comput. Sci. **749**, 2–16 (2018). https://doi.org/10.1016/j.tcs.2017.07.032
16. Yu, Y., Duan, Z., Tian, C., Yang, M.: Model checking C programs with MSVL. In: Liu, S. (ed.) SOFL 2012. LNCS, vol. 7787, pp. 87–103. Springer, Heidelberg (2013). https://doi.org/10.1007/978-3-642-39277-1_7
17. Zhang, N., Duan, Z., Tian, C.: A mechanism of function calls in MSVL. Theor. Comput. Sci. **654**, 11–25 (2016). https://doi.org/10.1016/j.tcs.2016.02.037

Specification and Verification

A Formal Approach to Secure Design of RESTful Web APIs Using SOFL

Busalire Emeka[1]([✉]), Soichiro Hidaka[1], and Shaoying Liu[2]

[1] Graduate School of Computer and Information Sciences, Hosei University, Tokyo, Japan
onesmus.busalire.5n@stu.hosei.ac.jp, hidaka@hosei.ac.jp
[2] School of Informatics and Data Science, Hiroshima University, Hiroshima, Japan
sliu@hiroshima-u.ac.jp

Abstract. A primary concern in the design and development of a RESTful Application Programming Interfaces (APIs) is API security. A RESTful API provides data over the network using HTTP and must not violate any of its security properties. When APIs are designed, the functional and security properties are inextricably linked thus security requirements of an API cannot be treated as afterthoughts. We therefore propose an approach to specifying and verifying APIs functional and security requirements with the practical formal method SOFL (Structured-Object-oriented Formal Language). We convert an API specification written in an API description language into SOFL while expressing security requirements as constraints on the APIs functional requirements and dataflow between the API's trust boundaries. The verification of the specifications can be carried out using specification-based conformance testing. We apply this approach to a model of an online banking API as a case study using Django REST Framework and analyze its results.

Keywords: RESTful APIs · API security requirements · Formal methods · Formal specification verification · SOFL

1 Introduction

A web API (Application Programming Interface) is a set of functions and procedures that allow users to access and build upon the data and functionality of an existing application available over the web through the HTTP protocol [1]. Many web APIs nowadays adopt REpresentational State Transfer (REST) [2] architectural style which allows building loosely coupled API designs relying on HTTP and the web friendly JSON data representation format. The loosely coupling approach makes client applications have flexibility and reusability of an API in terms of the fact that its elements can be easily added, replaced and changed.

However, REST is a design paradigm and protocol-agnostic. It does not rely on any set of defined standards to describe the implementation of a RESTful API. This poses a challenge in the development and testing for satisfiability of a RESTful API property such as security. Since REST APIs expose internal business services and data to a set

© Springer Nature Switzerland AG 2021
J. Xue et al. (Eds.): SOFL+MSVL 2020, LNCS 12723, pp. 105–125, 2021.
https://doi.org/10.1007/978-3-030-77474-5_8

of public and/or private heterogeneous client applications, the level of security offered by these APIs must be extremely high, since their breach may cause huge financial and business integrity losses on the part of the service providers.

An ideal and secure REST API must exactly and accurately function as intended and preserve its security properties during its operation. If a REST API is to provide access to some exposed business data to a requesting client application, it must fulfill the functional requirement of the client application without violation of its' security properties. It must also not violate the security properties of the system providing the data. In addition, while RESTful services can easily be invoked through a web browser or a client application, it is still difficult for users to fully understand and evaluate their functions with respect to the requirements in the context of target systems, because a few formal descriptions are provided with these services. Moreover, while each individual operation in an API may be secure on its own, combinations of operations might not be. Therefore, adopting a model that enables the capture and verification of precisely defined functional and security requirements of an API is crucial in the development of an API.

Formal methods have been proven to offer an approach to the construction and verification for precise, consistent and correct specifications using mathematical notations. Research reveals that formal methods have been effective in capturing requirements, identifying errors and transforming specifications to programs [3, 4]. However, in practice, there exists limitations in applying formal methods like VDM [5], B-Method and Z notation because they require high skills for abstraction and their notations offer a steep learning curve for most engineers in the industry. In addition, their formal proof techniques and refinements are difficult and expensive to apply in practice.

Our research proposes a model offering a formal practical approach to specify and verify security and functional requirements of RESTful APIs using SOFL (Structured-Object-oriented Formal Language) [3]. Our approach focusses on ensuring that all of the expected functional behaviors provided by an API and their related security requirements must be captured correctly, since a secure web API is expected both to deliver its business functions and to preserve its security features and that of the system it is interfacing. To achieve this, we construct SOFL formal but comprehensible functional and security requirement specifications from an API description written in RESTful API modelling Language (RAML)[1] [6].

We chose RAML since its mostly used to describe REST APIs and from our experience, it's easy to covert to SOFL specifications as its structure of describing an API request clearly defines the inputs, outputs and the requests associated constraints. This means it can be converted into its equivalent SOFL process representation directly either manually or semi-automatically with only a change in the syntax. We then ensure the consistency and correctness of the specification through formal verification and specification-based conformance testing. Our choice of SOFL for specification and verification is influenced by its user-friendliness and practicality in requirement specifications. It supports both structured and object-oriented methodologies as well as provides both graphical and textual formal notation for specifications [3, 4]. In this paper, we consider a model of an online banking application API, a security critical API, as an

---

[1] https://raml.org/about-raml.

example to describe how to specify both the functional and security requirements in an interweaving manner and, conduct the verification of the specifications for the assurance of its' security properties. We achieve this by carrying out API specification-based testing to assert the correctness of data flow across the API functions, with regards to the preservation of its security attributes. Our contributions of this research include:

- Providing a formal model for transforming RAML definitions to SOFL and for interweaving functional and security requirements of RESTful APIs. We use SOFL to model the structural and behavioral features of REST web service.
- Providing specification-based conformance testing techniques for assurance of the correct implementation of an API's functional and security requirements.
- Evaluating the effectiveness of SOFL in security requirement engineering of REST APIs by sharing our experience through a case study implemented in Django REST framework

The remainder of this paper is organized as follows. Section 2 describes briefly SOFL and REST architectural style. Section 3 describes our proposed approach that interweaves API's security and functional requirements. Section 4 covers the technique we adopt for specification-based conformance testing. Section 5 gives a brief discussion on the evaluation of our proposed approach. Section 6 focusses on related work and finally Sect. 7 gives conclusions and outlines areas for our future research.

2   REST and SOFL

2.1   REST

The concept of REST was introduced by Roy Fielding in his PhD dissertation, "Architectural Styles and the Design of Network-based Software Architectures" [2]. REST relies on HTTP protocol for data communication and revolves around the concept of resources where each and every component is considered as a resource. These resources are accessed via a common interface using HTTP methods such as GET for retrieving a resource, PUT for updating a resource, POST for creating a resource and DELETE for removing a resource. Contrary to other web services, REST is an architectural style and protocol agnostic.

The REST architecture focusses on providing access to a resource for a REST client to access and render it [1]. It utilizes Uniform Resource Identifiers (URIs) in identifying each resource and provides several resource representations such as XML, JSON, Text etc. to represent its type. For an API to be considered RESTful, it needs to satisfy the following design characteristics commonly referred to as REST constraints [1].

- *Client-server architecture* – separates concerns between user interfaces and data storage with the client sending requests for various types of services to the server and the server providing services to the client as per the requests.
- *Statelessness* – The client makes requests to the server with all information as stated so that the server understands the requests and treats them as independent. The client requests keep the server independent of any stored context.

- *Caching* – Frequently accessed data i.e., client responses are stored to reduce the need to generate the same response more than once until they need to be.
- *Uniform Interface* – REST-based services can use the HTTP interface, such as GET, PUT, POST and DELETE, to maintain uniformity across the web. The primary reason for a uniform interface is to retain some common vocabulary across the internet that can be mapped with CRUD operations i.e., Create, Read, Update, Delete. The services can independently evolve as their interfaces simplify and decouple the architecture.
- *Layered systems* – A layered system consists layers with different units of functionality. A layer communicates by means of predefined interfaces to only the layer above or the layer below. The layers above rely on the layers below to perform its functions. Layers can be added, removed, modified or reordered as the architecture evolves.
- *Code on Demand* - this is an optional constraint of REST that is intended to allow business logic within the client web browser.

Out of the six constraints, the first four mainly influence the design. The Layered System is more important to the deployment of Web APIs than to their design, and Code on Demand does not seem to be popular in application to web API's [1]. A detailed description of RESTful web APIs is given in [7].

2.2 SOFL

SOFL is a formal engineering method that provides a formal but comprehensible language for both requirements and design specifications, and a practical method for developing software systems [3]. SOFL is designed by integrating different notations and techniques on the basis that all are needed to work together effectively in a coherent manner for specification constructions and verifications. The SOFL specification language integrates Data Flow Diagrams [4] which describe comprehensibly the architecture of specifications, Petri nets [8] and VDM-SL [5]. A formalized Data Flow diagram resulting from the integration is called Condition Data Flow Diagram (CDFD). SOFL also uses classes to model complicated data flows and stores. A data store offers data that can be accessed by processes in a CDFD. SOFL adopts a three-step evolutionary approach to developing formal specifications, starting from informal specifications, to semi-formal specifications and finally to formal specifications. The informal specification usually written in a natural language serves as the basis for deriving the semi-formal specifications in which the SOFL syntax to some extent is enforced. The formal specification is then derived from the semi-formal specification through formalization of the informal parts in the semi-formal specifications. More details about the SOFL specifications language can be found from the SOFL book [3].

3   Our Proposed Approach

We describe a formal secured design approach that seeks to interweave the functional and security requirements of REST APIs using SOFL. Our approach uses RAML definitions as a base for informally describing the APIs functional and security requirements. The approach has three steps. The first step yields a set of informal functional and their related security requirements expressed in RAML security schemes definitions. The security requirements are defined as constraints upon the functional requirements. They express the APIs security goals in operational terms. The second step focus on transformation of RAML definitions to SOFL based semi-formal specifications by first modelling the API's behavioral features using SOFL's Conditional Data Flow Diagrams (CDFDs) and then express the REST specific request methods as SOFL module processes with informal pre-post conditions. Their related security requirements are defined as either SOFL module invariants or guard condition in the process' pre-post conditions. Finally, the last step involves formalization of the pre-post conditions and proving the satisfiability of the functional and security requirements through specification testing [8]. The formalized functional and security requirements can then be transformed into executable API code manually or semi-automatically with the help of a supporting tool. In the following sections, we explain each step-in detail.

3.1 Step 1: Identification of Informal Functional and Security Requirements

We define the API's functional requirements from the request methods (a program unit) that yield a response in the form of a resource. The request methods are simply HTTP methods which are mapped to specific REST API semantics as outlined in Table 1.

Table 1. HTTP methods

Method	Meaning
GET	Reads the representation of a resource state
POST	Creates new resource
PUT	Updates a resource
DELETE	Removes a resource
HEAD	Fetches metadata associated with a resource's state
OPTIONS	List the available methods

We express these informal functional requirements using RAML [6, 9] description language that allows defining the resources and operations of a REST API in JSON. We chose RAML because of its ease of transformation to SOFL syntax during the formalization process as well as its ability to strike a better balance between machine and human readability. Figure 1 shows an excerpt of the RAML definition of an online banking API with JSON representation of its resources. The online banking API allow customers access and manage their bank accounts. The paths objects e.g. */accounts/{accountid}* include relative paths to individual endpoints. Each path item includes operations using HTTP methods e.g. GET for */accounts/{accountid}*, which in turn include properties such as their parameters i.e. response status codes e.g. 200, and the media types they produce or consume e.g. application/json. The definition also includes JSON schema determining the response/request payload. A sample RAML API description excerpt for an online banking application is given below.

```
# RAML API description Language
title: Online_Banking
version: 1.0.0
baseURI : http://localhost:8000/onlinebanking/api
/accounts/{accountid}
  displayName: Individual User Account
  GET:
    description: Get Individual Account Details
    responses:
      200:
        body:
          application/json
            example: |
                [
                    {
                      'userid':'1',
                      'Account Number':'113345647',
                      'Available Balance':'KES 1500',
                      'Current Balance':'KES 1500',
                      'Account Currency':'KES',
                      'Account Name':'James J',
                      'Status':'Active',
                      'Uncleared Amount':'KES 1000'
                      }

                ]
      404:
        body:
          application/json:
            example: |
                {"message" : "User account not found"}
      securitySchemes:
        -BankingAPIScopes
              {"Customer": { <read>}}
/accounts/balance/{accountid}
  displayName: Individual User Account Balance
  GET:
    description: Get Individual Account balance
    responses:
      200:
        body:
          application/json:
            example: |
                [
                    {
                      'id':'1',
                      'Account Number':'11334567',
                      'Account Name':'James J',
                      'Currency':'KES',
                      'Current Balance':'KES 1500',
                      'Available Balance':'KES 1500'
                      }

                ]
      404:
        body:
          application/json:
            example: |
                {"message": " Account number | id not found"}
      securitySchemes:
        -BankingAPIScopes
              {"Customer":{<read>}}
```

Fig. 1. Sample RAML specification for an Online Banking API

We derive the informal API security requirements by considering the following aspects:

- The resources exposed by the API that are to be protected e.g. customer names and account details
- The security goals that are important such as confidentiality of target API resources
- The mechanisms that are available to achieve these goals such as authentication, access control, audit logging and rate limiting
- Common security vulnerabilities of RESTful APIs [7] as described in Table 2.

Table 2. Common REST API vulnerabilities and mitigations

REST API vulnerability	Vulnerability mitigation
Cross Site Request Forgery	Apply token-based approaches for PUT, POST, and DELETE request
Incorrect input	Reject incorrect input by validation on both client and server side. Log validation failures and limit processing rate if failure rate increases
URL modification	Validate all URLs servicing a request
Insecure message parsing	Check all incoming messages framed either as XML or JSON for security violations
Incoming content type validation	Explicitly validate all incoming content types for POST and PUT methods
Response types validation	Make clients specify which MIME types should be used in the reply message
XML signature wrapping	Securely parse XML messages for XML-based services
XML injection attacks	Construct XML messages using XML serializer
Tempering of message integrity	Use message digest algorithms to preserve message integrity e.g. JSON web token (JWT) for messages delivered in JSON format

- The set of threats relevant to the API. We identify these threats using S.T.R.I.D.E [10] threat modelling process, by analysing the flow of requests/responses across trust boundaries defined by the main logical components of the API, and the target environment for deployment.

These security requirements are mapped as constraints on the expressed functional requirements with an ultimate goal of arriving at a convincing argument to prove their satisfiability in the formalized specifications. The distinction between convincing and proof of satisfiability is important. Whereas we may not prove the negative, that a violation of an API's security requirement does not exist through specification testing; we can make a convincing argument that sufficient outcomes have been addressed. We propose to use formal proofs as argumentation to this end; to convince a reader that the security requirements can be satisfied.

3.2 Step 2: Transforming RAML Definitions to SOFL

In this step, we adopt the following rules of transformation from RAML definitions to SOFL semi-formal specifications

- *Rule 1*: Transform REST request definitions GET, POST, PUT and DELETE to SOFL processes specified with informal pre-post conditions.
- *Rule 2*: Construct CDFDs [4] for the textual semi-formal specifications so that the requirements can be visualized. The CDFDs describe the API's request input and output data flows.
- *Rule 3:* Define REST request parameters as inputs and their types to their respective SOFL processes, and responses as outputs of their associated SOFL processes. All data stores interacting with the inputs and outputs are also defined.
- *Rule 4*: Express the defined RAML security schemes (i.e. security requirements) as SOFL module invariants or guard conditions in the post-condition of the relevant processes. This rule achieves the interweaving of functional and security requirements.

The excerpt shows an example of SOFL module specification transformed from the RAML definitions defined in Sect. 3.1. For brevity, we give only the necessary parts of the module.

```
MODULE BANKING_API
type
Permissions = map userID to PermissionSet;
userID = nat;
accID = nat;
Permission = {<create>, <read>, <delete>} /* enumeration type for permis-
sions */
/* restricted subset drawn from the powerset of Permission */
PermissionSet = {{<create>, <read>, <delete>}, {<read>}, {<create>, <read>}}
Status = {<Active>,<Suspended>,<Closed>} /* enumeration type for account
status */
CustomerAccounts = composed of
                            userid : userID
                            account_number: nat
                            current_balance: real
                            account_currency: string
                            account_name: string
                            uncleared_amount: real
                        end;
Account = map accID to CustomerAccounts;
var
ext # accountset: set of CustomerAccounts
ext # account_table: Account
ext # permission_table : Permissions
```

```
inv
/* all accounts are associated with users with read and create permission */
forall[x:CustomerAccounts] | permission_table(x.user_id) inset PermissionSet
and permission_table(x.user_id) = {<read>}
/* different accounts have different account_number, so an account_number
uniquely determines an account */
forall[account₁, account₂ :accountset] |
   account₁ <> account₂ =>account₁.account_number <> account₂.account_number


process Account_Details (account_id: accID, userid: userID) account_info:
CustomerAccounts, response_msg: string

ext rd account_table, permission_table
pre true
/* guard condition for valid input and permission */
post account_info should have account details associated with account_id.
The response_msg should give a HTTP status message of code 200 or code 404
end_process;


process Account_Balance (account_id: accID, userid: userID) account_balance:
CustomerAccounts, response_msg: string
ext rd account_table, permission_table


pre account_id must map to a customer account and userid must have <read>
only permissions
post account_balance should have account details associated with account_id.
The response_msg should give a HTTP status message of code 200 or code 404
end_process;
end module;
```

The CDFD in Fig. 2 diagramatically represent two processes i.e. *Account_Balance* and *Account_Details*. *Account_Balance* takes 3 inputs i.e. *acc_bal* signal from an API request A(auth_req) conditional structure, *accID* and *userID*; and yields *account_balance* and *response_message* as outputs. The *Account_Details* process consumes *acc_det* signal, an output of B(auth_req) conditional structure, *accID* and *userID* and yields *account_info* and *response_msg* as outputs. Both processes read from *account_table* and *permission_table data* stores.

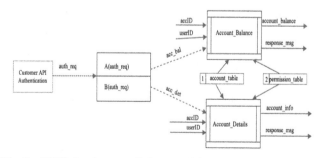

Fig. 2. CDFD for Account_Balance and Account_Details processes

We apply our transformation rules in converting the RAML API definitions in Fig. 1 into a SOFL module with two process definition albeit expressed informally. We convert the request GET /accounts?account_id = {account_id} into a SOFL module process *Account_Details* with its associated inputs and outputs, as well as their data types being explicitly declared. We also convert the request GET /accounts/balance? = {account_id} request into the process *Account_Balance* and declare all its inputs and outputs as well as their respective data types. Finally we express the RAML access control security scheme i.e. *securitySchemes:BankingAPIScopes {"Customer":{< read >}}* as an invariant that constrains the functionality of the two processes, formally expressed as *forall[x:CustomerAccounts] | permission_table(x.user_id) = {<read>}*, that is, a user instance must only have read permissions while servicing a request defined by the two processes.

3.3 Step 3: Formalization of API Specifications

So far, our API specification is expressed as a set of system modules encapsulating the functions, data resources and constraints. In particular, the API's request methods are specified as SOFL processes. The input and output data structures of these processes are formally defined while the pre- and post-conditions are expressed in informal language. To test for satisfiability of API's both functional and security requirements, the processes need to be completely formalized to lay a foundation for generating proper test cases to run specification-based conformance testing. The formalization process involves fully formalizing the pre- and post-conditions of these processes to precisely express the expected operational semantics upon their associated request methods. To formally define the pre- and post-conditions of these processes, we re-introduce the concept of a SOFL process.

A SOFL process is defined as a five-tuple: $(P, InPortSet, OutPortSet, preP, postP)$.

- P is the name of the process
- $InPortSet = \{inPort_1, inPort_2, \ldots, inPort_f\}$ defines the set of input ports of P where $inPort_i(i = 1, \ldots, f)$ is an input port. Each input port is defined as $inPort_i = \{v_{j_1}, \ldots, v_{j_{r_i}}\}$ where $v_k(k = j_1, \ldots, j_{r_i})$ is a variable of this port.
- $OutPortSet = \{outPort_1, inPort_2, \ldots, outPort_g\}$ defines the set of output ports of P where $outPort_i(i = 1, \ldots, g)$ is an output port. Each output port is defined as $outPort_i = \{v_{l_1}, \ldots, v_{l_{s_i}}\}$ where $v_k(k = l_1, \ldots, l_{s_i})$ is a variable of this port.
- $preP$ is the pre-condition of P, which specifies the condition that the input variables need to satisfy.
- $postP$ is the post-condition of P, which specifies the condition that the output variables are required to satisfy.

An interpretation of a process *P* is as follows. When one of the input ports in *inPortSet* e.g. *inPort$_i$* is available, all its input variables are bound to specific values in their types and the process *P* is executed. The results of the execution make one of the output ports in *OutPortSet* say *outPort$_j$* is made available and all of its output variables are bound to specific values of their types. If the input variables satisfy the pre-condition *preP* before the execution of *P*, the output variables are required to satisfy the post-condition *postP* after the execution of the process *P*, provided that the execution of P terminates and is deterministic. The SOFL excerpts below show the formal specification of the two processes *Account_Details* and *Account_Balance*. *Account_Details* takes two input parameters, *account_id* and *user_id* and yields either an output *account_info* of a composite data type and a response message of type string or a response error message of type string. To represent the necessary data resources to be shared by the processes, for example, the customer account details, the data stores *account_table* of map type and *permission_table* of map type are defined as external variables.

```
MODULE BANKING_API
type
/* type definitions omitted for brevity */
inv
forall[x:accountset] |
  permission_table(x.user_id) inset PermissionSet
    and permission_table(x.user_id) = {<read>}

forall[account₁, account₂ :accountset] |
  account₁ <> account₂ =>account₁.account_number <> account₂.account_number

function get_account(aid : accID) : account
  == get({a:accountset|a.account_number = aid })
end_function /* returns an account with given account_number */

process Account_Details(account_id:accID, userid:userID)
                        account_info: CustomerAccounts, response_msg:string

ext rd account_table, permission_table

pre true

post
```

```
        /* guard condition for valid input and permission */
        exists! [account:accountset] | account_id = account.account_number
                                  and permission_table(account.userid) = {<read>}
   /* read permission */
            and
            /* defining condition for valid input and permission */
        account_info = get_account(account_id)
            and response_msg = "200 OK" /* message indicates success */
       or
     /* guard condition for nonexisting account number */
        not exist[account:accountset] |
            account_id <> account.account_number
        and response_msg = "404 account not found"
       or
        exists![account:accountset] |
        account_id = account.account_number
            and permission_table(get_account(account_id).userid) <> {<read>}
            and response_msg = "401 permission denied"

end process;

...
process Account_Balance(account_id: accID, userid: userID) account_balance: Cus-
tomerAccount, response_msg: string

ext rd accountlist, permission_table

pre true

post exists![account:accountset] |
            account_id = account.account_number
            and permission_table(account.userid) = {<read>}
            and account_info = get_account(account_id)
            and response_msg = "200 OK"
       or
        not exist[account:accountset] |account_id = account.account_number
            and response_msg = "404 account not found"
       or
        exists![account:accountset] | account_id = account.account_number
            and permission_table(get_account(account_id).userid) <> {<read>}
            and response_msg="401 permission denied"

end process;
end module;
```

The pre- and post-conditions of process *Account_Details* precisely represents the functions of a request operation *Account_Details* and its related constraining functions. The constraining function check for permissions of the process' *userid* input parameter. The predicate *exists! [account:accountset] | account_id = account.account_number and permission_table(account.userid) = { <read> }* states that there exists a user account of the required Account type in the *accountset* datastore whose *account_number* matches the input parameter *account_id* and the user attached to the account has <*read*> only permissions. After formalizing all the pre-post-conditions, the next step is to check whether the formal API specifications satisfy their required functions and constraints. We apply specification-based conformance testing technique as described in the next section.

4 Specification Based Conformance Testing

A REST API offers a group of operations in form of request methods to perform its functions. These operations are stateless, and the execution results depend on the input data. To check whether a stateless operation implements its desired behavior, the developer needs to check whether the relations between its input and outputs are consistent with the defined formal pre- and post-conditions of its processes. The pre- and post-conditions of an API process can be transformed into a number of independent relations called functional scenarios [11]. Let the post-condition $P_{post} \equiv (C_1 \wedge D_1) \vee (C_2 \wedge D_2) \vee \ldots \vee (C_n \wedge D_n)$, where each $C_i (i = 1, \ldots, n)$ is a predicate called guard condition that contains no output variables and D_i a defining condition that contains at least one output variable but no guard condition. Then each $\sim P_{pre} \wedge C_i \wedge D_i$ is called a functional scenario, where $\sim F$ for logical formula F of the input/output variables of a process denotes the value of F before starting execution of the process. A process P can then be transformed into a functional scenario of the form $\equiv \sim P_{pre} \wedge C_1 \wedge D_1 \vee \ldots \vee \sim P_{pre} \wedge C_n \wedge D_n$. Each functional scenario $\sim P_{pre} \wedge C_i \wedge D_i$ independently defines how the output of P is defined using D_i under the condition $\sim P_{pre} \wedge C_i$. Therefore, to test whether a REST API request operation implements all the expected functions and its related constraints correctly, a developer will need to run adequate test data generated from all the functional scenarios of its associated process. In the publication [8], a scenario-coverage for test case generation is proposed. We introduce its detail as follows. Suppose a process $P \equiv \left(\sim P_{pre} \wedge C_1 \wedge D_1 \right) \vee \ldots \vee \left(\sim P_{pre} \wedge C_n \wedge D_n \right)$ where $(n \geq 1)$ and T is a test set. Then T is said to satisfy the scenario-coverage of iff $\forall_{i \in \{1, \ldots, n\}} \exists_{t \in T} \cdot \sim P_{pre}(t) \wedge C_i(t)$. That is, a test set T satisfies the scenario coverage for a process P *iff* for any functional scenario, there exists a test case in T such that it satisfies the conjunction of the precondition $\sim P_{pre}$ and the guard condition C_i.

The functional coverage allows us to generate sufficient test data for checking conformance of an API request operation o with respect to its associated process P. Suppose for each functional scenario $f_i \equiv \sim P_{pre} \wedge C_i \wedge D_i$ of process P, we define t to be a test case generated from f_i and r be the execution result of the associated request operation o using t, then we can assert o does not conform to P *iff* $\sim P_{pre}(t) \wedge C_t \wedge \neg D_i(t, r)$ holds. We use this condition as a test oracle to judge the conformance of a REST API request method to its associated process. For a test case t satisfying the pre-condition and guard condition of f_i, if the corresponding test result r of request operation o does not satisfy the defining condition D_i then we can determine that request operation o does not correctly satisfy the functional and security requirements of the API's request under test. The condition $\sim P_{pre}(t) \wedge C_t \wedge \neg D_i(t, r)$ serves as a test oracle that can be applied for judging the satisfiability of the functional and security requirements to their associated processes. For a given test case t satisfying the pre-condition and guard condition of f_i, if the corresponding test result r of operation o does not satisfy the defining condition D_i, then we can establish that the operation o does not correctly implement the functional and security requirement of the API request under test.

We can use a very simple example to demonstrate the application of the functional scenario-based test data generation. In Fig. 3, the required function for the *GET* API operation *Account_Details is* defined formally as shown below

```
process Account_Details(account_id:accID, userid:userID)
                        account_info: CustomerAccounts, response_msg:string

ext rd account_table, permission_table

pre true
post
/* guard condition for valid input and permission */
    exists![account:accountset] | account_id = account.account_number
                                and permission_table(account.userid) = {<read>}
/* read permission */
        and
        /* defining condition for valid input and permission */
        account_info = get_account(account_id)
        and response_msg = "200 OK" /* message indicates success */
    or
  /* guard condition for nonexisting account number */
        not exist[account:accountset] | account_id <> account.account_number
        and response_msg = "404 account not found"
    or
        exists![account:accountset] |
        account_id = account.account_number
        and permission_table(get_account(account_id).userid) <> {<read>}
        and response_msg="401 permission denied"
end process;
```

The process *Account_Details* takes *account_id* and *userid* as input variables and returns two output variables, *account_info* and *response_msg*. The pre- and post-conditions of the process are represented as three functional scenarios:

```
(1.)  FS1 exists! [account:accountset] |
      account_id = account.account_number
      and permission_table(account.userid) = {<read>}
          /* read permission */
      and
      /* defining condition for valid input and permission */
      account_info = get_account(account_id)
      and response_msg = "200 OK" /* message indicates success */

(2.)  FS2 not exist [account:accountset] |
          account_id <> account.account_number
      and response_msg = "404 account not found"

(3.)  FS3 exists! [account:accountset] |
      account_id = account.account_number
          and permission_table(get_account(account_id).userid) <> {<read>}
      and response_msg = "401 permission denied"
```

We can generate test data from each functional scenario. Table 3 shows some sample test cases covering the three functional scenarios and the corresponding test results.

Table 3. Sample Test Cases: Account_Details GET API operation

Functional scenario	Test case	Execution result	Expected result	Test oracle
FS1	(True, True)	True	True	False
FS2	(False, True)	False	False	False
FS3	(True, True)	False	True	True

To cover functional scenario 1 (FS1), we generate a sample test case *(true, true)* for the two input variables *account_id* and *userid* respectively. After executing the test case, the output value of *account_info* yields a truth value of *true* against the expected truth value of *true*. We proceed to generate test case *(false, true)* for the functional scenario 2 (FS2) and the output value of *account_info* yields a truth value of *false* against the expected truth value of *false*. Running the test case *(true,true)* for FS3 the output variable *account_info* yields a truth value of *false* which violates the expected truth value of *true*.

Considering that REST APIs are stateless, developers only need to observe the execution results and determine the conformance of the operations corresponding to their associated processes by analysing the defining conditions.

5 Case Study

We conducted a small experiment to validate our approach by using it to model specifications of a RESTful online banking API. The model API allows users to conduct banking operations, such as *view account details, view account balance, make utility bills payments, transfer money to other accounts.* The model specifications include 1 module containing 15 processes. The processes reflect the resources to be retrieved by the API via requests made by a client application for example.

```
/onlinebanking/accounts/{accountid}
/onlinebanking/accounts/balance/{accountid}
/onlinebanking/accounts
/onlinebanking/TransferBetweenMyAccounts/{transferaccountID}
/onlinebanking/TransferToOtherBankCustomers/customer/{customeraccID}
```

The REST architectural style requires that all resources should be addressable and connected. Thus, we require that our resource model should not contain an isolated resource. Since we are describing RESTful web interfaces, the allowed operations on resources are GET, POST, PUT, PATCH and DELETE. The GET method retrieves a representation of a resource without any side effects i.e., it does not cause a change in the state of the system. For example GET */onlinebanking/accounts?id = {id}* and GET */onlinebanking/CardsOverview?card_id = {cardid}* represent GET requests on resources accounts and *CardsOverview* respectively. Whenever a GET method is invoked on a resource, it gives the representation of the resource as a response if the resource is available, else a response code of 404 is sent back. The POST, PUT, PATCH or DELETE methods can have side effects i.e. they can cause a change in the state of the interacting resource. Adopting our proposed approach as described in Sect. 3, we first expressed the API's business functions (functional requirements) as well as their associated constraints (security requirements) in RAML. Next, we converted the RAML based specifications into SOFL based specifications by applying our RAML to SOFL transformation rules. We then formalized the specifications so as to have a base for testing and validating their conformance to their expected functional and security attributes as well as achieve inter-weaved functional and security requirements. Finally, we transformed this formalized specification into executable web service by implementing it in Django REST framework. Since the scope of the application is too large to be covered in this section, we shall use GET */onlinebanking/accounts?account_id = {accountid}* as an example. The SOFL excerpt in Sect. 4 shows a SOFL based representation of a contract generated for the HTTP method GET on accounts resource.

6   Case Study Implementation Using Django REST Framework

Django REST framework abstracts the complexities of developing RESTful web services in Python. Django REST frameworks works on top of Django web framework which can be understood with its three basic files that support separation of concerns i.e. *models.py, urls.py* and *views.py* where models.py contains descriptions of database tables, *views.py* contains the business logic and *urls.py* specifies which URI to map to which view. When using Django REST framework on top of Django web framework, an additional file serializers.py defines the representational format i.e. JSON or XML of the resources exposed by a RESTful API end point. The excerpt below gives an executable representation of the code manually generated from our formalized SOFL specifications on GET */onlinebanking/accounts?customeraccount = {account_id}* API endpoint

```python
from django.db import models
from django.contrib.auth.models import User
from . import countrylist, choicelists

# models.py
class CustomerAccount(models.Model):
    INACTIVE = 0
    ACTIVE = 1
    SUSPENDED = 2
    CLOSED = 3
    STATUS = ((INACTIVE, 'In-active account'),
              (ACTIVE, 'Active Account'),
              (CLOSED, 'CLosed Account'),
              (SUSPENDED, 'Suspended Account'),)

    account_owner = models.ForeignKey(User, on_delete=models.CASCADE)
    account_number = models.CharField(max_length=13, unique=True)
    account_name = models.CharField(max_length=40,
                            help_text="Maximum of 40 Characters")
    current_balance = models.FloatField(null=True)
    account_currency = models.IntegerField(
                        choices=choicelists.ACCOUNTCURRENCY,
                        default=choicelists.KES)
    account_status = models.IntegField(choices=STATUS, default=INACTIVE)
    uncleared_amount = models.FloatField(null=True)


    def __str__(self):
        return '{0}, {1}'.format(self.account_number,
                        self.account_name)
#api/serializers.py
#API serializers with business logic for account transfers
from django.urls import reverse
from rest_framework import serializers
from onlinebanking.models import  CustomerAccount

class CustomerAccountSerializer(serializers.ModelSerializer):
```

```
     class Meta:
       model = CustomerAccount
       fields = ('account_owner', 'account_number', 'account_name',\
                 'current_balance', 'account_currency',\
                 'account_status', 'uncleared_amount')
 class InternalAccountTransferSerializer(serializers.ModelSerializer):
     account_transfer = serializers.SerializerMethodField()
     class Meta:
         model = CustomerAccount
         fields = ('account_owner','account_number','account_name',\
                   'current_balance','account_currency','account_status')
     def get_account_transfer(self, transfer_amount):
             self.current_balance = self.current_balance
                                    - transfer_amount
      return reverse ('internaltransfer', args=(transfer_amount,))


 class CompleteInternalAccountTransferSerializer (
                         serializers.ModelSerializer):
     update_transfer = serializers.SerializerMethodField()
     class Meta:
       model = CustomerAccount
       fields = ('account_owner','account_number','account_name',\
                 'current_balance','account_currency','account_status',)
     def get_update_transfer(self, transfer_amount):
         self.current_balance = self.current_balance + transfer_amount
         return reverse('completetransfer', args=(transfer_amount,))


# API views excerpt. Lists customer accounts and view for
# Internal account transfers
from rest_framework import generics
from .models import CustomerAccount
from .serializers import CustomerAccountSerialize,
         CompleteInternalAccountTransferSerializer

class CustomerAccountAPIView(generics.ListAPIView):
    queryset = CustomerAccount.objects.all()
    serializer_class = CustomerAccountSerializer

class InternalAccountTransfersAPIView(generics.RetrieveUpdateAPIView):
    lookup_field = 'id'
    queryset = CustomerAccount.objects.all()
    serializer_class = CompleteInternalAccountTransferSerializer
```

Our approach of testing consisted of three steps. First, we generated test cases that included both input and output values for the process specifications. We achieved this by extracting independent paths from SOFL processes represented by the API's resource paths. We transformed the pre-, post-conditions of each process involved in each path to Functional Scenario Form (FSF), constructed Functional Scenario Sequence (FSS) of the involved processes and generated test cases from the FSS. Second, we evaluated the specifications with the test cases and finally we analyze the test results in order to determine whether violations of their functional and security attributes are detected. Since our specifications do not indicate algorithms for implementation but rather are expressed with predicate expressions such as pre- and post-conditions, we substituted all the variables involved with concrete values of their types while evaluating them. The results of such evaluations are Boolean values: true or false. We analyzed the test results by comparing the evaluation results with a predicate expression that represent the functional and /or security property to be verified for each process. Consistency between the evaluated results and the predicate expressions implied satisfiability of the properties in test.

7 Related Work

As far as the security of web APIs is concerned, several approaches have been studied according to published literature. Fett et al. [12] propose a rigorous, systematic formal analysis of OpenID Financial-grade API (FAPI) based on a web infrastructure model. They first develop a precise model of the FAPI in the web infrastructure model, including different profiles for read-only and read-write access, different types of clients, and different combinations of security features, capturing the complex interactions in a web-based environment. They then use their model of FAPI to precisely define central security properties of an API. Yamaguchi et al. [13] propose an API-based design approach that allows non-security experts easily configure and enable Web Services Security. Their design approach mainly focusses on abstraction of Web Services Security processing by providing a six-step programming model for configuring and testing Web Services Security. Alqahatni et al. [14] introduce an approach for automatically tracing source code vulnerabilities at the API level across project boundaries. Their approach takes advantage of Semantic Web and its technology stack to establish a unified knowledge representation that can link and analyze vulnerabilities across project boundaries. Woo et al. [15] introduce a security assessment framework for RESTful services in a Software Defined Network (SDN). The framework aims at automatically finding out security holes related to RESTful services in the SDN controller.

However, studies targeting formal requirement engineering approaches to specifying and testing RESTful APIs are limited. We seek to plug this research gap by providing a formal approach that offers a secure by design approach for RESTful APIs. We take advantage of formal specification-based conformance testing to infer the satisfiability of both security and functional requirements provided by an API operation.

8 Conclusion and Future Works

We have described an approach to interweaving the functional and security requirements of RESTful APIs and to testing whether the implementation of the requirements satisfies its specification. Our approach offers three steps. The first step yields a set of functional and security requirements of a RESTful API expressed in RAML definitions. The second step focus on transformation of the RAML definitions to SOFL based semi-formal specifications. We express the REST specific request methods as SOFL processes with informal pre-post conditions and their related security requirements as either SOFL module invariants or guard conditions in functional scenarios of the process. The third step involves formalization of the pre-post conditions and "proving" the satisfiability of the functional and security requirements through specification testing. We have confirmed the feasibility of our approach by using it to develop a model of an online banking API. In the future, we will extend the research by developing a supporting tool for semi-automatic conversion from RAML definitions to SOFL specifications and from formalized SOFL API specifications to executable API code.

References

1. Richardson, M.A.L., Ruby, S.: RESTful Web APIs. 1st edn. O'reilly Media Inc., Sebastopol (2013)
2. Fielding, R.T.: Architectural styles and the design of network-based software architectures - Ph.D. dissertation. University of California, Irvine (2000). https://www.ics.uci.edu/~fielding/pubs/dissertation/fielding_dissertation.pdf
3. Liu, S.: Formal Engineering for Industrial Software Development Using the SOFL Method. Springer-Verlag, Heidelberg (2004)
4. Liu, S., Offutt, A.J., Ho-Stuart, C., Sun, Y., Ohba, M.: SOFL: a formal engineering methodology for industrial applications. IIEEE Trans. Softw. Eng. **24**(1), 24–45 (1998). https://doi.org/10.1109/32.663996
5. Jones, C.B.: Systematic Software Development Using VDM, 2nd edn. Prentice Hall (1990)
6. Hunter, K.L.: Irresistible APIs- Designing Web APIs that Developers will Love. Manning Publications Co. (2017)
7. Harihara Subramanian, P.R.: Hands-On RESTful API Design Patterns and Best Practices. Packet Publishing (2019)
8. Miao, W., Liu, S.: A Formal Specification-based Integration Testing Approach, pp. 26–43. Japan, Kyoto (2012)
9. Biehl, M.: API Architecture: The Big Picture for Building APIs, vol. 2. API University Series (2015)
10. Jiang, L., Chen, H., Deng, F.: A security evaluation method based on STRIDE model for web service. In: 2010 2nd International Workshop on Intelligent Systems and Applications, Wuhan, China, May 2010, pp. 1–5 (2010). https://doi.org/10.1109/iwisa.2010.5473445
11. Liu, S.: Integrating specification-based review and testing for detecting errors in programs. In: The 9th International Conference on Formal Engineering Methods (ICFEM2007), pp. 136–150 November 2007
12. Fett, D., Hosseyni, P., Kusters, R.: An extensive formal security analysis of the OpenID Financial-Grade API. In: 2019 IEEE Symposium on Security and Privacy (SP), San Francisco, CA, USA, pp. 453–471 May 2019. https://doi.org/10.1109/sp.2019.00067
13. Yamaguchi, Y., Chung, H.-V., Teraguchi, M., Uramoto, N.: Easy-to-use programming model for web services security. In: The 2nd IEEE Asia-Pacific Service Computing Conference (APSCC 2007), Tsubuka Science City, Japan, pp. 275–282 December 2007. https://doi.org/10.1109/APSCC.2007.38

14. Alqahtani, S.S., Eghan, E.E., Rilling, J.: Recovering semantic traceability links between APIs and security vulnerabilities: an ontological modeling approach. In: 2017 IEEE International Conference on Software Testing, Verification and Validation (ICST), Tokyo, Japan, pp. 80–91 March 2017. https://doi.org/10.1109/icst.2017.15
15. Woo, S., Lee, S., Kim, J., Shin, S.: RE-CHECKER: towards secure RESTful service in software-defined networking. In: 2018 IEEE Conference on Network Function Virtualization and Software Defined Networks (NFV-SDN), Verona, Italy, pp. 1–5 November 2018. https://doi.org/10.1109/nfv-sdn.2018.8725649

Pointer Program Synthesis
as Non-deterministic Planning

Xu Lu and Bin Yu$^{(\boxtimes)}$

ICTT and ISN Lab, Xidian University, Xi'an 710071, People's Republic of China
byu@xidian.edu.cn

Abstract. Program synthesis is the task of automatically constructing programs that satisfy a given high-level formal specification (constraints). In this paper, we concentrate on the synthesis problem of a
special category of program, named pointer program that manipulate
heaps. Separation logic has been applied successfully in modular reasoning of pointer programs. There are many studies on formal analysis of
pointer programs using a form of symbolic execution based on a decidable proof theory of separation logic. Automatic specification checking
can be done efficiently by means of symbolic execution. With this basis,
we present a novel approach to simulate the symbolic execution process for the sake of synthesizing pointer programs. Concretely, symbolic
execution rules are compiled into a non-deterministic planning problem
which can be directly solved by existing planners. The reason of using
non-deterministic planning is that it enables to generate strong cyclic
plans where loop and branch connections (similar to basic program constructs) may appear. We show the preliminary experimental results on
synthesizing several programs that work with linked lists.

Keywords: Program synthesis · Non-deterministic planning ·
Separation logic · Symbolic execution

1 Introduction

Automatic synthesis of program has long been considered as one of the most
central problems in computer science. It is the task of automatically finding
programs from the underlying language that satisfy user intent expressed in
some form of (formal) constraints [15]. Usually, we need to perform certain kind
of search over the state space of all potential programs in order to generate one
that meets the constraints.

Fruitful studies have achieved a lot of progress for program synthesis in many
communities. Beginning in 1957, Alonzo Church defines the problem to synthesize a circuit from mathematical requirements. Reactive synthesis is a special

This research is supported by the National Natural Science Foundation of China under
Grant 61806158, China Postdoctoral Science Foundation under Grant 2019T120881
and Grant 2018M643585.

J. Xue et al. (Eds.): SOFL+MSVL 2020, LNCS 12723, pp. 126–141, 2021.
https://doi.org/10.1007/978-3-030-77474-5_9

case of program synthesis that aims to produce a controller that reacts to environment's inputs satisfying a given temporal logic specification [5]. An international competition called the Reactive Synthesis Competition is held annually since 2014.[1] Camacho et al. establish the correspondence of planning problems with temporally extended goals to reactive synthesis problems [8]. Building on this correspondence, synthesis can be realized more efficiently via planning. A pattern-based code synthesis approach is presented to assemble an application from existing components [12]. The code patterns are expressed by planning domain models. Recently, the application of AI techniques especially deep learning methods in program synthesis becomes an active research topic. DeepCoder, developed by Microsoft, is to train a neural network to predict properties of program that generated the outputs from the inputs [1]. Empirically, DeepCoder is able to help generate small programs only containing several lines. Gu et al. propose a deep learning based approach to generate API usage sequences for a given natural language query [14]. The work in [2] transforms a graphical user interface screenshot created by a designer into computer code by deep learning methods. Various codes for three different platforms can be generated with the accuracy over 77%. In addition, other techniques from different perspectives such as inductive programming [16] and genetic programming [20] are also applied in program synthesis. However, synthesizing a program is still a challenging problem due to the large search space.

AI planning, or planning for short, has been successfully applied in many fields. Planning is the problem of finding a sequence of actions that leads from an initial state to a goal state [13]. Classical planning is the problem such that each action has deterministic outcome. If the outcomes of some actions are uncertain, the problem is referred to as a non-deterministic planning problem. The non-deterministic actions give rise to the exponential growth in the search space and hence make the problem more difficult even in the simplest situation where the states of the world are full observable. A plan to a non-deterministic planning problem may have loops or branches which are similar to basic programming language constructs. Inspired by this, we obtain the idea to bridge the gap between program synthesis and non-deterministic planning.

Programs that manipulate heaps are called pointer programs. Pointer operations allow dynamic heap allocation and deallocation, pointer reference and dereference etc. These characteristics make pointer programs more error prone. Separation logic is an extension of Hoare logic addressing the task of reasoning about pointer programs [19]. Its key power lies in the separating conjunction $\Sigma_1 * \Sigma_2$, which asserts that Σ_1 and Σ_2 hold for separate portions of heaps, leading the reasoning in a modular way. Starting from the pioneer work [4], which presents a symbolic execution of a fragment of separation logic formulas called symbolic heaps, many researchers exploit symbolic execution techniques to build formal proofs of pointer programs [7,10,17]. The most famous tool, Infer [6], is a static analyzer developed at Facebook rooting on symbolic execution.

---

[1] http://www.syntcomp.org/.

This paper focusses on the pointer program synthesis. We propose a compilation based approach to simulate the symbolic execution process of pointer programs by non-deterministic planning. The compilation result is specified in the Planning Domain Definition Language (PDDL) [11] that is a standard input to the state-of-the-art planners. The major contribution of our work is the encoding approach from symbolic execution rules to non-deterministic planning models. To the best of our knowledge, it is unique in using non-deterministic planners as program synthesizers.

The rest of the paper is organized as follows. Section 2 and Sect. 3 review the notations of non-deterministic planning and symbolic heaps; Sect. 4 shows symbolic execution theory of pointer programs with symbolic heaps; Sect. 5 describes how to compile symbolic execution rules into non-deterministic planning problems; Sect. 6 gives the experimental results; the last section concludes our work.

2   FOND Planning

We assume environments are fully observable. Following [13], a *Fully Observable Non-Deterministic* (FOND) planning problem $\mathcal{P}$ is a tuple $(\mathcal{F}, \mathcal{I}, \mathcal{G}, \mathcal{A})$, where $\mathcal{F}$ is a set of *fluents*, $\mathcal{I} \subseteq F$ characterizes what holds initially, $\mathcal{G} \subseteq \mathcal{F}$ characterizes the goal, and $\mathcal{A}$ is the set of actions. The set of literals of $\mathcal{F}$ is $Lits(\mathcal{F}) = \mathcal{F} \cup \{\neg f \mid f \in \mathcal{F}\}$. Each action $a \in \mathcal{A}$ is associated with a pair $(pre(a), eff(a))$, where $pre(a) \subseteq Lits(\mathcal{F})$ is the precondition and $eff(a)$ is a set of outcomes of a. An outcome $o \in eff(a)$ is a set of conditional effects (with, possibly, an empty condition), each of the form $C \rhd l$, where $C \subseteq Lits(\mathcal{F})$ and $l \in Lits(\mathcal{F})$. Briefly speaking, $C \rhd l$ expresses the meaning that after applying a in the current state, l becomes true in the next state if current state satisfies C. A planning state s is a subset of $\mathcal{F}$ that are true.[2] Given $s \subseteq \mathcal{F}$ and $f \in \mathcal{F}$, we say that s satisfies f, denoted $s \models f$ iff $f \in s$. In addition, $s \models \neg f$ iff $f \notin s$, and $s \models L$ for a set of literals L, if $s \models l$ for every $l \in L$. An action a is *applicable* in state s if $s \models pre(a)$. We say s' is a result of applying a in s iff for one outcome o in $eff(a)$, $s' = s \setminus \{f \mid (C \rhd \neg f) \in o, s \models C\} \cup \{f \mid (C \rhd f) \in o, s \models C\}$.

Solutions to a FOND planning problem are referred to as *policies*. A policy p is a partial mapping from states to actions. We say a is applicable in s if $p(s) = a$. An *execution* σ of a policy p in state s is a finite sequence $\langle(s_0, a_0), \ldots, (s_{n-1}, a_{n-1}), s_n\rangle$ or an infinite sequence $\langle(s_0, a_0), (s_1, a_1), \ldots\rangle$, where $s_0 = s$, and all of its state-action-state substrings s, a, s' satisfy $p(s) = a$ and s' is a result of applying a in s. Finite executions ending in a state s if $p(s)$ is undefined. A state trace π can be *yielded* from an execution σ by removing all the action symbols from σ.

---

[2] Fluents in $\mathcal{F} \setminus \mathcal{I}$ are implicitly assumed to be false according to the closed world assumption.

An infinite execution σ is *fair* iff whenever s, a occurs infinitely often within σ, then for every s' that is a result of applying a in s, s, a, s' occurs infinitely often. A solution to $\mathcal{P}$ is *strong cyclic* iff each of its executions in $\mathcal{I}$ is either finite and ends in a state that satisfies $\mathcal{G}$ or is infinite and unfair [9]. Intuitively speaking, the execution fairness of a strong cyclic solution guarantees that a goal state can eventually be reached from every reachable state with no effect that is always ignored. There are also *strong* solutions and *weak* solutions to a FOND planning problem, but we will not need those definitions in this paper.

3   Symbolic Heaps

We assume a set of programs variables Var (ranged over by $x, y, \ldots$), and a set of primed variables Var' (ranged over by $x', y', \ldots$). All variables are restricted as pointer type. The primed variables can only be used within logical formulas. The concrete heap models contain a set of locations Loc and a special notation nil which indicates a null pointer value. Let $Val = Loc \cup \{nil\}$. We then define stack $\mathcal{S}$ and heap $\mathcal{H}$ as:

$$\mathcal{S} : (Var \cup Var') \rightharpoonup Val \qquad\qquad \mathcal{H} : Loc \rightharpoonup Val$$

A heap maps a location to a location or nil representing a heap cell. The syntax of symbolic heap is defined below [4] which is a strict subset of separation logic [19].

$$
\begin{array}{ll}
e ::= x \mid x' \mid nil & \text{expression} \\
\Pi ::= e_1 = e_2 \mid e_1 \neq e_2 \mid true \mid \Pi_1 \wedge \Pi_2 & \text{pure formula} \\
\Sigma ::= emp \mid e_1 \mapsto e_2 \mid ls(e_1, e_2) \mid true \mid \Sigma_1 * \Sigma_2 & \text{spatial formula} \\
P ::= \Pi \wr \Sigma \mid \exists x' : P & \text{symbolic heap}
\end{array}
$$

Note that the assertions are restricted without negations and universal quantifiers. A symbolic heap $\Pi \wr \Sigma$ can be divided into pure part Π (heap independent) and spatial part Σ (heap dependent), where Π is essentially an $\wedge$-separated sequence of pure formulas, and Σ a $*$-separated sequence of spatial formulas. The pure part is straightforward to understand, and the spatial part characterize spatial features of heaps. $e_1 \mapsto e_2$ is read as e_1 points-to e_2. It can hold only in a singleton heap, where e_1 is the only active cell holding the value e_2. $ls(e_1, e_2)$ denotes a linked list segment with head pointer e_1 and e_2 holding in the tail cell. A complete linked list is one that satisfies $ls(e, nil)$.

The semantics of symbolic heaps is given by a relation $\mathcal{S}, \mathcal{H} \models_{\text{SH}} P$. $\mathcal{H} = \mathcal{H}_1 \bullet \mathcal{H}_2$ indicates that the domains of $\mathcal{H}_1$ and $\mathcal{H}_2$ are disjoint, and $\mathcal{H}$ is their union.

$[\![x]\!]s \stackrel{\text{def}}{=} s(x)$ $\quad$ $[\![x']\!]s \stackrel{\text{def}}{=} s(x')$ $\quad$ $[\![nil]\!]s \stackrel{\text{def}}{=} nil$

$\mathcal{S}, \mathcal{H} \models_{\text{SH}} e_1 = e_2$ $\quad$ iff $\quad$ $[\![e_1]\!]s = [\![e_2]\!]s$.

$\mathcal{S}, \mathcal{H} \models_{\text{SH}} e_1 \neq e_2$ $\quad$ iff $\quad$ $[\![e_1]\!]s \neq [\![e_2]\!]s$.

$\mathcal{S}, \mathcal{H} \models_{\text{SH}} true$ $\quad$ iff $\quad$ always.

$\mathcal{S}, \mathcal{H} \models_{\text{SH}} \Pi_1 \wedge \Pi_2$ $\quad$ iff $\quad$ $\mathcal{S}, \mathcal{H} \models_{\text{SH}} \Pi_1$ and $\mathcal{S}, \mathcal{H} \models_{\text{SH}} \Pi_2$.

$\mathcal{S}, \mathcal{H} \models_{\text{SH}} emp$ $\quad$ iff $\quad$ $\mathcal{H} = \emptyset$.

$\mathcal{S}, \mathcal{H} \models_{\text{SH}} e_1 \mapsto e_2$ $\quad$ iff $\quad$ $\mathcal{H} = [([\![e_1]\!]s, [\![e_2]\!]s)]$.

$\mathcal{S}, \mathcal{H} \models_{\text{SH}} ls(e_1, e_2)$ $\quad$ iff $\quad$ there is a nonempty acyclic path from $[\![e_1]\!]s$ to $[\![e_2]\!]s$ in $\mathcal{H}$ and this path contains all heaps cells in $\mathcal{H}$.

$\mathcal{S}, \mathcal{H} \models_{\text{SH}} \Sigma_1 * \Sigma_2$ $\quad$ iff $\quad$ $\exists \mathcal{H}_1, \mathcal{H}_2 : \mathcal{H} = \mathcal{H}_1 \bullet \mathcal{H}_2$ and $\mathcal{S}, \mathcal{H}_1 \models_{\text{SH}} \Sigma_1$ and $\mathcal{S}, \mathcal{H}_2 \models_{\text{SH}} \Sigma_2$.

$\mathcal{S}, \mathcal{H} \models_{\text{SH}} \Pi \wr \Sigma$ $\quad$ iff $\quad$ $\mathcal{S}, \mathcal{H} \models_{\text{SH}} \Pi$ and $\mathcal{S}, \mathcal{H} \models_{\text{SH}} \Sigma$.

$\mathcal{S}, \mathcal{H} \models_{\text{SH}} \exists x' : P$ $\quad$ iff $\quad$ $\exists v \in Val : \mathcal{S}, \mathcal{H} \models_{\text{SH}} P(v/x')$.

For simplicity, symbolic heap we define only allows to reason about linked lists. The field can be regarded as the next pointer. For other linked shapes such as binary trees, we can extend the points-to assertion as $e_1 \mapsto e_2, e_3$. The semantics of list segment is given informally, saying that it holds of given heap containing at least one heap cell. Therefore it is equivalent to the least predicate satisfying:

$$ls(e_1, e_2) \Leftrightarrow e_1 \mapsto e_2 \vee \exists x' : e_1 \neq e_2 \wedge e_1 \mapsto x' * ls(x', e_2)$$

4   Symbolic Execution

In this section we give symbolic execution rules for a pointer programming language. The grammar of commands is given by:

$b ::= e_1 = e_2 \mid e_1 \neq e_2$ $\hfill$ Boolean terms

$c ::= x := e \mid x := [e] \mid [e] := e' \mid new(x) \mid dispose(e)$ $\hfill$ Primitive commands

$\mathcal{C} ::= c \mid \mathcal{C}_1; \mathcal{C}_2 \mid while\ (b)\ do\ \{\mathcal{C}\} \mid if\ (b)\ then\ \{\mathcal{C}_1\}\ else\ \{\mathcal{C}_2\}$ $\hfill$ Commands

The heap dereferencing operator $[\cdot]$ is similar to symbolic heaps, that refers to the "next" field. $x := e$ is the assignment, $x := [e]$ and $[e] := e'$ are called lookup and mutation respectively, $new(x)$ and $dispose(e)$ are heap allocation and deallocation commands.

Shown in Table 1, the symbolic execution semantics $P, \mathcal{C} \implies P'$ takes a symbolic heap P and a primitive command $\mathcal{C}$ as input, and transforms it into a new symbolic heap P' as an output. The primed variables x', y' are fresh primed variables in these rules.

Table 1. Symbolic execution rules

$\Pi \wr \Sigma$	$new(x)$	$\implies$	$\exists x', y' : (\Pi \wr \Sigma)(x'/x) * x \mapsto y'$
$\Pi \wr \Sigma * e_1 \mapsto e_2$	$dispose(e_1)$	$\implies$	$\Pi \wr \Sigma$
$\Pi \wr \Sigma$	$x := e$	$\implies$	$\exists x' : x = e(x'/x) \wedge (\Pi \wr \Sigma)(x'/x)$
$\Pi \wr \Sigma * e_1 \mapsto e_2$	$[e_1] := e_3$	$\implies$	$\Pi \wr \Sigma * e_1 \mapsto e_3$
$\Pi \wr \Sigma * e_1 \mapsto e_2$	$x := [e_1]$	$\implies$	$\exists x' : x = e_2(x'/x) \wedge (\Pi \wr \Sigma * e_1 \mapsto e_2)(x'/x)$

We use notation $A(e)$ for primitive commands that access heap cell e:

$$A(e) ::= [e] := e' \mid x := [e] \mid dispose(e)$$

When executing $A(e)$, we expect its precondition to be in a particular form $\Pi \wr \Sigma * e \mapsto e'$. That is, the value holds in e should be explicitly exposed in order to fire the rule. Therefore, we have to equivalently rearrange the precondition whenever current symbolic heap do not match the rule.

Rearrangement rules are listed below. The Switch rule simply makes use of equalities to recognize that a dereferencing step is possible. The other two rules correspond to unrolling a list segment. To do so, we need to unroll the list to be a single heap cell (Unroll List2) or more cells (Unroll List1).

Rearrangement Rules

$$\text{Switch} \quad \frac{\Pi_1 \wr \Sigma_1 * e_1 \mapsto e_3, A(e_1) \implies \Pi_2 \wr \Sigma_2}{\Pi_1 \wr \Sigma_1 * e_2 \mapsto e_3, A(e_1) \implies \Pi_2 \wr \Sigma_2} \quad \Pi_1 \vdash e_1 = e_2$$

$$\text{Unroll List1} \quad \frac{\exists x' : e_1 \neq e_2 \wedge \Pi_1 \wr \Sigma_1 * e_1 \mapsto x' * ls(x', e_2), A(e_1) \implies \Pi_2 \wr \Sigma_2}{\Pi_1 \wr \Sigma_1 * ls(e_1, e_2), A(e_1) \implies \Pi_2 \wr \Sigma_2}$$

$$\text{Unroll List2} \quad \frac{\Pi_1 \wedge e_1 \mapsto e_2 \wr \Sigma_1, A(e_1) \implies \Pi_2 \wr \Sigma_2}{\Pi_1 \wr \Sigma_1 * ls(e_1, e_2), A(e_1) \implies \Pi_2 \wr \Sigma_2}$$

Generally, the number of symbolic heaps is infinite since primed variables can be introduced during symbolic execution. For example, in a loop that includes allocation (e.g., $while \ (true) \ do \ \{\ldots; new(x); \ldots\}$). An arbitrary length of symbolic heap can be generated, i.e., $x \mapsto x' * x' \mapsto x'' \cdots$. In order to achieve fixed-point convergence, abstraction rules $\Pi_1 \wr \Sigma_1 \rightsquigarrow \Pi_2 \wr \Sigma_2$ are introduced.

The main effort of abstraction rules is to reduce primed variables. The abstraction rules are reported below. On one hand, we can remove primed variables from the pure parts of formulas (Abs1). On the other hand, we can gobble up primed variables by merging lists, swallowing single cells into lists, and abstracting two cells by a list (Abs2 and Abs3). We use the notation $H(e_1, e_2)$ to stand for a formula in either of the form $e_1 \mapsto e_2$ or $ls(e_1, e_2)$.

Abstraction Rules

Abs1 $e = x' \wedge \Pi \wr \Sigma \rightsquigarrow (\Pi \wr \Sigma)(e/x')$ or $x' = e \wedge \Pi \wr \Sigma \rightsquigarrow (\Pi \wr \Sigma)(e/x')$

Abs2 $\dfrac{\Pi \vdash e_2 = nil \qquad x' \text{ not in } \{\Pi, \Sigma, e_1, e_2\}}{\Pi \wr \Sigma * H_1(e_1, x') * H_2(x', e_2) \rightsquigarrow \Pi \wr \Sigma * H(e_1, nil)}$

Abs3 $\dfrac{\Pi \vdash e_2 = e_3 \qquad x' \text{ not in } \{\Pi, \Sigma, e_1, e_2, e_3, e_4\}}{\Pi \wr \Sigma * H_1(e_1, x') * H_2(x', e_2) * H_3(e_3, e_4) \rightsquigarrow \Pi \wr \Sigma * ls(e_1, e_2) * H_3(e_3, e_4)}$

The $*$-conjunct $H_3(e_3, e_4)$ cannot be left out by considerations of soundness as Berdine and Calcagno pointed out [3,4]. If we want to abstract $H_1(-, -)$ and $H_2(-, -)$ into one, the end of the second should not point back into the first.

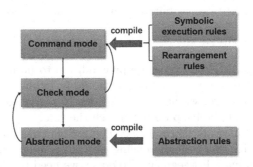

Fig. 1. The encoding approach

5   Compiling Symbolic Execution into FOND Planning

In this section we compile a pointer program synthesis problem into a FOND planning problem. The former is formalized as follows.

Definition 1 (Pointer Program Synthesis). *Given symbolic heaps P_{in} and P_{out} as input and output respectively, the task of pointer program synthesis is to generate a pointer program C that satisfies P_{in} and P_{out}.*

Figure 1 illustrates the key idea of our approach. There are three modes after compilation, i.e., Command mode, Check mode and Abstraction mode. The order of their executions is reflected by black arrows. The Command mode contains a set of planning actions encoded from primitive command. We do not encode the rearrangement rules into a separate phase. Instead, the rearrangement step is embedded in the encoding of $A(e)$. The actions in the Check mode are used to check the existence of an abstraction action that can fire. The abstraction rules are compiled into a set of abstraction actions.

Suppose the resulting FOND planning problem is $\mathcal{P} = (\mathcal{F}, \mathcal{I}, \mathcal{G}, \mathcal{A})$, where each component is described as follows. The initial state $\mathcal{I}$ and goal $\mathcal{G}$ are determined by P_{in} and P_{out} of specific synthesis problems.

Fluents: The set of fluents $\mathcal{F}$ is listed in Table 2, where int_0 represents the null value. Moreover, we use the fluents $command()$, $check()$, $choose()$, $abstraction()$ to represent different phases, and $abs_1()$, $abs_2()$, $abs_3()$ to denote which abstraction rule can be activated.

Table 2. Fluents of the encoded problem

Fluent	Meaning
$pvar(x)$	x is a program variable
$lvar(x')$	x' is a logical variable
$auxiliary(x')$	x' is a logical variable in use
$pt(x_1, x_2)$	A single heap cell
$ls(x_1, x_2)$	A linked list segment
$equal(x_1, x_2)$	Equality of x_1 and x_2
$var\text{-}num(x, v)$	Value of x is v in $\{int_i \mid 0 \le i \le n\}$
$active(v)$	Value v is allocated

Command Mode: Command mode is the first phase that a primitive command action is performed along with a possible rearrangement. Different from symbolic execution, here we do not distinguish rearrangement and command execution, only do rearrangement when it is needed. The encoded actions are shown in Table 3. For instance, there are two dispose actions corresponding to the dispose command, i.e., $dispose_1$ and $dispose_2$. The precondition of the former includes an explicit heap cell $pt(x_2, x_3)$, and that of the latter includes a list $ls(x_2, x_3)$ which needs to be unrolled as non-deterministic effects. The keyword "**oneof**" is used to express the non-deterministic effects in a planning model.

Table 3. Compilation of primitive commands

Action	Preconditions	Effects
$new(x_1, x_2, v_1, v_2)$	$command()$, $pvar(x_1)$, $lvar(x_2)$, $\neg auxiliary(x_2)$, $var\text{-}num(x_1, v_1)$, $var\text{-}num(x_2, int_0)$, $\neg active(v_2)$	$\neg command()$, $check()$, $pt(x_1, nil)$, $active(v_2)$, $var\text{-}num(x_1, v_2)$, $\neg var\text{-}num(x_1, v_1)$, $\forall y : \{equal(x_1, y)\} \rhd \{auxiliary(x_2), \neg equal(x_1, y), \neg equal(y, x_1), equal(x_2, y), equal(y, x_2), \neg var\text{-}num(x_2, int_0), var\text{-}num(x_2, v_1)\}$, $\forall y : \{pt(x_1, y)\} \rhd \{auxiliary(x_2), \neg pt(x_1, y), pt(x_2, y), \neg var\text{-}num(x_2, int_0), var\text{-}num(x_2, v_1)\}$, $\forall y : \{pt(y, x_1)\} \rhd \{auxiliary(x_2), \neg pt(y, x_1), pt(y, x_2), \neg var\text{-}num(x_2, int_0), var\text{-}num(x_2, v_1)\}$, $\forall y : \{ls(x_1, y)\} \rhd \{auxiliary(x_2), \neg ls(x_1, y), ls(x_2, y), \neg var\text{-}num(x_2, int_0), var\text{-}num(x_2, v_1)\}$, $\forall y : \{ls(y, x_1)\} \rhd \{auxiliary(x_2), \neg ls(y, x_1), ls(y, x_2), \neg var\text{-}num(x_2, int_0), var\text{-}num(x_2, v_1)\}$
$dispose_1(x_1, x_2, x_3, v)$	$command()$, $pvar(x_1)$, $active(v)$, $var\text{-}num(x_1, v)$, $var\text{-}num(x_2, v)$, $pt(x_2, x_3)$	$\neg command()$, $\neg pt(x_2, x_3)$, $\neg active(v)$, $\forall y : \{var\text{-}num(y, v)\} \rhd \{\neg var\text{-}num(y, v), var\text{-}num(y, int_0)\}$
$dispose_2(x_1, x_2, x_3, x_4, v_1, v_2)$	$command()$, $pvar(x_1)$, $lvar(x_4)$, $active(v_1)$, $\neg active(v_2)$, $var\text{-}num(x_1, v_1)$, $var\text{-}num(x_2, v_1)$, $ls(x_2, x_3)$, $\neg auxiliary(x_4)$, $var\text{-}num(x_4, int_0)$	$\neg command()$, $check()$, $\neg ls(x_2, x_3)$, $\neg active(v_1)$, $\forall y : \{var\text{-}num(y, v_1)\} \rhd \{\neg var\text{-}num(y, v_1), var\text{-}num(y, int_0)\}$, $\textbf{oneof}(\emptyset, \{auxiliary(x_4), ls(x_4, x_3), active(v_2), \neg var\text{-}num(x_4, int_0), var\text{-}num(x_4, v_2)\})$
$assign(x_1, x_2, x_3, v_1, v_2)$	$command()$, $pvar(x_1)$, $pvar(x_2)$, $lvar(x_3)$, $var\text{-}num(x_1, int_1)$, $var\text{-}num(x_2, int_2)$, $\neg auxiliary(x_3)$, $var\text{-}num(x_3, int_0)$	$\neg command()$, $check()$, $equal(x_1, x_2)$, $equal(x_2, x_1)$, $\{v_1 \neq v_2\} \rhd \{\neg var\text{-}num(x_1, v_1), var\text{-}num(x_1, v_2)\}$, $\forall y : \{equal(x_1, y)\} \rhd \{auxiliary(x_3), \neg equal(x_1, y), \neg equal(y, x_1), equal(x_3, y), equal(y, x_3), \neg var\text{-}num(x_3, int_0), var\text{-}num(x_3, v_1)\}$, $\forall y : \{pt(x_1, y)\} \rhd \{auxiliary(x_3), \neg pt(x_1, y), pt(x_3, y), \neg var\text{-}num(x_3, int_0), var\text{-}num(x_3, v_1)\}$, $\forall y : \{pt(y, x_1)\} \rhd \{auxiliary(x_3), \neg pt(y, x_1), pt(y, x_3), \neg var\text{-}num(x_3, int_0), var\text{-}num(x_3, v_1)\}$, $\forall y : \{ls(x_1, y)\} \rhd \{auxiliary(x_3), \neg ls(x_1, y), ls(x_3, y), \neg var\text{-}num(x_3, int_0), var\text{-}num(x_3, v_1)\}$, $\forall y : \{ls(y, x_1)\} \rhd \{auxiliary(x_3), \neg ls(y, x_1), ls(y, x_3), \neg var\text{-}num(x_3, int_0), var\text{-}num(x_3, v_1)\}$
$mutation_1(x_1, x_2, x_3, x_4, v)$	$command()$, $pvar(x_1)$, $pvar(x_4)$, $var\text{-}num(x_1, v)$, $var\text{-}num(x_2, v)$, $pt(x_2, x_3)$	$\neg command()$, $check()$, $\neg pt(x_2, x_3)$, $pt(x_2, x_4)$
$mutation_2(x_1, x_2, x_3, x_4, x_5, v_1, v_2)$	$command()$, $pvar(x_1)$, $pvar(x_4)$, $lvar(x_5)$, $\neg active(v_2)$, $var\text{-}num(x_1, v_1)$, $var\text{-}num(x_2, v_1)$, $ls(x_2, x_3)$, $\neg auxiliary(x_5)$, $var\text{-}num(x_5, int_0)$	$\neg command()$, $check()$, $\neg ls(x_2, x_3)$, $\textbf{oneof}(\{pt(x_2, x_4)\}, \{auxiliary(x_5), pt(x_2, x_4), ls(x_5, x_3), active(v_2), \neg var\text{-}num(x_5, int_0), var\text{-}num(x_5, v_2)\})$

(continued)

Table 3. (*continued*)

Action	Preconditions	Effects
$lookup_1(x_1, x_2, x_3, x_4,$ $x_5, v_1, v_2, v_3)$	$command(),$ $pvar(x_1),$ $pvar(x_2),$ $lvar(x_5),$ $var\text{-}num(x_1, v_1),$ $var\text{-}num(x_4, v_2),$ $var\text{-}num(x_2, v_3),$ $var\text{-}num(x_3, v_3),$ $pt(x_3, x_4),$ $\neg auxiliary(x_5),$ $var\text{-}num(x_5, int_0)$	$\neg command(), check(), equal(x_1, x_4), equal(x_4, x_1),$ $\{v_1 \neq v_2\} \rhd \{\neg var\text{-}num(x_1, v_1), var\text{-}num(x_1, v_2)\},$ $\forall y : \{equal(x_1, y)\} \rhd \{auxiliary(x_5), \neg equal(x_1, y),$ $\neg equal(y, x_1), equal(x_5, y), equal(y, x_5),$ $\neg var\text{-}num(x_5, int_0), var\text{-}num(x_5, v_1)\},$ $\forall y : \{pt(x_1, y)\} \rhd \{auxiliary(x_5), \neg pt(x_1, y), pt(x_5, y),$ $\neg var\text{-}num(x_5, int_0), var\text{-}num(x_5, v_1)\},$ $\forall y : \{pt(y, x_1)\} \rhd \{auxiliary(x_5), \neg pt(y, x_1), pt(y, x_5),$ $\neg var\text{-}num(x_5, int_0), var\text{-}num(x_5, v_1)\},$ $\forall y : \{ls(x_1, y)\} \rhd \{auxiliary(x_5), \neg ls(x_1, y), ls(x_5, y),$ $\neg var\text{-}num(x_5, int_0), var\text{-}num(x_5, v_1)\},$ $\forall y : \{ls(y, x_1)\} \rhd \{auxiliary(x_5), \neg ls(y, x_1), ls(y, x_5),$ $\neg var\text{-}num(x_5, int_0), var\text{-}num(x_5, v_1)\}$
$lookup_2(x_1, x_2, x_3, x_4,$ $x_5, x_6, v_1, v_2, v_3, v_4)$	$command(),$ $pvar(x_1),$ $pvar(x_2),$ $lvar(x_5),$ $lvar(x_6),$ $var\text{-}num(x_1, v_1),$ $var\text{-}num(x_4, v_2),$ $var\text{-}num(x_2, v_3),$ $var\text{-}num(x_3, v_3),$ $ls(x_3, x_4),$ $\neg active(v_4),$ $\neg auxiliary(x_5),$ $var\text{-}num(x_5, int_0),$ $\neg auxiliary(x_6),$ $var\text{-}num(x_6, int_0)$	$\neg command(), check(), \neg ls(x_3, x_4),$ $\{v_1 \neq v_5\} \rhd \{\neg var\text{-}num(x_1, v_1), var\text{-}num(x_1, v_5)\},$ $\forall y : \{equal(x_1, y)\} \rhd \{auxiliary(x_5), \neg equal(x_1, y),$ $\neg equal(y, x_1), equal(x_5, y), equal(x_5, y),$ $\neg var\text{-}num(x_5, int_0), var\text{-}num(x_5, v_1)\},$ $\forall y : \{pt(x_1, y)\} \rhd \{auxiliary(x_5), \neg pt(x_1, y), pt(x_5, y),$ $\neg var\text{-}num(x_5, int_0), var\text{-}num(x_5, v_1)\},$ $\forall y : \{pt(y, x_1)\} \rhd \{auxiliary(x_5), \neg pt(y, x_1), pt(y, x_5),$ $\neg var\text{-}num(x_5, int_0), var\text{-}num(x_5, v_1)\},$ $\forall y : \{ls(x_1, y)\} \rhd \{auxiliary(x_5), \neg ls(x_1, y), ls(x_5, y),$ $\neg var\text{-}num(x_5, int_0), var\text{-}num(x_5, v_1)\},$ $\forall y : \{ls(y, x_1)\} \rhd \{auxiliary(x_5), \neg ls(y, x_1), ls(y, x_5),$ $\neg var\text{-}num(x_5, int_0), var\text{-}num(x_5, v_1)\},$ $\textbf{oneof}(\{pt(x_3, x_4), equal(x_1, x_4), equal(x_4, x_1),$ $\neg var\text{-}num(x_1, v_1), var\text{-}num(x_1, v_2)\}, \{auxiliary(x_6),$ $active(v_4), equal(x_1, x_6), equal(x_6, x_1),$ $\neg var\text{-}num(x_1, v_1), var\text{-}num(x_1, v_4), pt(x_3, x_6),$ $ls(x_6, x_4), \neg var\text{-}num(x_6, int_0), var\text{-}num(x_6, v_4)\})$

Check Mode: The definition actions in Check mode are shown in Table 4. Action *check-act* alters the truth value of flags $abs_i(), i = 1, 2, 3$ according to the current state whenever a corresponding abstraction rule is enabled. Then the *choose-act* will be executed to determine the next phase to be switched with respect to $abs_i()$. When no abstraction rules can be applied, the next phase is the command mode, otherwise it is still turned to the abstraction mode.

Table 4. Actions in Check mode

Action	Preconditions	Effects
check-act()	check()	$\neg check(), choose(),$ $\{\exists x_1, x_2 : pvar(x_1) \wedge lvar(x_2) \wedge equal(x_1, x_2))\} \rhd \{abs_1()\},$ $\forall x_1, x_2, x_3 : \{pt(x_1, x_2), pt(x_2, x_3), auxiliary(x_2),$ $\exists v : var\text{-}num(x_1, v) \wedge \neg var\text{-}num(x_3, v), \forall y : \neg equal(y, x_2) \wedge$ $\neg ls(y, x_2) \wedge \neg ls(x_2, y), \forall y : y \neq x_1 \rightarrow \neg pt(y, x_2),$ $\forall y : y \neq x_3 \rightarrow \neg pt(x_2, y)\} \rhd \{abs_2()\},$ $\forall x_1, x_2, x_3 : \{pt(x_1, x_2), ls(x_2, x_3), auxiliary(x_2),$ $\exists v : var\text{-}num(x_1, v) \wedge \neg var\text{-}num(x_3, v), \forall y : \neg equal(y, x_2) \wedge$ $\neg ls(y, x_2) \wedge \neg pt(x_2, y), \forall y : y \neq x_1 \rightarrow \neg pt(y, x_2),$ $\forall y : y \neq x_3 \rightarrow \neg ls(x_2, y)\} \rhd \{abs_2()\},$ $\forall x_1, x_2, x_3 : \{ls(x_1, x_2), pt(x_2, x_3), auxiliary(x_2),$ $\exists v : var\text{-}num(x_1, v) \wedge \neg var\text{-}num(x_3, v), \forall y : \neg equal(y, x_2) \wedge$ $\neg pt(y, x_2) \wedge \neg ls(x_2, y), \forall y : y \neq x_1 \rightarrow \neg ls(y, x_2),$ $\forall y : y \neq x_3 \rightarrow \neg pt(x_2, y)\} \rhd \{abs_2()\},$ $\forall x_1, x_2, x_3 : \{ls(x_1, x_2), ls(x_2, x_3), auxiliary(x_2),$ $\exists v : var\text{-}num(x_1, v) \wedge \neg var\text{-}num(x_3, v), \forall y : \neg equal(y, x_2) \wedge$ $\neg ls(y, x_2) \wedge \neg ls(x_2, y), \forall y : y \neq x_1 \rightarrow \neg ls(y, x_2),$ $\forall y : y \neq x_3 \rightarrow \neg ls(x_2, y)\} \rhd \{abs_2()\},$ $\{\exists x : auxiliary(x) \wedge \forall y : \neg equal(x, y)) \wedge \neg pt(x, y) \wedge$ $\neg pt(y, x) \wedge \neg ls(x, y) \wedge \neg ls(y, x)\} \rhd \{abs_3()\},$
choose-act()	choose()	$\neg choose(), \neg abs_1(), \neg abs_2(), \neg abs_3(),$ $\{abs_1(), abs_2(), abs_3()\} \rhd \{command()\}$ $\{\neg abs_1(), \neg abs_2(), \neg abs_3()\} \rhd \{abstraction()\}$

Abstraction Mode: Table 5 shows the set of abstraction actions encoded from abstraction rules. The first two actions correspond to the abstraction rules. The last rule is used to free a logical variable in use, and make it available. When after applying an abstraction rule, we will go back to the Check mode until no abstraction rules can fire.

Table 5. Compilation of abstraction rules

Action	Preconditions	Effects
$abstract_1(x_1, x_2)$	$abstraction(),$ $pvar(x_1),$ $auxiliary(x_2),$ $equal(x_1, x_2)$	$\neg abstraction(), check(),$ $\neg equal(x_1, x_2), \neg equal(x_2, x_1),$ $\forall y : (equal(x_2, y) \wedge x_1 \neq y) \rhd$ $\{\neg equal(x_2, y), \neg equal(y, x_2),$ $equal(x_1, y), equal(y, x_1)\},$ $\forall y : pt(x_2, y) \rhd \{\neg pt(x_2, y),$ $pt(x_1, y)\},$ $\forall y : pt(y, x_2) \rhd \{\neg pt(y, x_2),$ $pt(y, x_1)\},$ $\forall y : ls(x_2, y) \rhd \{\neg ls(x_2, y),$ $ls(x_1, y)\},$ $\forall y : ls(y, x_2) \rhd \{\neg ls(y, x_2),$ $ls(y, x_1)\}$
$abstract_2(x_1, x_2, x_3, v)$	$abstraction(),$ $auxiliary(x_2),$ $var\text{-}num(x_1, v),$ $\neg var\text{-}num(x_3, v),$ $equal(x_3, nil) \vee x_3 = nil,$ $(pt(x_1, x_2) \wedge pt(x_2, x_3)) \vee$ $(pt(x_1, x_2) \wedge ls(x_2, x_3)) \vee$ $(ls(x_1, x_2) \wedge pt(x_2, x_3)) \vee$ $(ls(x_1, x_2) \wedge ls(x_2, x_3)),$ $\forall y : \neg equal(y, x_2),$ $\forall y : (y \neq x_1 \wedge y \neq x_2 \wedge$ $y \neq x_3) \rightarrow$ $(\neg pt(x_2, y) \wedge \neg pt(y, x_2) \wedge$ $\neg ls(x_2, y) \wedge \neg ls(y, x_2)),$	$\neg abstraction(), check(),$ $ls(x_1, x_3),$ $pt(x_1, x_2) \rhd \neg pt(x_1, x_2),$ $ls(x_1, x_2) \rhd \neg ls(x_1, x_2),$ $pt(x_2, x_3) \rhd \neg pt(x_2, x_3),$ $ls(x_2, x_3) \rhd \neg ls(x_2, x_3)$
$abstract_3(x, v)$	$abstraction(),$ $auxiliary(x),$ $var\text{-}num(x, v),$ $\forall y : \neg equal(x, y) \wedge$ $\neg pt(x, y) \wedge \neg pt(y, x) \wedge$ $\neg ls(x, y) \wedge \neg ls(y, x)$	$\neg abstraction(), check(),$ $\neg auxiliary(x),$ $v \neq int_0 \rhd var\text{-}num(x, int_0)$

6   Case Study and Experiment

In this section, we conduct a series of experiments to evaluate our approach. Further, we illustrate an example on synthesis of a disposal program which aims to dispose a linked list. The following code is the disposal program.

```
while (x ≠ nil) do {
  y := x;
  x := [x];
  dispose(y)
}
```

The initial state of this program is $ls(x, nil)$. Using the symbolic execution rules, the symbolic execution process is shown in Fig. 2. Note that the loop arrow from bottom to up means that $ls(x, nil)$ is the invariant of the program. At the beginning, we know x does not equal to nil since $ls(x, nil)$ at least contains one cell. Hence the first assignment command in the loop body is executed. When executing the second command, we do not know what holds in address x according to the spatial part $ls(x, nil)$ of the symbolic heap. Therefore a rearrangement step should be applied to distinguish the symbolic heap into a couple of situations. After executing $x := [x]$, we need to try to abstract the obtained symbolic heap since some primed variables are introduced. Then the last deallocation command is executed. In one situation, the loop exits. In the other, we find an invariant that is the same to the initial state. At this time the process terminates.

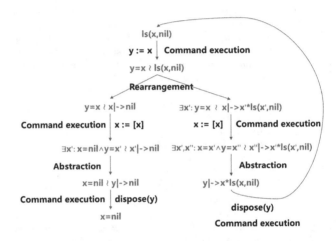

Fig. 2. Symbolic execution process for disposal program

In practice, we encode the program into standard PDDL which can be accepted by existing planners. The details are omitted here. We evaluate our approach on several list manipulated program. The non-deterministic planner PRP [18] is used as the FOND planner. Experiments are conducted on a laptop running Ubuntu 16.04 on an Intel® Core™ i7-8550U CPU 1.80 GHz and 8 GB of RAM. The results are shown in Table 6. "Insert" is to synthesize a program that inserts a cell before the head, "Remove" is the list disposal program, "Traverse" is to travel a list, "Append" is to append two lists into one. Sometimes we cannot synthesize a list program by our approach. For instance, reversing a list is impossible to be synthesized since the initial state and the goal are both an abstract list. Whether the list is reversed or not finally is never known. The second column is the search time in seconds. The third column is length of a policy. Note that the length includes additional actions (check actions and abstraction actions) except primitive command actions.

Table 6. Experimental results on list program

Program	Time(s)	Length
Insert	1.94	49
Remove	25.18	31
Traverse	16.56	25
Append	258.18	86

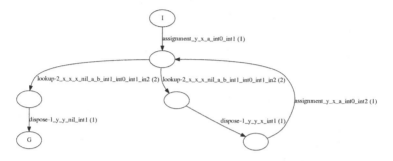

Fig. 3. Policy for synthesizing the disposal program

PRP generates a sequential plan for "Insert" and constructs loops for the other three programs. Consider the performance, we can see that synthesizing loop programs is not easy since the search time is much more than synthesizing sequential ones. More efforts needs to be made in order to find a loop for a planner. The essential reason is the quantifiers in the encoded actions especially in the effects of abstractions and preconditions of check actions. In practice, the quantifiers are expanded that will result in the explosion of the state space.

The solution generated for disposal program is shown in Fig. 3. We preserve the command actions and remove rest. Therefore, we obtain a compact policy much closer to a pointer program. Obviously, the policy is similar to the disposal program mentioned before. The boolean condition at the start of the loop must be specified manually.

7   Conclusion

Synthesizing programs is a difficult and central problem in computer science. In this paper, we propose an automated planning based method for pointer program synthesis. Inspired by symbolic execution of separation logic, we compile this process into a FOND planning problem, mainly including primitive command compilation, rearrangement compilation and abstraction compilation. In future work, we plan to synthesize larger scale programs. This is feasible from the theoretical point of view because of the modular reasoning feature of separation logic. Furthermore, we have to find a way that can reduce the number of quantifiers in the encoded actions to improve the performance of planners.

References

1. Balog, M., Gaunt, A.L., Brockschmidt, M., Nowozin, S., Tarlow, D.: Deepcoder: learning to write programs. In: 5th International Conference on Learning Representations, ICLR 2017, Toulon, France, 24–26 April 2017, Conference Track Proceedings. OpenReview.net (2017). https://openreview.net/forum?id=ByldLrqlx
2. Beltramelli, T.: pix2code: generating code from a graphical user interface screenshot. In: Proceedings of the ACM SIGCHI Symposium on Engineering Interactive Computing Systems, EICS 2018, Paris, France, 19–22 June 2018. pp. 3:1–3:6. ACM (2018). https://doi.org/10.1145/3220134.3220135
3. Berdine, J., Calcagno, C., O'Hearn, P.W.: A decidable fragment of separation logic. In: FSTTCS 2004: Foundations of Software Technology and Theoretical Computer Science, 24th International Conference, Chennai, India, 16–18 December 2004, Proceedings, pp. 97–109 (2004). https://doi.org/10.1007/978-3-540-30538-5_9
4. Berdine, J., Calcagno, C., O'Hearn, P.W.: Symbolic execution with separation logic. In: Programming Languages and Systems, Third Asian Symposium, APLAS 2005, Tsukuba, Japan, 2–5 November 2005, Proceedings, pp. 52–68 (2005). https://doi.org/10.1007/11575467_5
5. Bloem, R., Jobstmann, B., Piterman, N., Pnueli, A., Sa'ar, Y.: Synthesis of reactive(1) designs. J. Comput. Syst. Sci. **78**(3), 911–938 (2012). https://doi.org/10.1016/j.jcss.2011.08.007
6. Calcagno, C., et al.: Moving fast with software verification. In: Havelund, K., Holzmann, G.J., Joshi, R. (eds.) NASA Formal Methods - 7th International Symposium, NFM 2015, Pasadena, CA, USA, 27–29 April 2015, Proceedings. Lecture Notes in Computer Science, vol. 9058, pp. 3–11. Springer (2015). https://doi.org/10.1007/978-3-319-17524-9_1
7. Calcagno, C., Distefano, D., O'Hearn, P.W., Yang, H.: Compositional shape analysis by means of bi-abduction. J. ACM **58**(6), 26:1–26:66 (2011). https://doi.org/10.1145/2049697.2049700
8. Camacho, A., Bienvenu, M., McIlraith, S.A.: Towards a unified view of AI planning and reactive synthesis. In: Benton, J., Lipovetzky, N., Onaindia, E., Smith, D.E., Srivastava, S. (eds.) Proceedings of the Twenty-Ninth International Conference on Automated Planning and Scheduling, ICAPS 2018, Berkeley, CA, USA, 11–15 July 2019, pp. 58–67. AAAI Press (2019). https://aaai.org/ojs/index.php/ICAPS/article/view/3460
9. Cimatti, A., Pistore, M., Roveri, M., Traverso, P.: Weak, strong, and strong cyclic planning via symbolic model checking. Artif. Intell. **147**(1–2), 35–84 (2003). https://doi.org/10.1016/S0004-3702(02)00374-0
10. Distefano, D., O'Hearn, P.W., Yang, H.: A local shape analysis based on separation logic. In: Hermanns, H., Palsberg, J. (eds.) Tools and Algorithms for the Construction and Analysis of Systems, 12th International Conference, TACAS 2006 Held as Part of the Joint European Conferences on Theory and Practice of Software, ETAPS 2006, Vienna, Austria, March 25 - April 2, 2006, Proceedings. Lecture Notes in Computer Science, vol. 3920, pp. 287–302. Springer (2006). https://doi.org/10.1007/11691372_19
11. Fox, M., Long, D.: PDDL2.1: an extension to PDDL for expressing temporal planning domains. J. Artif. Intell. Res. **20**, 61–124 (2003). https://doi.org/10.1613/jair.1129

12. Fu, J., Bastani, F.B., Yen, I.: Automated AI planning and code pattern based code synthesis. In: 18th IEEE International Conference on Tools with Artificial Intelligence (ICTAI 2006), 13–15 November 2006, Arlington, VA, USA, pp. 540–546. IEEE Computer Society (2006). https://doi.org/10.1109/ICTAI.2006.37

13. Ghallab, M., Nau, D.S., Traverso, P.: Automated Planning - Theory and Practice. Elsevier (2004)

14. Gu, X., Zhang, H., Zhang, D., Kim, S.: Deep API learning. In: Zimmermann, T., Cleland-Huang, J., Su, Z. (eds.) Proceedings of the 24th ACM SIGSOFT International Symposium on Foundations of Software Engineering, FSE 2016, Seattle, WA, USA, 13–18 November 2016, pp. 631–642. ACM (2016). https://doi.org/10.1145/2950290.2950334

15. Gulwani, S., Polozov, O., Singh, R.: Program synthesis. Found. Trends Program. Lang. 4(1–2), 1–119 (2017). https://doi.org/10.1561/2500000010

16. Kitzelmann, E.: Inductive programming: A survey of program synthesis techniques. In: Schmid, U., Kitzelmann, E., Plasmeijer, R. (eds.) Approaches and Applications of Inductive Programming, Third International Workshop, AAIP 2009, Edinburgh, UK, 4 September 2009. Revised Papers. Lecture Notes in Computer Science, vol. 5812, pp. 50–73. Springer (2009). https://doi.org/10.1007/978-3-642-11931-6_3

17. Magill, S., Nanevski, A., Clarke, E., Lee, P.: Inferring invariants in separation logic for imperative list-processing programs. SPACE 1(1), 5–7 (2006)

18. Muise, C.J., McIlraith, S.A., Beck, J.C.: Improved non-deterministic planning by exploiting state relevance. In: McCluskey, L., Williams, B.C., Silva, J.R., Bonet, B. (eds.) Proceedings of the Twenty-Second International Conference on Automated Planning and Scheduling, ICAPS 2012, Atibaia, São Paulo, Brazil, 25–19 June 2012. AAAI (2012). http://www.aaai.org/ocs/index.php/ICAPS/ICAPS12/paper/view/4718

19. Reynolds, J.C.: Separation logic: A logic for shared mutable data structures. In: 17th IEEE Symposium on Logic in Computer Science (LICS 2002), 22–25 July 2002, Copenhagen, Denmark, Proceedings, pp. 55–74 (2002). https://doi.org/10.1109/LICS.2002.1029817

20. Vanneschi, L., Poli, R.: Genetic programming - introduction, applications, theory and open issues. In: Rozenberg, G., Bäck, T., Kok, J.N. (eds.) Handbook of Natural Computing, pp. 709–739. Springer (2012). https://doi.org/10.1007/978-3-540-92910-9_24

Runtime Verification of Ethereum Smart Contracts Based on MSVL

Bin Yu[1], Xu Lu[1], Hao Chen[2,3], Ming Lei[4], and Xiaobing Wang[1(✉)]

[1] School of Computer Science and Technology, Xidian University, Xi'an 710071, China
{byu,xlu}@xidian.edu.cn, xbwang@mail.xidian.edu.cn
[2] Beijing Edutainment World Education Technology Co., Ltd., Beijing 100000, China
chenhao@stemedu.cn
[3] Xi'an CoolMi Technology Co., Ltd., Xi'an 710077, China
[4] School of Computer Science, Shaanxi Normal University, Xi'an 710062, China
leiming@snnu.edu.cn

Abstract. Ethereum has become the most widely used underlying platform of blockchain smart contracts in the world. Compared with traditional software, the security problem of Ethereum smart contracts is more prominent due to its characteristics. Being a lightweight formal verification technique, runtime verification is pursued to check whether one monitored program execution obeys a desired property. In this paper, we propose a runtime verification method for smart contract security based on modeling, simulation and verification language (MSVL). First, a smart contract program is modeled by MSVL and a translator SOL2M is developed to convert a Solidity program to MSVL program. Then Propositional Projection Temporal Logic (PPTL) formulas are used to describe the security properties of smart contracts. Finally, runtime verification is used to verify whether the modeling program conforms to the given security properties. As a case study, a voting smart contract is employed to show the efficiency and effectiveness of the proposed approach.

Keywords: Ethereum smart contract · Runtime verification · Solidity · PPTL · MSVL

1 Introduction

Blockchain uses cryptography knowledge to store all digital assets on the point-to-point network, and provides a trusted channel for information and value transfer and exchange in untrusted network, which has the characteristics of decentralization, open autonomy and non tampering [1]. Cisco research shows that it is estimated that more than 10%

This research is supported by the Fundamental Research Funds for the Central Universities under Grant XJS210305, Natural Science Basic Research Program of Shaanxi (Program No. 2021JQ-208 and No. 2021JQ-314), National Natural Science Foundation of Shaanxi Province under Grant 2020GY-043, National Natural Science Foundation of China under Grant 61972301 and Grant 61806158, China Postdoctoral Science Foundation under Grant 2019T120881 and Grant 2018M643585.

© Springer Nature Switzerland AG 2021
J. Xue et al. (Eds.): SOFL+MSVL 2020, LNCS 12723, pp. 142–153, 2021.
https://doi.org/10.1007/978-3-030-77474-5_10

of the global GDP will be stored on the blockchain by 2027 [2]. As the application layer core of the blockchain, Ethereum [3] is the first open source public blockchain platform with smart contract function, which supports the smart contracts deployed on it. It uses a Turing's complete high-level programming language, Solidity, to realize complex business logic [4], based on the proof of work (POW) consensus mechanism and Ethereum virtual machine, (EVM) execution environment, in the case of no third party for digital asset transactions [5].

At present, Ethereum has become the most widely used underlying platform of blockchain smart contracts in the world, and has been highly concerned by top financial institutions and technology enterprises such as JPMorgan Chase, Microsoft and IBM. Ethereum smart contracts are utilized to realize the core logic of different business scenarios such as financial audit [6], contract signing [7] and supply chain management [8]. In 2020, the number of newly created Ethereum smart contracts exceeded 10 million, and the number of transfers based on Ethereum smart contracts was nearly 350 million. With such a large scale of funds, the security of Ethereum smart contracts must be highly valued.

Compared with traditional software, the security problems of Ethereum smart contracts are more prominent due to its characteristics [9]. Firstly, smart contracts are open-source, and the security defects of deployed contracts will be directly exposed to potential malicious attackers. Secondly, smart contracts are non tamperable, and the losses caused by the defects can not be made up. What is more, the reuse rate of Ethereum smart contract code deployed on the blockchain is more than 90%. Due to the digital storage and management of the key information such as assets and identity, once the copied contract code has defects, it will bring huge security risks to the whole system. For example, the attacker took advantage of the script code vulnerability of the Dao smart contract to steal more than 3 million Ethernet coins in 2016. In 2018, the attacker used the integer overflow problem in the batch transfer function of the BEC smart contract to generate tokens indefinitely, resulting in a loss of about 6 billion RMB.

In current detection methods, the traditional code testing and manual audit methods have certain limitations. The incompleteness of these methods makes them impossible to verify all the state space of the contract, and it is difficult to find the hidden logic defects. In view of the above problems, Ethereum community has repeatedly recommended formal verification methods, which have been successfully used in many safety critical fields. Formal verification method is based on logic calculus, formal language, automata and other theoretical computer science. It can strictly deduce whether a smart contract meets the temporal properties of the specified business logic, which has become an important way to ensure the temporal correctness of Ethereum smart contracts.

Being a lightweight formal verification technique, runtime verification is pursued to check whether one monitored program execution obeys a desired property [10]. In this paper, we propose a runtime verification method for Ethereum smart contracts based on modeling, simulation and verification language (MSVL). First, a smart contract program is modeled by MSVL. In order to reduce a lot of manual operations in modeling, SOL2M is developed to convert Solidity to MSVL. Then Propositional Projection Temporal Logic (PPTL) formulas are used to describe the security properties of smart contracts. Because of the projection and temporal operators, PPTL has a stronger expressive power than the general propositional logics. Finally, runtime verification is used to verify whether the modeling program conforms to the given security properties. As a case study, a voting smart contract is employed to show the efficiency and effectiveness of the proposed approach.

This paper is organized as follows. The next section briefly presents the language MSVL used for the implementation of the model and PPTL used for the description of properties. Section 3 gives the proposed runtime verification approach for Ethereum smart contracts. Then, a verification case is described in Sect. 4. Finally, the conclusion is drawn in Sect. 5.

2 Preliminaries

In this section, we will introduce programming language MSVL and property language PPTL, both of which are subsets of Projection Temporal Logic (PTL) [11]. The contents in this section are borrowed from [12–14].

2.1 MSVL

The arithmetic expression e and boolean expression b are inductively defined as follows:

$$e ::= c \mid x \mid g(e_1,\ldots,e_m) \mid ext\ f(e_1,\ldots,e_n) \mid \ominus e \mid \bigcirc e$$
$$b ::= true \mid false \mid \varepsilon \mid \ni \mid \neg b \mid b_0 \wedge b_1 \mid e_0 = e_1 \mid e_0 < e_1$$

In the arithmetic expression, c is a constant, x a variable, m and n integers, g a state function, and f a function. A state function $g(e_1,\ldots,e_m)$ contains no temporal operators. $ext\ f(e_1,\ldots,e_n)$ is an external call of function f meaning that we only concern the return value of function f rather than the interval over which the function is executed. $\ominus e$ and $\bigcirc e$ respectively stand for the value of e at the previous state and the next state. In the boolean expressions, $\ni \overset{\text{def}}{=} \bigcirc true$ and $\varepsilon \overset{\text{def}}{=} \neg \ni$.

The following are the elementary statements in MSVL:

1. Termination	`empty`	2. Assignment	`x<==e`
3. Unit Assignment	`x:=e`	4. Interval Frame	`frame(x)`
5. Selection	`p or q`	6. Conjunction	`p and q`
8. Always	`alw(p)`	7. Next	`next p`
9. Sequence	`p;q`	10. Local variable	`local x:p`
11. Projection	`{p₁,...,pₘ} prj q`	12. Parallel	`p ‖ q`
13. Conditional	`if(b)then{p}else{q}`	14. While	`while(b){p}`
15. Await	`await(b)`	16. Function call	`g(e₁,...,eₘ)`
17. External function call `ext f(e₁,...,eₙ)`			

where x is a variable, e and b denote an arithmetic expression or a boolean expression, respectively. $p_1,\ldots,p_m$, p and q are programs of MSVL. The meaning of each statement is given in [12] and omitted here.

2.2 PPTL

Syntax: Over a countable set *Prop* of atomic propositions, the syntax of a PPTL formula P is inductively defined as follows:

$$P ::= p \mid \bigcirc P \mid \neg P \mid P_1 \vee P_2 \mid (P_1, \ldots, P_m) \, prj \, P \mid P^+$$

where $p \in Prop$ is an atomic proposition; $P_1, \ldots, P_m$ and P are all well-formed PPTL formulas.

Semantics: The boolean domain $\mathcal{B} = \{true, false\}$. A state s is a mapping from *Prop* to $\mathcal{B}$. $s[p]$ represents the value of the atomic proposition p at state s. A non-empty sequence of states $\sigma = \langle s_0, s_1, \ldots \rangle$ is called an interval. $|\sigma|$ denotes the length of σ. If σ is finite, $|\sigma|$ equals the number of states minus 1. Otherwise, $|\sigma|$ equals ω. In order to consider both finite and infinite intervals in a unified way, the integers is extended as $N_\omega = N_0 \cup \{\omega\}$, where N_0 denotes the set of non-negative integers. Besides, the comparison operators $=, <, \leq$ to N_ω is also extended by considering $\omega = \omega$ and $i < \omega$ for all $i \in N_0$. Further, $\preceq$ is defined as $\leq -\{(\omega, \omega)\}$. A sub-interval $\langle s_i, \ldots, s_j \rangle$ can be denoted as $\sigma_{(i..j)}$ for simplicity. For an interval σ and integers $r_1, \ldots, r_h$ such that $0 \leq r_1 \leq r_2 \leq \ldots \leq r_h$, the operation $\downarrow$ can be utilized to obtain the projected interval, $\sigma \downarrow (r_1, \ldots, r_h) = \langle s_{t_1}, s_{t_2}, \ldots, s_{t_l} \rangle$, where $t_1, \ldots, t_l$ are obtained from $r_1, \ldots, r_h$ by deleting the duplicates. $\sigma_1 \cdot \sigma_2 = \langle s_0, \ldots, s_n, s_0', \ldots \rangle$ denotes the concatenation of a finite interval $\sigma_1 = \langle s_0, \ldots, s_n \rangle$ with another interval $\sigma_2 = \langle s_0', \ldots \rangle$.

For an interval σ, $i \in N_0$, $j \in N_\omega$, and $i \leq j \leq |\sigma|$, an interpretation of a PPTL formula is $\mathcal{I} = (\sigma, i, j)$. The satisfaction relation $\models$ is inductively defined as follows:

$\mathcal{I} \models p$ iff $s_i[p] = true$, and $p \in Prop$ is an atomic proposition.
$\mathcal{I} \models \bigcirc P$ iff $i < j$ and $(\sigma, i + 1, j) \models P$.
$\mathcal{I} \models \neg P$ iff $\mathcal{I} \not\models P$.
$\mathcal{I} \models P \wedge Q$ iff $\mathcal{I} \models P$ and $\mathcal{I} \models Q$.
$\mathcal{I} \models (P_1, \ldots, P_m) \, prj \, P$ iff there exist integers $r_0, \ldots, r_m$, and $i = r_0 \leq \ldots \leq r_{m-1} \leq r_m \leq j$ such that $(\sigma, r_{l-1}, r_l) \models P_l, 1 \leq l \leq m$, and $(\sigma', 0, |\sigma'|) \models P$ for one of the following σ':
  (a) $r_m < j$ and $\sigma' = \sigma \downarrow (r_0, \ldots, r_m) \cdot \sigma_{(r_m+1..j)}$,
  (b) $r_m = j$ and $\sigma' = \sigma \downarrow (r_0, \ldots, r_h)$ for some $0 \leq h \leq m$.
$\mathcal{I} \models P^+$ iff there exist finitely many integers $r_0, \ldots, r_n$ and $i = r_0 \leq \ldots \leq r_{n-1} \leq r_n = j$ ($n \geq 1$) such that $(\sigma, r_{l-1}, r_l) \models P, 1 \leq l \leq n$; or $j = \omega$ and there are infinitely many integers $k = r_0 \leq r_1 \leq \ldots$ such that $\lim_{i \to \infty} r_i = \omega$ and $(\sigma, r_{l-1}, r_l) \models P, l \geq 1$.

The abbreviations *true, false* and $\wedge$ are defined as usual. The following exhibits some derived formulas from elementary PPTL formulas, which have been explained in [11, 14].

$$\varepsilon \stackrel{def}{=} \neg \bigcirc true \qquad more \stackrel{def}{=} \neg \varepsilon$$
$$\Diamond P \stackrel{def}{=} true; P \qquad P_1; P_2 \stackrel{def}{=} (P_1, P_2) \, prj \, \varepsilon$$
$$P^* \stackrel{def}{=} P^+ \vee \varepsilon \qquad \Box P \stackrel{def}{=} \neg \Diamond \neg P$$
$$len(n) \stackrel{def}{=} \bigcirc^n \varepsilon \qquad fin(P) \stackrel{def}{=} \Box(\varepsilon \to P)$$

With Example 1 in the following, we intuitively illustrate two PPTL formulas whose contained operators are frequently used in this paper.

Example 1. The first PPTL formula is $P'; len(5)$, where P' can also be a PPTL formula. It means that after property P' holds, there also exists an interval whose length is 5. The second PPTL formula is $\bigcirc(p \wedge ((len(2); (p \wedge \varepsilon))^*))$, meaning that the atomic property p must hold at every odd state ignoring even ones. Their intuitive semantics are respectively shown in Fig. 1(a) and Fig. 1(b).

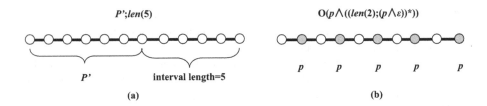

Fig. 1. Two examples of PPTL formulas

In order to explicitly illustrate the model of a PPTL formula P, we can construct its corresponding LNFG. An LNFG is defined as a tuple $G = (CL(P), EL(P), V_0, \mathbb{L} = \{\mathbb{L}_1, \cdots, \mathbb{L}_k\})$, where $CL(P)$ denotes the set of nodes and $EL(P)$ denotes the set of directed edges among $CL(P)$, V_0 is the set of initial nodes, and each $\mathbb{L}_i \subseteq CL(P)$, $1 \leq i \leq k$, is the set of nodes with l_i being the label. Each node is specified by a PPTL formula; each edge is labeled with a state formula; and the extra propositions l_k labeled on some nodes are used to identify an infinite acceptable path. In an LNFG, a finite path, $\pi = \langle n_0, p_0, \cdots, \varepsilon \rangle$, is an alternating sequence of nodes and edges from an initial node to the ε node, while an infinite path, $\pi = \langle n_0, p_0, \cdots, (n_i, p_i, \cdots, n_j, p_j)^\omega \rangle$, is an infinite alternate sequence of nodes and edges emanating from an initial node. In an infinite path, the set of nodes which infinitely often occur is denoted by $Inf(\pi)$. If a path π is finite or infinite with all the nodes in $Inf(\pi)$ not sharing a same label, it is called acceptable. Theories relative to LNFGs can be referred to [15].

Example 2. In order to show how an LNFG looks like, Fig. 2 illustrates the LNFG of PPTL formula $\Diamond(p \wedge \Box(\neg q))$ as an example. In this LNFG, $\pi = \langle 1, p \wedge \neg q, 3, \neg q, 4 \rangle$ is a finite path, while $\pi = \langle 1, true, (2, true)^\omega \rangle$ is an infinite path. In this infinite path, we have $Inf(\pi) = \{2\} \subseteq \mathbb{L}_1 = \{2\}$, which means that the nodes occurring infinitely often have the same label l_1. Hence, this path is unacceptable.

3 Runtime Verification of Ethereum Smart Contracts

3.1 Framework

Figure 3 shows the framework of our runtime verification approach. First, a smart contract program is modeled by MSVL with the translator SOL2M. Then PPTL formulas

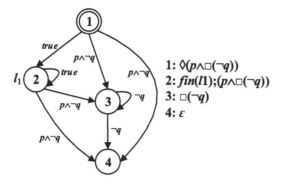

1: $\Diamond(p \wedge \Box(\neg q))$
2: $fin(l1);(p \wedge \Box(\neg q))$
3: $\Box(\neg q)$
4: ε

Fig. 2. LNFG of formula $\Diamond(p \wedge \Box(\neg q))$

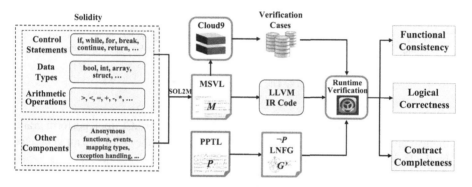

Fig. 3. The framework of our runtime verification approach

are used to describe the security properties of smart contracts, including functional consistency, logical correctness and contract completeness. After that, Cloud 9 is employed to generated as many verification cases as possible. Finally, runtime verification is used to verify whether the modeling program conforms to the given properties.

3.2 SOL2M Converter

MSVL is employed to model the smart contract program written by Solidity. In order to reduce a large number of manual operations in the modeling process, an equivalent conversion tool SOL2M realizing the translation from Solidity to MSVL is developed, which achieves the automation of the modeling process. The specific structure and workflow are shown in Fig. 4. The SOL2M converter is mainly divided into four parts:

1. Preprocessing: Process the version identification statement in the Solidity source program and import other source file statements;
2. Lexical analysis: Generate a lexical analyzer through the JavaCC tool, perform lexical analysis on the Solidity program, and identify the source program as a specific word stream;

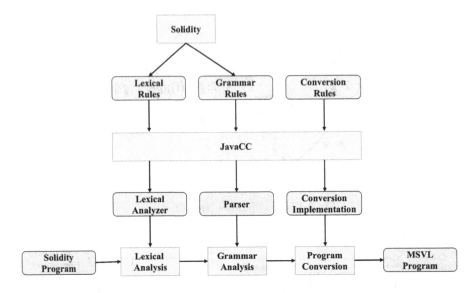

Fig. 4. The structure of SOL2M

3. Syntax analysis: Generate a syntax analyzer through the JavaCC tool, perform grammatical analysis on the Solidity program, and recognize the word stream generated by the lexical analysis as a program statement;
4. Program conversion: By analyzing the lexical and grammatical similarities and differences between Solidity and MSVL, formulate the conversion rules from Solidity to MSVL, nest the conversion code in the BNF paradigm of grammatical analysis, and realize the dynamic conversion from Solidity to MSVL.

Since the first three parts have been given in detail in [16, 17], we just introduce the last part. Semantic analysis is a logical stage in the compilation process. Its function is to analyze the context-sensitive nature of the source program, examine whether there are semantic errors, and finally translate the source program into a language that can be read by the machine. SOL2M analyzes the semantics of the Solidity source program after syntax analysis, and formulates the equivalent conversion rules between Solidity and MSVL according to the actual meaning of each statement, and realizes the program conversion in the process of semantic analysis.

Through the analysis and comparison of Solidity and MSVL language, the conversion rules between them are formulated. The following two aspects are introduced from the conversion rules of contract and basic statements, and some conversion rules are shown in Fig. 5.

In Solidity, integer variables are declared with "int8" or "uint256", which are converted to "int" in MSVL. Similarly the "bytes" in Solidity are equivalent to the "char" in MSVL. The address variable "address" in Solidity is also converted to the "char". The mapping variable "mapping" is converted to structure. If there is nested mapping, the mapping variable will be converted to multiple nested structs. In Solidity. the declaration of struct is the same as MSVL so that we only need to add the corresponding temporal operators in the struct. Meanwhile, the usage of function declaration in Solidity and MSVL are same, but we need to add a frame operator in function to ensure variables remain the same value over an interval unless it is explicitly assigned.

For the basic statements. if there is an approximate statement of Solidity in MSVL, it can be replaced directly, such as "while" statement and "if" statement. If there is no approximate statement in MSVL, abstract conversion is required, e.g. "throw" statement. Since there is no statement throwing exception in MSVL, we abstract the "throw" statement into "skip" with interval length of 1, and execute the empty statement in the next state. That is, when an exception is thrown, the subsequent statement will not be executed.

According to the characteristics of JavaCC, semantic analysis and program conversion are carried out simultaneously in the process of syntactic analysis. The semantic action of conversion is predefined in each parsing function according to the conversion rules. The basic flow of program conversion is as follows: First, the Solidity program file is read by SOL2M converter (solidity.sol). Then it enters the syntactic analysis stage. The semantic information of the syntax unit of Solidity program is extracted based on the conversion rules, and the Solidity program is also converted into MSVL program which is equivalent in function. The converted MSVL program is temporarily stored in the recreated Java collection object. After the syntactic analysis is completed, the temporary collection is traversed and written into the MSVL program file (msvl.m).

3.3 Runtime Verification

With the traditional runtime verification approach, finding counterexamples amounts to sequentially exploring acceptable paths in the automaton constructed for the negation of a desired property. In order to take full advantage of hardware resources supplied by a multi-core machine, a parallel approach has been proposed in [18] to verify full regular temporal properties for real-world programs.

In this approach, the produced trace (possibly incomplete) is first divided into several segments which can be verified in parallel. Then, a thread pool is created for each segment. The thread pool provides an opportunity for each thread to track nondeterministic branches in the LNFG of the negation of the property concurrently. When some of the segments have been verified, the obtained results are merged to show whether the trace satisfies or violates the desired property. If we know that the property is valid or invalid with the already verified segments, it is unnecessary to keep on executing the program and verifying more segments. Otherwise, the verification module continues working until a conclusive result is given or all the segments are verified.

4   Case Study: Runtime Verification for a Vote Smart Contract

This section takes the voting smart contract as an example, and gives the detailed process of modeling and verification procedure. As shown in Fig. 6, the voting contract mainly includes three parts: state variables, structures, and functions. The name of the contract is voteContract. The contract first declares the Candidate structure, which contains two member variables, the candidate name and the number of votes obtained.

Struct	struct Candidate{
	bytes8 name ;
	uint voteCount;
	}
		struct Candidate {
		char name and
		int voteCount
		};

Declaration statement	uint public a=0; uint[] public arr;	int a and a<== 0 and skip; int arr[MAX] and skip;

Function	function vote(uint id) public {
	uint a= id;
	}
	
	throw;
	block;
		function vote (int id){
		frame(a) and (
		int a and a<== id and skip
		)
		};
		
		skip;

Return
statement
	function fun() {
	return 0;
	}
		function fun(int return_value) {
		frame(return_flag)(
		int return_flag <== 0 and skip;
		return_flag :=1 and return_value:=0)
		};

Conditional
statement
	if(expression){
	block
	}else{
	block
	}
		if(expression) then {
		block
		}else{
		block
		}

Loop
statement
	for(statedef;e1;e2){
	block
	}
		while(e1) {
		block
		e2;
		}

Expressions with arithmetic operators	e1[+,-,*,/,%]e2 e1[++,--]	e1[+,-,*,/,%]e2 e1:=e1[+,-]1
Expressions with assignment operators	e1=e2 e1[+,-,*,/,%]=e2	e1:=e2 e1:=e1[+,-,*,/,%]e2
Expressions with logical operators	e1&&e2 e1||e2	e1 AND e2 e1 OR e2

Fig. 5. Conversion rules from Solidity to MSVL

Secondly, a mapping type from the candidate to the number of votes is created, and the array Candidate is used to store all candidates. Two functions are also declared in the contract: function vote implements the voting for a specific candidate and function winner selects the winner with the highest number of votes from all candidates.

The voting smart contract is modeled and automatically stored in the solidity.sol file as the input of the SOL2M converter. The Solidity code is converted to the MSVL code, and the result is stored in the msvl.m file. We summarize the properties of smart contracts into three levels: functional consistency, logical correctness, and contract completeness. The following describes the properties of the voting smart contract that should be satisfied from these three aspects.

Functional consistency: The basic requirements that each smart contract should meet refer to the consistency between the functions of the smart contract and the design requirements, that is, the functions of the contract to be verified should meet the actual requirements. For the voting smart contract, function winner needs to select the winner with the highest number of votes from all candidates. If there is a candidate with a higher number of votes than the winner, it means that function winner does not meet the actual requirements. In this case, the smart contract does not meet the functional consistency.

```
1   contract voteContract{
2     struct Candidate{
3       bytes8 name ;
4       uint voteCount;
5     }
6     uint public winnerId=0;
7     mapping(address=>uint) public voters;
8     Candidate[] public candidates;
9     function vote(address sender,uint id) public{
10      if(voters[sender]==0){
11        return;
12      }else{
13        voters[sender] = voters[sender] - 1;
14        candidates[id].voteCount = candidates[id].voteCount + 1;
15      }
16    }
17    function winner() public{
18      uint maxCount = 0;
19      for(uint i = 0; i< candidates.length; i++){
20        if(candidates[i].voteCount > maxCount){
21          maxCount = candidates[i].voteCount;
22          winnerId = i;
23        }
24      }
25    }
26  }
```

Fig. 6. The vote smart contract

The PPTL formula used to describe the property can be specified as $P_1 \equiv fin(!m)$, meaning that after the voting, there is no candidate with higher votes than the winner.

Logical correctness: The security issue of smart contracts refers to ensuring that the logic of the functions in the contract is correct, that is, there are no logical loopholes. For the voting smart contract, function vote is the logical core part of the whole contract. One of the desired property is that when a person calls function vote to initiate a vote, the number of votes he has in his hand is at least 1. The property can be specified as $P_2 \equiv \Box(q \rightarrow r)$.

Contract completeness: It is the comprehensive expression of functional consistency and logical correctness. Only when both of the functional consistency and logical correctness are satisfied, can the contract be considered to meet the completeness. For the voting smart contract, it can be specified as $P_3 \equiv P_1 \wedge P_2 \equiv fin(!m) \wedge \Box(q \rightarrow r)$.

After the smart contract is implemented in MSVL and all of the properties are specified in PPTL formulas, runtime verification is performed to check whether the program satisfies the desired properties. The runtime verification results show that the voting smart contract satisfies all of these three properties. The verification time is 356 ms, 475 ms and 687 ms, respectively.

5 Conclusion

In this paper, we propose a runtime verification method for Ethereum smart contracts based on MSVL. To achieve this, a smart contract program is first modeled by MSVL. In order to reduce a lot of manual operations in modeling, a translator tool, SOL2M, is developed to convert the Solidity program to MSVL program. Then PPTL formulas are used to describe the security properties of smart contracts from three aspects. After that, runtime verification is used to verify whether the modeling program conforms to the given security properties. Finally, a voting smart contract is employed as a case study to show the efficiency and effectiveness of the proposed approach.

References

1. Lao, L., Li, Z., Hou, S., Xiao, B., Guo, S., Yang, Y.: A survey of iot applications in blockchain systems: architecture, consensus, and traffic modeling. ACM Comput. Surv. **53**(1), 1–32 (2020)
2. Yuan, Y., Wang, F.Y.: Blockchain and cryptocurrencies: model, techniques, and applications. IEEE Trans. Syst. Man Cybern.: Syst. **48**(9), 1421–1428 (2018)
3. Wood, G., et al.: Ethereum: a secure decentralised generalised transaction ledger. Ethereum Proj. Yellow Pap. **151**(2014), 1–32 (2014)
4. Peng, C., Akca, S., Rajan, A.: SIF: a framework for solidity contract instrumentation and analysis. In: 26th Asia-Pacific Software Engineering Conference (APSEC). IEEE, vol. 2019, pp. 466–473 (2019)
5. Belotti, M., Božić, N., Pujolle, G., Secci, S.: A vademecum on blockchain technologies: wwhen, which, and how. IEEE Commun. Surv. Tutor. **21**(4), 3796–3838 (2019)
6. Fan, K., Bao, Z., Liu, M., Vasilakos, A.V., Shi, W.: Dredas: decentralized, reliable and efficient remote outsourced data auditing scheme with blockchain smart contract for industrial iot. Futur. Gener. Comput. Syst. **110**, 665–674 (2020)
7. Zhang, L., Zhang, H., Yu, J., Xian, H.: Blockchain-based two-party fair contract signing scheme. Inf. Sci. **535**, 142–155 (2020)
8. Song, A.Q., Chen, Y., Zhong, Y., Lan, K., Fong, S., Tang, B.R.: A supply-chain system framework based on internet of things using blockchain technology. ACM Trans. Internet Technol. **21**(1), 1–24 (2021)
9. Tolmach, P., Li, Y., Lin, S.W., Liu, Y., Li, Z.: A survey of smart contract formal specification and verification. arXiv:2008.02712 (2020)
10. Leucker, M., Schallhart, C.: A brief account of runtime verification. J. Logic Algebraic Program. **78**(5), 293–303 (2009)
11. Duan, Z.: Temporal Logic and Temporal Logic Programming. Science Press (2005)
12. Duan, Z., Yang, X., Koutny, M.: Framed temporal logic programming. Sci. Comput. Program. **70**(1), 31–61 (2008)
13. Duan, Z., Koutny, M.: A framed temporal logic programming language. J. Comput. Sci. Technol. **19**(3), 341–351 (2004)
14. Duan, Z.: An extended interval temporal logic and a framing technique for temporal logic programming. Ph.D. thesis, University of Newcastle upon Tyne (1996)
15. Duan, Z., Tian, C.: A practical decision procedure for propositional projection temporal logic with infinite models. Theor. Comput. Sci. **554**, 169–190 (2014)

16. Wang, X., Yang, X., Li, C.: A formal verification method for smart contract. In: 2020 7th International Conference on Dependable Systems and Their Applications (DSA), pp. 31–36, IEEE (2020)
17. Wang, X., Yang, X., Shu, X., Zhao, L.: Formal verification of smart contract based on MSVL. Ruan Jian Xue Bao/J. Softw. **32**(6), 1–20 (2021)
18. Yu, B., Duan, Z., Tian, C., Zhang, N.: Verifying temporal properties of programs: a parallel approach. J. Parallel Distrib. Comput. **118**, 89–99 (2018)

Automatic Generation of Specification from Natural Language Based on Temporal Logic

Xiaobing Wang[1], Ge Li[1], Chunyi Li[1], Liang Zhao[1(✉)], and Xinfeng Shu[2(✉)]

[1] Institute of Computing Theory and Technology and ISN Laboratory,
Xidian University, Xi'an 710071, People's Republic of China
xbwang@mail.xidian.edu.cn, 0902140226@csu.edu.cn, lzhao@xidian.edu.cn
[2] School of Computer Science and Technology, Xi'an University of Posts
and Communications, Xi'an 710061, People's Republic of China
shuxf@xupt.edu.cn

Abstract. Formal specifications are usually used for describing safety system properties and play an important role in formal verification. In order to improve the effectiveness of formal specification generation and formal verification, this paper proposes a framework for automatic conversion from natural language describing properties to temporal logic formulas, and implements a tool PPTLGenerator (Propositional Projection Temporal Logic formula Generator) for the conversion. First, PPTL-Generator is developed based on JavaCC for automatic conversion from natural language to PPTL. Then, the satisfiability of a PPTL formula generated by PPTLGenerator is checked by a tool PPTLSAT. Finally, to illustrate the principle and effectiveness of the framework, a case study of the safety property of Level 3 autonomous car is provided.

Keywords: PPTL · Natural language processing · Temporal logic specification · Formal methods

1 Introduction

With increase in the scale and complexity of software systems, the probability of exposing software errors grows obviously. The software safety has been focused in industry and academic circles [13,20]. To verify software correctness, the formal method is proposed to check properties of the software which is an important approach based on rigorous mathematical theories [10]. In particular, a formal specification is specified by a temporal logic formula, and then the formal verification is employed to check whether or not the software meets the formal specification.

This research is supported by National Natural Science Foundation of China Grant Nos. 61672403 and 61972301, National Natural Science Foundation of Shaanxi Province Grant No. 2020GY-043, and Shaanxi Key Science and Technology Innovation Team Project Grant No. 2019TD-001.

J. Xue et al. (Eds.): SOFL+MSVL 2020, LNCS 12723, pp. 154–171, 2021.
https://doi.org/10.1007/978-3-030-77474-5_11

The unified model checking approach based on MSVL (Modeling, Simulation and Verification Language) [14] and PPTL (Propositional Projection Temporal Logic) [5] has been widely applied in software systems, such as neural networks, social networks, etc. [25,26]. In general, the steps of model checking in the UMC4M (Unified Model Checker for MSVL) [4] are as follows: An MSVL program M is used to describe the model, and a PPTL formula P is used to describe properties [27]. Then $\neg P$ is converted into an MSVL program P' and a program M and P' is input into MC (MSVL Compiler). In this way, the model checking problem is transformed into whether or not the program M and P' can be executed successfully. If the program is executed successfully, it means that the property is unsatisfied, otherwise it is satisfied.

In the unified model checking approach, it is essential to formalize the desired properties. Experts need to understand specifications and use PPTL formulas to describe properties. Generally, software requirements are informal and written in natural languages. Hence, it is very difficult for untrained analysts to use logic formulas to formalize properties. For this reason, it is crucial to study the technique for automatic generation of specification from natural languages based on PPTL.

There are three research techniques on the conversion from natural language to formal specification. The first technique is to define a structured subset of natural language and simplify the acquisition of semantics through the subset [27]. At present, this technique is not suitable for processing complex sentences. The second technique is to use semi-formal templates to analyze natural language [7,21]. However, templates have to be manually summarized by professional designers. The third technique is to use NLP (Natural Language Processing) and machine learning for extracting requirements. Nevertheless, it is problematic to learn all temporal sequences for analyzers without enough computational abilities [12,22].

To solve the above problems, we propose a PPTL generation framework for automatic generation of specification based on PPTL. First, a tool PPTLGenerator implements the conversion from natural language to PPTL specification, and generates the formal specification with a full regular expressiveness for describing behaviors of sequence, loop and concurrency. Then a tool PPTLSAT is used to decide the satisfiability of the generated PPTL formula. If the formula is valid, the unified model checking is unnecessary. If the formula is a contradiction, it should be modified. After that, the formula can be input into the UMC4M at a code level based on MSVL for model checking. Remarkably, to avoid learning all temporal sequences for analyzers, our framework uses a natural language processing tool Stanford CoreNLP [15] which includes trained models for word segmentation and part-of-speech tagging. In addition, to support compound sentences, structured English grammar we defined has the capability of parsing complex sentences. In the end, a typical case study illustrates the principle and proves effectiveness of the framework.

The rest of the paper is organized as follows. Section 2 briefly introduces the theoretical basis and tools of the method. Section 3 defines the rules for the automatic conversion from a natural language describing properties to PPTL formulas. Section 4 illustrates the practicality and effectiveness of the method with a specific case. Section 5 discusses the current related work. Finally, Sect. 6 gives conclusions and future work.

2   Background

2.1   PPTL

Temporal logic is usually used as a formal specification language for describing system properties in model checking. PTL (Projection Temporal Logic) [3,6] extends ITL (Interval Temporal Logic) [18,19] which includes a new temporal operator prj. PPTL is a propositional subset of PTL, and a PPTL formula can be reduced to NF (Normal Form) and LNFG (Labeled Normal Form Graph). The finite and infinite paths in LNFG correspond to the finite and infinite models of the PPTL formula respectively. Then, the decidability of PPTL is proved and a decision procedure is obtained.

Generally, we use capital letters, possibly with subscripts, to represent PPTL formulas. The syntax of PPTL is defined as follows:

$$P ::= p \mid \neg P \mid P_1 \wedge P_2 \mid \bigcirc P \mid (P_1, \ldots, P_m)\, prj\, P$$

where p is a proposition, $\bigcirc$ (next) and prj (projection) are temporal operators.

The derived formulas of PPTL are defined in the following, where the $\neg$, $\rightarrow$, $\leftrightarrow$ operators have the same meaning as the corresponding ones in classical logic, and $\Box$ (always) and $\Diamond$ (sometimes) are temporal operators in PPTL.

$$\varepsilon \stackrel{\text{def}}{=} \neg \bigcirc true \qquad\qquad more \stackrel{\text{def}}{=} \neg\varepsilon$$

$$P; Q \stackrel{\text{def}}{=} (P, Q)\, prj\, \varepsilon \qquad\qquad skip \stackrel{\text{def}}{=} \bigcirc\varepsilon$$

$$len(0) \stackrel{\text{def}}{=} \varepsilon \qquad\qquad len(n) \stackrel{\text{def}}{=} len(n-1), n \geq 1$$

$$\Diamond P \stackrel{\text{def}}{=} (true, P)\, prj\, \varepsilon \qquad\qquad \Box P \stackrel{\text{def}}{=} \neg\Diamond\neg P$$

$$fin(P) \stackrel{\text{def}}{=} \Box(\varepsilon \rightarrow P) \qquad\qquad halt(P) \stackrel{\text{def}}{=} \Box(\varepsilon \leftrightarrow P)$$

$$keep(P) \stackrel{\text{def}}{=} \Box(\neg\varepsilon \rightarrow P)$$

The satisfiability of a PPTL formula is decided by the tool PPTLSAT. If a PPTL formula p has an LNFG, it means that p is satisfiable, otherwise p is a contradiction and unsatisfiable. In addition, the satisfiability of $\neg p$ is also checked in the PPTLSAT. If $\neg p$ has no LNFG, it means that $\neg p$ is unsatisfiable and p is a tautology. If the formula is neither a contradiction nor a tautology, it can be regarded as a property and input into the UMC4M for model checking.

2.2 NLP Tools

Three NLP tools are used in the framework for automatic generation of specification based on PPTL, such as Stanford CoreNLP, WordNet and JavaCC. They are briefly introduced in the following paragraphs.

Stanford CoreNLP is a natural language processing toolkit [15], which integrates several practical modules, including word segmentation, part-of-speech tagging, named entity recognition, syntax analysis and dependency analysis. Its models are trained by deep learning techniques, and the accuracy of an automatic natural language translation has been greatly improved compared with original tools. In recent years, several natural language processing toolkits have been developed, which can provide convenience to formalize properties of natural language during the automatic generation. Word segmentation and part-of-speech tagging in Stanford CoreNLP are used in our framework.

WordNet is an English dictionary based on cognitive linguistics jointly designed by psychologists, linguists and computer engineers from Princeton University [17]. It not just arranges words in an alphabetical order, but also forms a "word-net" according to the meaning of the words. It is a semantic web of English vocabulary covering a wide range [1,16]. Nouns, verbs, adjectives and adverbs are organized into a synonym network. Each synonym set represents a basic semantic concept, and these sets are also connected by various relationships. WordNet is utilized to extract words or phrases with the same semantic information.

JavaCC is a parser generator for Java applications which is widely used in formal language processing. A grammar specification is input into JavaCC and converted to a top-down parser in a Java program that can recognize matches to the grammar. Compared with YACC in generating bottom-up parsers [11], JavaCC has a more general and readable grammar. In a JavaCC file, regular expressions and BNF are used in lexical specifications and grammar specifications respectively. A grammar analyser is generated by JavaCC for lexical analysis and syntax analysis in our framework.

3 Automatic Generation of Specification from Natural Language to Temporal Logic

This section introduces the implementation process of the automatic conversion based on the PPTLGenerator and the implementation of checking satisfiability in detail. The overall structure of the thesis work is shown in Fig. 1. The specific implementation of the tool can be divided into four parts:

a. **Natural Language Tagging**. Use the Stanford CoreNLP tool to implement word segmentation and part-of-speech tagging of the input natural language texts.
b. **Tag Recognition**. Recognize the clauses from the marked natural language sentences, and extract information such as atomic propositions, logical operators, and temporal semantics to generate a standardized syntax tree by the PPTLGenerator.

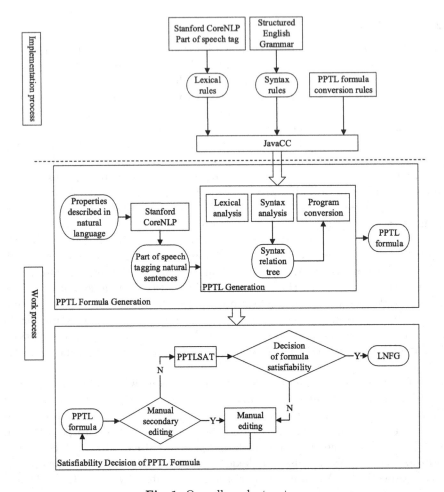

Fig. 1. Overall work structure

c. **Formula Generation**. Traverse the tree paths and convert the information of each clause node into atomic propositions according to the conversion template. Then, a complete PPTL specification is generated by extracting the temporal and logic information of the syntax tree. If necessary, the PPTL formula can be modified secondary manually.

d. **Formula Satisfiability Decision**. Apply a tool PPTLSAT for checking satisfiability of the PPTL formula, then generate an LNFG state transition diagram and feedback the result to users.

3.1   Definition of Structured English Grammar

The structured English grammar is defined as a specification scheme to handle semantic ambiguity in the complex sentence structures [27]. Instead of providing translations for the full set of natural languages, we chose a special structured subset which can meet requirements in the automatic conversion. In this subset, it only supports the present tense and the future tense, and the correct grammar, i.e. positive grammatical forms. In addition, the structured grammar allows to extract temporal semantics from tenses, adverbs and prepositional phrases. The definition of the structured English grammar is shown in Table 1.

*(Star) indicates the existence of zero or more subcomponents. ?(Question mark) indicates the existence of 0 or 1 sub-components. +(Plus sign) indicates the existence of one or more sub-components. For nouns, verbs, participles, adjectives and adverbs, we will not decompose them. Moreover, according to the definition of the structured grammar, a sentence consists of at least one clause which consists of at least two components: a subject and a predicate. Clauses are used to express the core interpretation to a sentence and we can also use the complex clause to expand the interpretation of a sentence.

3.2 Formal Specification Generation

The descriptive properties of sentences in natural language can be expressed by logic formulas through the PPTLGenerator. A general overview of Fig. 1, the generation step of PPTL formula can be divided in four sub-steps. First, we use a Stanford CoreNLP tool to decompose and tokenize each sentence in natural language, which aims to extract all grammatical components. Then PPTLGenerator extracts atomic propositions after tag recognition, and infers the tense operators of each atomic proposition according to tenses, adverbs and prepositional phrases. With the syntax analysis according to the structured English grammar, a syntax tree is constructed simultaneously. Next, the satisfiability of a PPTL formula is generated by PPTLGenerator and finally checked by the tool PPTLSAT. The following is the specific operation process:

Step 1. Natural Language Tagging In order to process the input texts in natural language, the Stanford CoreNLP tool is called to perform word segmentation and part-of-speech tagging. Word segmentation is to split the text string into the basic token unit of grammatical analysis. Part-of-speech tagging is the process of marking up a word in a text as corresponding to a particular part of speech based on both its definition and its context. In specific, we use a tag module in the Stanford CoreNLP tool to generate the tagged results at a character level. The tag module utilizes both preceding and following tag context, and many lexical features technologies. The part-of-speech tag is a special label assigned to each token in a text corpus to indicate the part of speech and often also other grammatical categories such as tense, number, case, etc. The part-of-speech tags are used in corpus searches and in text analysis tools and algorithms. The list of part-of-speech tags is shown in Table 2.

In the identification of part-of-speech tags, we ignore the symbols such as ",", ";", "%" and <CD>, because they have less specific impact on the identification of the following recognition tasks.

Table 1. Structured English grammar

sentence	::= subclauses((","conjunction)?subclauses)*"."
clause	::= (modifier)?subject(predicates)(subject)?(temporal)?
subordinator	::= (markprj|(<IN>)|(<WRB>)
markprj	::= (<END><MONITORING><WITH>)
	|(<START><MONITORING><WITH>)
conjunction	::= (<CC>)|(<RB>)
modifier	::= <RB>
void subject	::= substantives
temporal	::= (<RB>(<CC><RB>)?)
	|((<IN>(<DT>)?(<JJ>)?((<NN>|<NNS>))+)
	|(<PDT><DT><NN>))
substantives	::= substantive
substantive	::= (((<CD>|<DT>))?(participle)?
	(<NN>|<NNS>))+
predicates	::= (modality)?predicate
modality	::= <MD>
predicate	::= (verb(<CONSTANT>)?)
	|(be((participle|complement|preposition)(<CONSTANT>)?))
be	::= <BE>|<IS>|<ARE>
complement	::= adjective|adverb
adjective	::= <JJ>
adverb	::= <RB>
preposition	::= <IN>
participle	::= <VBD>|<VBG>|<VBN>|<VBP>
verb	::= <VB>|<VBD>|<VBN>|<VBP>|< VBZ >

Step 2. Tag Recognition

The tag recognition module has the ability to recognize the components and tenses of sentences that conform to the structured English grammar. More precisely, the module recognizes the tagged sentences and extracts information including atomic propositions, logical semantics, temporal semantics, etc. Then the tagged sentences are converted into a structured syntax tree in which tree nodes are generated and connected according to the syntax structure of the

Table 2. Part-of-speech tags

Tag	Description	Tag	Description
WRB	Wh-adverb	VBN	Verb, past participle
NN	Noun, singular or mass	VBP	Verb, non-3rd person singular present
NNS	Noun, plural	VBZ	Verb, 3rd person singular present
CD	Cardinal number	IN	Preposition or subordinating connector
CC	Coordinating connector	JJ	Adjective
MD	Modal	RB	Adverb
VB	Verb, base form	DT	Determiner
VBD	Verb, past tense	PDT	Predeterminer
VBG	Verb, gerund or present participle		

clauses. In the extraction of clause components and compound sentence structure, we also need to perform semantic analysis. We construct and modify syntax tree nodes based on logical and temporal semantics, so as to complete the generation of the syntax tree.

In the process of logical semantic analysis, when at least two independent clauses are connected by coordinating connectors, a new connector node will be created and marked. When analyzing attributive clauses, it will first determine whether the antecedent is a time noun. Remarkably, we use the synonym set in the WordNet tool for synonym analysis. For example, if a word or a phrase is synonymous with a time noun, it means that the word or phrase also needs to be treated as a time noun. We should create a new antecedent node of attributive clause, which connects the principal and subordinate sentences and describes the logical relationship between the two clauses.

In the process of temporal semantic analysis, the recognition rule is for an adverb, a prepositional phrase or a sentence tense. If the recognized string is an adverb or a prepositional phrase, WordNet performs the synonym search function that the corresponding temporal semantics will be matched according to the search results. If it is a tense word, we mark the sentence according to the tense type. To improve the performance of extracting logical semantics, we define the priority for the extraction of adverbs, prepositional phrase semantics and sentence tense semantics. The recognition priority of phrase semantics is higher than the extraction of tense semantics, that is, if the current sentence does not have adverbs or prepositional phrases that define temporal semantics, the sentence tense will be extracted as the temporal semantics of the sentence. Specially for the adverbial clause connectors, whenever the antecedent of an adverbial clause are identified, such as when, whenever, while, if, etc. They have the dual semantics of logical connectives and temporality. Therefore, when the leading words of the adverbial clause are recognized, we use the antecedent to describe the logical connectives and temporal semantic relations between the two clauses.

Through the lexical analysis and the syntax analysis, a syntax tree is constructed with the data structure includes: left and right subtree nodes, the node value, the node type and the node label. The process of constructing a syntax tree is shown as follow, and the syntax tree data structure is shown in Table 3.

Table 3. The syntax tree data structure

```
public class TreeNode {
      public int ivalue;        //Node number: marking proposition
      public int type;          //Node type: 0, sentence 1, connector
      public String svalue;     //Node label: proposition content or connector
      public TreeNode left;     //Left or right subtree
      public TreeNode right;
      public int mark;
      public TreeNode(){
         this.ivalue=0;
         this.type=0;           ////Node type: 0, sentence 1, connector
         this.svalue=null;
         this.left=null;
         this.right=null;
         this.mark=-1;
      }
}
```

i) **Whenever a clause is identified**, we will create a new node, and assign it to the svalue label of the node with removing the temporal information from the identified clause. Meanwhile, we set the node type to 0 which indicates that the node denotes a proposition node.

ii) **Whenever a connective is identified**, we will create a new node and assign the identified connective to the node's label svalue. Moreover, we set the node type to 1, in order to indicate that the node is a connective node.

iii) **Whenever an adverb, a prepositional phrase or a sentence tense is recognized.** If it is an adverb or a prepositional phrase, the temporal tag of the sentence will be set according to the synonym recognition by the WordNet. If it is a sentence tense, we will set the temporal tag of the sentence according to the tense type, and modify the temporal tag of the node according to the identified temporal semantic information.

Step 3. Formula Generation

The post-order traversal algorithm is used to access the syntax tree and the PPTL formula is generated based on the accessed the node information. The syntax tree traversal has two cases shown as follows:

i) **If we encounter a proposition node**, we need to decide whether the node timing table is empty. If it is not empty, add a sequence operator to the proposition according to the tag, take out the proposition description information, and then store the argument and description of the proposition in a hashmap.

ii) **If we encounter a connector node**, we need to analyze the description information of the linked parent node, determine the logical operator based on the description information, and connect the corresponding propositions.

In general, an atomic proposition in the syntax tree is derived from a subject and corresponding predicate, that is, an atomic proposition is expressed in the form of a subject-predicate. For multiple clauses connected with connectors, they are decomposed to generate different atomic propositions which are connected by logical operators. When the syntax tree traversal is completed, the final PPTL formula is obtained with the corresponding atomic propositions preserved in the hashmap. If the PPTL formula generated by the formula generation module does not meet the user's expectations, it can be modified manually. For example, we can directly add PPTL operators in our developed software.

Step 4. Formula Satisfiability Decision

We apply a tool PPTLSAT for formula decision. In specific, a PPTL formula is provided as a input parameter to the PPTLSAT, then a decision result is output which can decide the satisfiability of the generated PPTL formula. The tool PPTLSAT can create a folder to store the generated files automatically, in which decision.txt and lnfg.bmp store results in text and image format separately. To observed intuitively, the decision result can be displayed in an LNFG state transition diagram.

4   Case Study

In recent years, many scholars have carried out research on the autonomous driving takeover behavior. The takeover request time is an important factor that affects the takeover behavior. It is usually defined as the time to collision (TTC) between the vehicle and the obstacle ahead when the takeover request warning signal of the automatic driving system is issued. Takeover time is one of the important takeover performance indicators, which is usually defined as the time interval from the start of the takeover request time to when the driver turns off the autopilot mode. The closing mode of automatic driving is mainly realized through the buttons on the steering wheel, braking and steering (setting the brake pedal or steering wheel angle to exceed a certain threshold).

A natural language sentence in Table 4 aims to evaluate the safety of L3 autonomous vehicle takeover [8].

Table 4. L3 autonomous vehicle takeover

When an anchor vehicle appears in front, the system sets the time in the next state,

then the system will send the message, then when the driver presses the switch button,

the vehicle switches modes.

Next, we will follow the steps mentioned above to process the sentence and explain the principle of our work. Figure 2 shows the main interface and running results of our tool.

Table 5. Part of speech tagging results

WRB When DT an NN anchor NN vehicle VBZ appears IN in NN front, DT the

NN system VBZ sets DT the NN time IN in DT the JJ next NN state, RB then

DT the NN system MD will VB send DT the NN message, RB then WRB when

DT the NN driver VBZ presses DT the NN switch NN button, DT the NN vehicle

VBZ switches NNS modes.

4.1 Natural Language Tagging

Stanford CoreNLP is utilized to quickly and painlessly get linguistic annotations for the sentence, which performs word segmentation, part-of-speech tagging. A part of tagging results corresponding to the sentence through word segmentation is shown in Table 5, from which we can observe that each word has been tokenized with a part-of-speech tag added before.

4.2 Tag Recognition

Then the tagged results are input into the tag-recognizing module in PPTL-Generator. It can realize the function of recognizing tagged sentences: identify components and tenses of the sentence, as well as extract atomic propositions to construct a syntax tree through syntax analysis. The corresponding syntax tree is shown in Fig. 3.

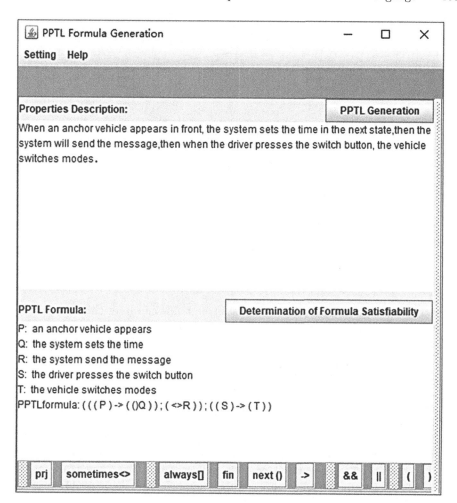

Fig. 2. PPTL formula generation

As shown in Fig. 3, the leaf nodes store atomic propositions and temporal description information about the autonomous driving behaviors. In addition, the internal nodes and root nodes store subordinate connectors and coordinating connectors separately. In our case, we set different node types and node labels to distinguish the role of nodes:

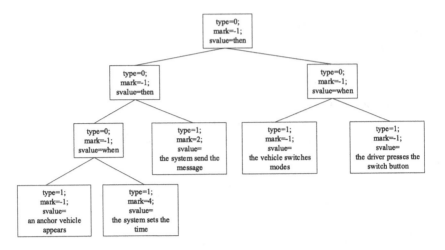

Fig. 3. The syntax tree

i) **when**: The proposition in the left subtree holds can infer that the proposition in the right subtree holds. It corresponds to a logical symbol $\rightarrow$ which connects the left and right subtrees of the **when** node, and the normal form is written as: $P_{left-subtree} \rightarrow P_{right-subtree}$.

ii) **then**: If the proposition in the left subtree holds, the proposition in the right subtree will hold in the next state. It have the sequential semantics which is described as $P_{left-subtree}; P_{right-subtree}$ corresponding to the logical symbol; (chop).

iii) **in the next state**: WordNet is used to recognize the synonym of this phrase. The phrase is found synonymous with next and defined as **next**. The semantics of the **next** tree node indicates that the current proposition is established in the next state with the logical symbol $\bigcirc$ (next).

iv) **will**: The proposition in the current tree node holds in a certain future state, and the current atomic proposition is defined with the logic symbol $\Diamond$ (sometimes).

4.3   Formula Generation

The generated syntax tree is traversed in a post order, and formulas are generated according to the information of tree nodes. When traversing the syntax tree, we map the **when** connector node to a logical symbol $\rightarrow$. The **then** node is mapped to a logical symbol; (chop). The phrase **in the next state** is mapped to $\bigcirc$ (next). The tense verb **will** is mapped to $\Diamond$ (sometimes). Then we split a sentence into several atomic propositions, and compose PPTL formulas according to conversion rules. The generated atomic propositions and formulas are shown in Table 6.

We can see from the result that connectors and temporal description information have been removed from the generated atomic propositions. The proposi-

Table 6. Formula generation result

P: an anchor vehicle appears

Q: the system sets the time

R: the system send the message

S: the driver presses the switch button

T: the vehicle switches modes

PPTL formula: (((P) -> (()Q)) ; (<>R)) ; ((S) -> (T))

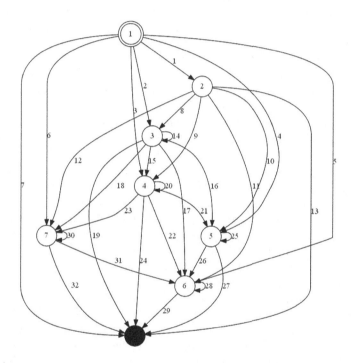

Fig. 4. LNFG

tional argument is marked. The generated formula that describes the properties of the sentence about the automatic driving vehicle conforms to the information of tree nodes expressed in the syntax tree.

4.4 Decision of Formula Satisfiability

In the end, the PPTLSAT is applied to check the satisfiability of the PPTL formula. Meanwhile, an LNFG is generated to show the decision result in Fig. 4.

Through the state transition diagram, the process that the satisfiability of the PPTL formula is checked by the PPTLGenerator can be observed obviously. Simultaneously, satisfiability decision can also provide the basis for inputting into the UMC4M with an MSVL program for model checking in the follow-up work.

5   Related Work

In order to help identify natural language effectively, there are three main branches of current work. The first is the definition of a natural language structured English grammar subset, with the help of structured form to simplify semantic acquisition. The second is to use semi-formal template to analyze natural language, and the third is using NLP technology and machine learning to realize automatic extraction of requirements analysis.

In the use of structured English grammar, Fei Wang et al. [24] devise an automatic transformation method from restricted natural language requirements to AADL model. The ambiguity and uncertainty in requirement specification can be reduced through restricted natural language. Rongjie Yan et al. [27] implement the automatic translation from natural language describing properties to abstract temporal logic. It expands pure syntax analysis by adding semantic reasoning and the division of input and output variables. The structured grammar defined in this study focuses on defining some simple sentences, which is slightly insufficient for describing the nature of complex requirements. Rongjie Yan et al. [9] create a grammar which has the capability of capturing the writing style and sentence structure of a specification and facilitating the automatic translation of English specification sentences into formal SystemVerilog Assertions. In general, methods can reduce the ambiguities of automatic conversion by structured English grammar with the technologies of structured data dictionary, domain thesaurus and limited sentence description, etc.

A common writing style used in formal specification causes the number of assertions in these clusters too large. To solve this problem, Mathias Soeken et al. [21] propose an algorithm that uses natural language processing technology to automatically convert natural language assertions into SystemVerilog Assertions. It divides all assertions into subsets based on sentence similarity, and then provides a translation template for each subset. Shalini Ghosh et al. [7] propose a framework for the automatic extraction of requirement specifications from natural language. The structure of natural language processed in this research is semi-formal, and the Symbolic Analysis Laboratory(SAL) model generated in the middle is a unified template defined manually. Fei Wang et al. [23] propose a semi-structured restricted natural language requirement template for requirement specification in component-based embedded software and realizes the transformation between software requirements based on the semi-structured template and AADL model. Though multiple assertions can be translated using the same template, which greatly reduces the verification work, the templates in most methods are still summarized by professional designers manually.

Natural language requirement extraction using NLP technology performs syntactic reconstruction to split a complex sentence into simple sentences to extract assertions from the requirements document. Deva Kumar Deeptimahanti et al. [2] normalize NL requirements and develop UML models for natural language requirements using efficient Natural Language Processing. Brian Keng et al. [12] propose a method that uses failed assertions, counter examples, and mutation models to generate alternative attributes for design verification, which can effectively find high-quality alternative assertions for empirical cases by NLP. However, this process has not yet been automated. Moreover, in the field of machine learning, Shobha Vasudevan et al. [22] propose a method to automatically extract assertions based on simulation tracking using NLP techniques. The assertion will be presented to the user (design or verification engineer) to determine whether the assertion is a suitable for designing, but the difficulty of learning all temporal sequences increases over time in this method.

6   Conclusions

This paper elaborates two main issues on the automatic generation of temporal logic converted by natural language. The first problem is abstracting the automatic conversion from properties described by natural language to PPTL formulas. The second problem is using the formula satisfiability decision tool to decide the satisfiability of PPTL formulas. In response to these two issues, we propose four specific steps to implement: First, tag the input natural language texts by the Stanford CoreNLP tool, and save tagged results. Second, process and identify the results, implement syntax analysis to build a syntax tree. Then, convert the syntax tree into a PPTL formula according to the defined rules and edit the obtained PPTL formula with necessary. Finally, call a tool PPTLSAT to decide the satisfiability of the PPTL formula. In addition, an example is used to illustrate the working principle of the method in detail. Our method reduces the manual work on generating formal specifications in the formal verification method. Future work will focus on extending structured natural languages to general natural languages, making them more suitable for ordinary users.

References

1. Brown, K.: Encyclopedia of Language and Linguistics, vol. 1. Elsevier (2005)
2. Deeptimahanti, D.K., Babar, M.A.: An automated tool for generating UML models from natural language requirements. In: 2009 IEEE/ACM International Conference on Automated Software Engineering, pp. 680–682. IEEE (2009)
3. Duan, Z.: An extended interval temporal logic and a framing technique for temporal logic proing. Ph.D. thesis, Newcastle University, Newcastle upon Tyne, UK (1996). http://hdl.handle.net/10443/2075
4. Duan, Z., Tian, C.: A unified model checking approach with projection temporal logic. In: Liu, S., Maibaum, T., Araki, K. (eds.) ICFEM 2008. LNCS, vol. 5256, pp. 167–186. Springer, Heidelberg (2008). https://doi.org/10.1007/978-3-540-88194-0_12

5. Duan, Z., Tian, C., Zhang, L.: A decision procedure for propositional projection temporal logic with infinite models. Acta Informatica **45**(1), 43–78 (2008)

6. Duan, Z., Yang, X., Koutny, M.: Semantics of framed temporal logic programs. In: Gabbrielli, M., Gupta, G. (eds.) ICLP 2005. LNCS, vol. 3668, pp. 356–370. Springer, Heidelberg (2005). https://doi.org/10.1007/11562931_27

7. Ghosh, S., Elenius, D., Li, W., Lincoln, P., Shankar, N., Steiner, W.: ARSE-NAL: automatic requirements specification extraction from natural language. In: Rayadurgam, S., Tkachuk, O. (eds.) NFM 2016. LNCS, vol. 9690, pp. 41–46. Springer, Cham (2016). https://doi.org/10.1007/978-3-319-40648-0_4

8. Gold, C., Happee, R., Bengler, K.: Modeling take-over performance in level 3 conditionally automated vehicles. Accid. Anal. Prev. **116**, 3–13 (2018)

9. Harris, C.B., Harris, I.G.: GLAsT: learning formal grammars to translate natural language specifications into hardware assertions. In: 2016 Design, Automation & Test in Europe Conference & Exhibition (DATE), pp. 966–971. IEEE (2016)

10. Huang, S.Y., Cheng, K.T.: Formal Equivalence Checking and Design Debugging, vol. 12. Springer, New York (1998). https://doi.org/10.1007/978-1-4615-5693-0

11. Johnson, S.C., et al.: YACC: Yet Another Compiler-Compiler, vol. 32. Bell Laboratories Murray Hill (1975)

12. Keng, B., Safarpour, S., Veneris, A.: Automated debugging of systemverilog assertions. In: 2011 Design, Automation & Test in Europe, pp. 1–6. IEEE (2011)

13. Koopman, P., Wagner, M.: Autonomous vehicle safety: an interdisciplinary challenge. IEEE Intell. Trans. Syst. Mag. **9**(1), 90–96 (2017)

14. Ma, Y., Duan, Z., Wang, X., Yang, X.: An interpreter for framed tempura and its application. In: First Joint IEEE/IFIP Symposium on Theoretical Aspects of Software Engineering, TASE 2007, Shanghai, China, 5–8 June, pp. 251–260. IEEE Computer Society (2007). https://doi.org/10.1109/TASE.2007.10

15. Manning, C.D., Surdeanu, M., Bauer, J., Finkel, J.R., Bethard, S., McClosky, D.: The Stanford CoreNLP natural language processing toolkit. In: Proceedings of the 52nd Annual Meeting of the Association for Computational Linguistics, ACL 2014, Baltimore, MD, USA, 22–27 June, pp. 55–60. The Association for Computer Linguistics (2014). https://doi.org/10.3115/v1/p14-5010

16. Miller, G.A.: WordNet: a lexical database for English. Commun. ACM **38**(11), 39–41 (1995). https://doi.org/10.1145/219717.219748

17. Miller, G.A.: WordNet: An Electronic Lexical Database. MIT Press, Cambridge (1998)

18. Moszkowski, B.C.: Compositional reasoning about projected and infinite time. In: 1st IEEE International Conference on Engineering of Complex Computer Systems (ICECCS 1995), Fort Lauderdale, Florida, USA, 6–10 November, pp. 238–245. IEEE Computer Society (1995). https://doi.org/10.1109/ICECCS.1995.479336

19. Moszkowski, B.C.: Reasoning about digital circuits (1983)

20. Praitheeshan, P., Pan, L., Yu, J., Liu, J.K., Doss, R.: Security analysis methods on ethereum smart contract vulnerabilities: a survey. CoRR (2019). http://arxiv.org/abs/1908.08605

21. Soeken, M., Harris, C.B., Abdessaied, N., Harris, I.G., Drechsler, R.: Automating the translation of assertions using natural language processing techniques. In: Proceedings of the 2014 Forum on Specification and Design Languages, FDL 2014, Munich, Germany, 14–16 October, pp. 1–8. IEEE (2014). https://doi.org/10.1109/FDL.2014.7119356

22. Vasudevan, S., Sheridan, D., Patel, S.J., Tcheng, D., Tuohy, W., Johnson, D.R.: GoldMine: automatic assertion generation using data mining and static analysis. In: Design, Automation and Test in Europe, DATE 2010, Dresden, Germany, 8–12 March, pp. 626–629. IEEE Computer Society (2010). https://doi.org/10.1109/DATE.2010.5457129
23. Wang, F., et al.: Approach for generating AADL model based on restricted natural language requirement template. J. Softw. **29**(8), 2350–2370 (2018). http://www.jos.org.cn/1000-9825/5530.html
24. Wang, F., Yang, Z.B., Huang, Z.Q., Liu, C.W., Zhou, Y., Bodeveix, J.P., Filali, M.: An approach to generate the traceability between restricted natural language requirements and AADL models. IEEE Trans. Reliab. **69**(1), 154–173 (2019)
25. Wang, X., Guo, W., Zhao, L., Shu, X.: Runtime verification method for social network security based on source code instrumentation. In: Duan, Z., Liu, S., Tian, C., Nagoya, F. (eds.) SOFL+MSVL 2018. LNCS, vol. 11392, pp. 55–70. Springer, Cham (2019). https://doi.org/10.1007/978-3-030-13651-2_4
26. Wang, X., Yang, K., Wang, Y., Zhao, L., Shu, X.: Towards formal verification of neural networks: a temporal logic based framework. In: Miao, H., Tian, C., Liu, S., Duan, Z. (eds.) SOFL+MSVL 2019. LNCS, vol. 12028, pp. 73–87. Springer, Cham (2020). https://doi.org/10.1007/978-3-030-41418-4_6
27. Yan, R., Cheng, C., Chai, Y.: Formal consistency checking over specifications in natural languages. In: Proceedings of the 2015 Design, Automation & Test in Europe Conference & Exhibition, DATE 2015, Grenoble, France, 9–13 March, pp. 1677–1682. ACM (2015). http://dl.acm.org/citation.cfm?id=2757200

Testing and Formal Verification

Software Testing with Statistical Partial Oracles
- Application to Neural Networks Software -

Shin Nakajima[✉]

National Institute of Informatics, Tokyo, Japan
nkjm@nii.ac.jp

Abstract. With the advent of Bigdata analytics or machine learning software, the characteristics of test target programs become more divergent than before. It brings about two issues on the test oracle problems, uncertainties of the testing conditions and unknown correctness criteria. This paper proposes a new testing framework, which is general enough to account for the existing statistical metamorphic testing and is further amenable to adapt itself to the machine learning software testing. The proposed approach is illustrated with an experiment of testing neural network programs.

1 Introduction

Software testing [2] is a practical approach to assuring quality of computer programs, but the characteristics of test targets are more divergent than before. Software systems are often data-intensive, such as CPS/IoT or Bigdata analytics, working on large sets of digital *data* that represent real-world phenomena on human behavior or industrial Bigdata. These programs are not free from *uncertainties* due to fluctuations in observed values or to data distributions. Therefore, testing under the uncertainties [8] is one of the major research topics in software testing of data-intensive systems including deep neural networks (DNN) [10,13].

Quality assurance of DNN programs is a challenging research topic [20,32]. Those programs extract valuable pieces of information from a given collection of data. The trained DNN models are not predictable before the development, always suffering from the uncertainties of the data distributions. Further the prediction or inference results cannot be definite, but may be accompanied with probabilistic certainties. These characteristics bring about new challenges to software testing methods, in particular to test oracles [14].

A standard method for quantifying uncertainties is the probabilistic modeling of the test target behavior, and adapts notions in statistics as a basis for testing; the methods may employ statistical hypothesis tests to refute the correctness of test target programs [17,26]. In addition, Metamorphic Testing (MT) [5], originally proposed in [4], is a practical testing methodology for programs that require derived test oracles [3]. MT is, indeed, successful in testing of machine learning classifiers [19,21,30]. Although those two notions, the hypothesis tests

© Springer Nature Switzerland AG 2021
J. Xue et al. (Eds.): SOFL+MSVL 2020, LNCS 12723, pp. 175–192, 2021.
https://doi.org/10.1007/978-3-030-77474-5_12

and MT, are combined to be Statistical Metamorphic Testing (SMT) [11], the method is introduced informally, and thus is not clear how it is instantiated to the cases of DNN software testing, which involves programs of two different roles, training and prediction [10,13].

This paper proposes a new testing framework general enough to account for the SMT. The framework is amenable to adapt itself to testing of DNN software. The proposed approach is illustrated with an experiment of testing DNN-based machine learning classifier programs.

2   Statistical Approach to Software Testing

This section presents background materials on test oracles and statistical approaches to software testing.

2.1   Test Oracles

A test oracle is informally a systematic method to check whether the test target program is correct with respect to its expected behavior. Software testing is a dynamic checking of programs, and the method consists of three technical aspects; (a) selecting test input data, (b) determining a correct output value for the input data, and (c) checking if the result of the execution satisfies the correctness criteria. The checking method is either manual or automatic.

For simplicity, in this paper, a test target program is modeled as a function $f \in D \rightarrow D'$, where D and D' are the sets of data. An automatic test oracle is a predicate $\mathcal{G}_T^{[N]}(C_a, f(a)) \stackrel{def}{=} (C_a = f(a))$, where $a \in D$ is a test input and $C_a \in D'$ is a correct output value for the particular input a. In addition, $_- =_- \in D' \times D'$ is the equality relation. The correct value may be given as a specification or determined by means of theoretical considerations. Let $S_a \in D'_A$ be such a value, whose domain D'_A may be more abstract than D'. A specified test oracle [3] needs a method of concretizing S_a to C_a. An abstraction function $abs \in D' \rightarrow D'_A$ helps this translation; $S_a = abs(C_a)$. The oracle now takes a form that $\mathcal{G}_T^{[S]}(S_a, f(a)) \stackrel{def}{=} (abs^{-1}(S_a) = f(a))$.

Correct values may not be known beforehand, and those programs are *non-testable* [29]. C_a is replaced by an output from a program different from the test target [6]. A derived test oracle $\mathcal{G}_T^{[D]}$ [3] involves two programs, $f(x)$ and $g(x)$; $\mathcal{G}_T^{[D]}(g(a), f(a)) \stackrel{def}{=} (g(a) = f(a))$. The program $g(x)$ is another implementation of the same specification as the test target $f(x)$, and is developed by means of an N-version programming methodology or design diversity [1] approach. This notion of $\mathcal{G}_T^{[D]}$ requires developing at least two versions of programs, namely involves tremendous manual efforts. The testing method can be complex and costly.

Metamorphic testing (MT), originally proposed in [4], is a property-based testing method based on the notion of partial oracles [5]. The method checks whether a program $f(_-)$ satisfies a metamorphic relation $MR \in D^N \times D'^N$ $(N>1)$,

$$MR(x^{(1)}, \ldots, x^{(N)}, f(x^{(1)}), \ldots, f(x^{(N)}))$$

denoting a $2N$-relationship on the N inputs $x^{(n)}$ and N outputs $f(x^{(n)})$.

A specific class of MRs is appropriate in practice. Such an MR consists of an input sub-relation in the form of a mapping T_f, and an output sub-relation R_T involving the outputs of the source input data and a follow-up one[1].

$$MR(x^{(1)}, x^{(2)}, f(x^{(1)}), f(x^{(2)})) \overset{def}{=} (x^{(2)} = T_f(x^{(1)})) \Rightarrow R_T(f(x^{(1)}), f(x^{(2)}))$$

This subclass of MRs can further be specialized to be a basis of derived test oracles; $\mathcal{G}_T^{[M]}(f(a), f(T_f(a))) \overset{def}{=} (f(a) = f(T_f(a)))$. T_f is a follow-up test generation function $(T_f \in D \rightarrow D)$, and the accompanying relation $R_T(f(a), f(T_f(a)))$ is chosen as an equality. As seen in the above, the oracle $\mathcal{G}_T^{[M]}$, based on the MT methodology, includes T_f and R_T referring to two executions of the test target $f(\_)$.

Up to now, the behavior of test targets is assumed to be *deterministic*; $f(a)$ always returns the same result for the same input data a. Some programs, however, violate this assumption. They, even for the same input data, may behave differently resulting in different outputs from execution to execution. Such behavior may be *probabilistic*, and is amenable to statistical analysis methods, which requires extending the notion of test oracles as well.

2.2 Statistical Test Oracles

Next presents a brief review of test oracles based on statistical methods [17,26], which is referred to statistical test oracles in this paper.

Hypothesis Testing. Basically, a statistical test oracle $\mathcal{G}_T$ adapts the statistical hypothesis testing method.

For simplicity, a test target program, showing probabilistic behavior, is modeled as a function relying on a certain probabilistic variable p internally. Such a program is denoted as $f_p \in D \rightarrow D'$, where p follows a probabilistic distribution ρ, written as $p \sim \rho$. For a certain input data $a \in D$, the output $f_p(a)$ is not definite, but differs from execution to execution. If y_a denotes an output for the input data a, then a series of such executions form a set $Y_a = \{y_a^{(j)}\}$ that follows a certain probabilistic distribution as well. Further, the statistical average of the output values $(\overline{y_a})$ is supposed to be a good observer, against which a known correct value C_a is checked.

The hypothesis testing is one of the methods to reason about statistical properties of a sample (a collection of data). First introduces a null hypothesis H_0 together with an alternative hypothesis H_1; H_0 states that $\overline{y_a} = C_a$, while H_1 is that $\overline{y_a} \neq C_a$. Second decides a significance level (α), defining a critical region which is a set of statistic values to show evidence against H_0. Third calculates a

---

[1] For simplicity, it is assumed that $N = 2$.

test statistic t_a to summarize the information of the sample distribution. Fourth shows that the test statistic t_a falls in the critical region. Then, H_0 is rejected at the certainty level of α, which implies that the test target program to produce $\overline{y_a}$ may be *faulty* because of H_1 ($\overline{y_a} \neq C_a$).

Now, a statistical test oracle $\mathcal{G}_T(Y_a, C_a)$ is defined in terms of the statistical hypothesis testing procedure $H_T(\langle \overline{y_a}, s_a^2, N \rangle, C_a)$. In particular, for cases where the sample distribution is Gaussian, written as $Norm(\mu, \sigma^2)$, the test statistic,

$$t_a = \frac{\overline{y_a} - C_a}{\sqrt{s_a^2/N}}$$

follows the t-distribution. With this t_a, the procedure H_T is written as

$$H_T(\langle \overline{y_a}, s_a^2, N \rangle, C_a) \stackrel{def}{=} \textbf{if } |t_a| > t_{\alpha/2}(N-1) \textbf{ then } error \textbf{ else } unknown$$

where *error* indicates that the H_0 is rejected at the certainty level α. $|t_a|$ is an absolute value of t_a, and $t_{\alpha/2}(N-1)$ denotes the critical value of the t-distribution of $N-1$ degrees of freedom at the confidence level α; the test is two-tailed as understood from the introduced hypotheses.

An auxiliary function $\mathcal{U}$ accepts a set of data or a sample (Y_a), and returns a tuple consisting of the average $(\overline{y_a})$, the standard variation (s_a^2), and the sample size (N). Let V be a set of y_a, then $Y_a \in \mathbb{P}V$, and thus $\mathcal{U} \in \mathbb{P}V \rightarrow \mathcal{R} \times \mathcal{R} \times \mathcal{N}$, where $\mathcal{R}$ is real numbers and $\mathcal{N}$ is natural numbers. For a set Y_a, $|Y_a|$ denotes its size.

$\mathcal{U}(Y_a \textbf{ as } \{y_a^{(j)}\}) \stackrel{def}{=}$
    $\textbf{let val } \overline{y_a} = \frac{1}{N}\sum y_a^{(j)} \textbf{ and } s_a^2 = \frac{1}{N-1}\sum (y_a^{(j)} - \overline{y_a})^2 \textbf{ and } N = |Y_a|$
    $\textbf{in } \langle \overline{y_a}, s_a^2, N \rangle \textbf{ end}$

These lead to the oracle; $\mathcal{G}_T(Y_a, C_a) \stackrel{def}{=} \neg(H_T(\mathcal{U}(Y_a), C_a) = error)$.

Statistical Metamorphic Testing. Statistical Metamorphic Testing (SMT) [11] is a refinement of the statistical test oracle to the case of the metamorphic testing. Let $f_p(x)$ be a non-testable program to exhibit probabilistic behavior. Given a test data a, a sample $\{y_a^{(j)}\}$ (or Y_a) is a set of executions of $f_p(a)$, and $\{y_{T(a)}^{(j)}\}$ (or $Y_{T(a)}$) is for $f_p(T_f(a))$. SMT adopts the two-sample t-test. The two samples, gathered from executions of a single test target program $f_p(\_)$, may have the same population variance. Therefore, the test statistic is that

$$t_a = \frac{\overline{y_a} - \overline{y_{T(a)}}}{\sqrt{s^2/N + s^2/M}}, \quad and \quad s^2 = \frac{(N-1)s_a^2 + (M-1)s_{T(a)}^2}{N+M-2}$$

where $N = |Y_a|$ and $M = |Y_{T(a)}|$. Finally, the test oracle for SMT is that

$$\mathcal{G}_T(Y_a, Y_{T(a)}) \stackrel{def}{=} \neg(H_S(\mathcal{U}(Y_a), \mathcal{U}(Y_{T(a)})) = error).$$

The hypothesis testing procedure $H_S(\langle \overline{y_a}, s_a^2, N \rangle, \langle \overline{y_{T(a)}}, s_{T(a)}^2, M \rangle)$ is similar to H_T, but refers to $t_{\alpha/2}(N+M-2)$ instead. As seen from the definition of t_a above, the null hypothesis H_0 represents that $\overline{y_a} = \overline{y_{T(a)}}$. This is consistent with the fact that the predicate R_T in the MR refers to equality relations.

3   Proposed Testing Framework

3.1   General Framework

This section starts with discussions on two extensions to SMT [11] (explained in Sect. 2.2), and then introduces the proposed testing framework.

Two Extensions. First, a program showing probabilistic behavior is denoted as $f_p(x)$ (Sect. 2.2), where p stands for a probabilistic variable $p \in P$ and $p \sim \rho$. The program may also take a form of $f \in D \to (P \to D')$ when p is made explicit. Then, $f(a) \in P \to D'$ forms Y_a if $f(a)(\_)$ accepts repeatedly an input data from a set of values $I_\rho = \{p \in P \mid p \sim \rho\}$. With another function $\mathcal{O}' \in (P \to D') \to (\mathbb{P}P \to \mathbb{P}D')$, the executions $\mathcal{O}'(f(a))(I_\rho)$ result in a set Y_a. A statistical test oracle similar to $\mathcal{G}_T$ is applicable to $f(a)(\_)$ as well.

Second, $\mathcal{O}'$ plays an important role in testing of machine learning (ML) software. As in Sect. 3.2, ML software usually involves two kinds of *non-testable* programs, a training program $\mathcal{L}_f$ and a prediction program $\mathcal{I}_f$. $\mathcal{L}_f$ accepts a training dataset and generates a trained machine learning model to provide the functional behavior of $\mathcal{I}_f$. If $\mathbb{P}V$ refers to the type of training dataset, $\mathcal{L}_f$ is schematically a function of $\mathbb{P}V \to (D \to D')$, and $\mathcal{I}_f$ is of type $D \to D'$. Software testing of $\mathcal{L}_f(\_)$ is indirect and may be conducted only with $\mathcal{I}_f(\_)$. When $\mathcal{L}_f$ is a test target program, $\mathcal{I}_f$ is, in a sense, an *observer*. A function $\mathcal{O}'$ is so defined as to play a role of the observer, to which the statistical test oracle $\mathcal{G}_T$ refers.

Statistical Partial Oracle. Now introduces a general testing framework which extends the notion of statistical metamorphic testing. A test target program is modeled as a function $\mathcal{F} \in V \to V'$. Additionally, an auxilary function may take a form such as $obs \in (V \to V') \to (V \to (D \to D'))$. In some cases, V' is identified with $D \to D'$. For a set of evaluation data of size N, $ES = \{e^{(n)} \in D \mid e^{(n)} \sim \rho\}$ with a certain probability distribution ρ, an observer $\mathcal{O} \in (V \to V') \to (V \to (\mathbb{P}D \to \mathbb{P}D'))$ is defined as

$$\mathcal{O}(\mathcal{F})(a)(ES \text{ as } \{e^{(n)}\}) = \{obs(\mathcal{F})(a)(e^{(n)})\},$$

where $a \in V$ is an input test data to the test target $\mathcal{F}$. Then, $\mathcal{U}(\,\mathcal{O}(\mathcal{F})(a)(ES)\,)$ returns a tuple of the statistical indicators (Sect. 2.2).

Some test targets may require partial test oracles. Two programs $\mathcal{F}_{(1)}$ and $\mathcal{F}_{(2)}$ are involved together with a single set of evaluation data ES. As ES is common, a revised statistical hypothesis testing procedure may take a form of

$$H'_S(\,\mathcal{U}(\,\mathcal{O}(\mathcal{F}_{(1)})(A_{(1)})(ES)\,),\,\mathcal{U}(\,\mathcal{O}(\mathcal{F}_{(2)})(A_{(2)})(ES)\,)\,)$$

where $A_{(j)} \in V$ is a test input to $\mathcal{F}_{(j)}$ ($j = 1$ or 2). Because $\mathcal{F}(a)(\_) = (\mathcal{F}(a))(\_)$, the proposed statistical test oracle $\mathcal{G}_S$ is

$$\mathcal{G}_S(\,\mathcal{F}_{(1)}(A_{(1)}),\,\mathcal{F}_{(2)}(A_{(2)})\,)\ \stackrel{def}{=}\ \neg(\,H'_S(\ldots)\ =\ error\,)$$

which encapsulates in itself the hypothesis testing procedure for a given pair of partial oracles ($\mathcal{F}_{(1)}(A_{(1)})$ and $\mathcal{F}_{(2)}(A_{(2)})$) and the common evaluation dataset ES whose data follow a certain probabilistic distribution.

Note, in this case, that the predicate R_T in the MR is the equality between the statistical averages of two series of executions (Sect. 2.2).

3.2   Framework for Neural Networks Testing

Testing of Deep Neural Networks (DNN) software is formulated as an instantiation of the proposed general framework $\mathcal{G}_S$. In particular, in order to present technical discussions concretely, the example case below concerns with the DNN software of supervised classifier tasks. Note that standard practices of DNN software [10,13] involve a training program $\mathcal{L}_f$ and a prediction program $\mathcal{I}_f$.

Let $Y(W; x)$ be a machine learning model and W be a set of weight parameters. Alternatively, the DNN model is written as $Y_W(x)$ to represent a W-indexed family of functions. Given definite values of weights W^c, $Y_{W^c} \in V \to T$ is a function. Then, the machine learning model is $Y \in W \to (V \to T)$ or $Y \in \mathbb{P}(V \to T)$ if W is made implicit.

A training dataset LS is a set of data-points or tuples; each data-point consists of a multi-dimensional vector data and a supervisor tag. The training dataset is $LS \in \mathbb{P}(V \times T)$ and $LS = \{\langle x^{(n)}, t^{(n)} \rangle\}$. A data-point is considered to be sampled from a data distribution, $\langle x^{(n)}, t^{(n)} \rangle \sim \rho^{EMP}$, where ρ^{EMP} is the empirical distribution of LS.

The training program $\mathcal{L}_f$ accepts LS, written as $\mathcal{L}_f(LS)$, and generates a trained DNN model (a function): $\mathcal{L}_f \in \mathbb{P}(V \to T) \to (\mathbb{P}(V \times T) \to (V \to T))$. $\mathcal{L}_f$ is essentially a program to solve a numerical optimization problem and returns $Y_{W^*} \in V \to T$.

$$W^* = \arg\min_{W} \mathcal{E}_{\langle x,t \rangle \sim \rho^{EMP}} [\![\ell(Y(W;x), t)]\!]$$

where $\ell(\_, \_)$ is an appropriate loss function, and $\mathcal{E}_{\langle x,t \rangle \sim \rho^{EMP}} [\![\cdot]\!]$ represents an average over the probability distribution ρ^{EMP}.

The prediction program $\mathcal{I}_f$, if trained machine learning models Y_{W^*} are made explicit, takes a form of $\mathcal{I}_f(Y_{W^*})(\_)$. It uses the trained DNN model, and returns the calculated result for an input data vector ($\mathcal{I}_f \in (V \to T) \to (V \to V')$).

The observer function $\mathcal{O}_f$, that the oracle $\mathcal{G}_S$ refers to, employs the trained DNN model and calculates a sample with a specified set of the evaluation data ES. With appropriate sets D and D', $\mathcal{O}_f \in (V \to T) \to (\mathbb{P} D \to \mathbb{P} D')$. Additionally, using an auxiliary function obs_f working on an individual data $e \in D$, $\mathcal{O}_f(Y_{W^*})(ES \text{ as } \{e^{(j)}\}) = \{obs_f(Y_{W^*})(e^{(j)})\}$.

Because $Y_{W^*} = \mathcal{L}_f(Y)(LS)$, the above definition of $\mathcal{O}_f$ is rewritten to be $\mathcal{O}_f(\mathcal{L}_f(Y)(LS))(\_)$, which illustrates the fact that the observer depends on the DNN model Y and training dataset LS.

This revised form can capture two different notions of partial oracles from a unified viewpoint for testing of machine learning programs. First, in a design diversity approach in which the testing of $\mathcal{L}_f$ involves two alternative DNN models, an instantiation of the framework refers to $\mathcal{O}_f(\mathcal{L}_f(\underline{Y_{(1)}})(LS))(\_)$

and $\mathcal{O}_f(\mathcal{L}_f(Y_{(2)})(LS))(\_)$. Second, in a metamorphic testing approach in which the training datasets are constructed systematically with the notion of the dataset diversity [21], the framework refers to $\mathcal{O}_f(\mathcal{L}_f(Y)(\underline{LS}))(\_)$ and $\mathcal{O}_f(\mathcal{L}_f(Y)(\underline{T_f(LS)}))(\_)$. T_f is a follow-up test generation function, but is actually a dataset transformer, $T_f \in \mathbb{P}(V \times T) \to \mathbb{P}(V \times T)$.

3.3   Observers for Monitoring Neural Network States

Concrete examples of $\mathcal{O}_f$ or obs_f monitor the states of a trained DNN model against an input data vector. Below introduces two of such observer functions, taking a form of $\mathcal{O}_f \in (V \to T) \to (\mathbb{P}(V \times T) \to \mathbb{P}[0, 1])$.

External Indices. The discussion here assumes that the machine learning task is to classify data into one of the C classes. The prediction program, $\mathcal{I}_f(Y_{W^*}) \in V \to [0, 1]^C$, accepts a vector data $x^{(j)} \in V$, which is an element of a tuple in an evaluation dataset $ES \in \mathbb{P}(V \times T)$ ($\langle x^{(j)}, t^{(j)} \rangle \in ES$), and returns a C-dimensional vector π; each component $\pi[c] \in [0, 1]$ represents a probability that the input data $x^{(j)}$ belongs to the category c for $c = 1, \ldots, C$. Furthermore, c^* is the category that it makes π maximum ($c^* = \underset{c \in [1, C]}{argmax}\ \pi[c]$). An observer function $obj_{prob}(Y_{W^*})(x^{(j)})$ is defined to return a value $\pi[c^*]$;

$$\mathcal{O}_{prob}(Y_{W^*})(ES \textbf{ as } \{\langle x^{(j)}, \_ \rangle\}) = \{\ \pi[c^*]\ \}.$$

The accuracy is sometimes regarded as a good indicator to study whether the search, in the training phase, proceeds as expected [13]. The supervisor tag may adopt the one-hot vector representation, $t^{(j)} \in \{0, 1\}^C$; $t^{(j)}[c_0] = 1$ if the corresponding data $x^{(j)}$ is categorized to c_0, and $t^{(j)}[c'] = 0$ for $c' \in [1, \ldots, C]$ and $c' \neq c_0$.

An accuracy, $Acc \in (V \to T) \to (\mathbb{P}(V \times T) \to [0, 1])$, is defined as a ratio to show how many data in ES reconstruct the corresponding supervisor tag;

$$Acc(Y_{W^*})(ES \textbf{ as } \{\langle x^{(j)}, t^{(j)} \rangle\}) = \frac{|\ \{\langle x^{(j)}, t^{(j)} \rangle\ |\ t^{(j)}[c^*] = 1\}\ |}{|\ ES\ |}.$$

However, this paper does not consider Acc as an observer, because its type is different from that of $\mathcal{O}_f$.

Internal Indices. The second observer introduced here is based on the notion of the neuron coverage [24], and is independent of the machine learning tasks. A trained DNN model Y_{W^*} consists of neurons, which form a set denoted as $\{\nu_k\}$. A neuron ν_k is a function to define an input-output relationship such that $o_k = \sigma_k(\sum_j w_j^* \times in_j)$. Given a threshold th, a neuron is said *active* if $o_k > th$ holds when present the input signals in_j at ν_k; the signals are propagated along the network from the vector data (x) input to the trained DNN model $(Y_{W^*}(x))$. The neuron coverage NC is a ratio of the active neurons.

An observer function $obs_{act} \in (V \to T) \to (V \to [0,1])$ is the neuron coverage for neurons at the penultimate layer of Y_{W^*} when an input vector data is presented. Let PL be a set of neurons at the penultimate layer.

$$obs_{act}(Y_{W^*})(x) = \frac{|\ \{\nu_k \in PL | o_k > th\}\ |}{|\ PL\ |}$$

The observer is that $\mathcal{O}_{act}(Y_{W^*})(ES \text{ as } \{\langle x^{(j)}, \_\rangle\}) = \{\ obs_{act}(Y_{W^*})(x^{(j)})\ \}$. Note that obs_{act} is defined to look at the neurons in the penultimate layer only.

4   A Case Study

This section presents results of an experiment, in which the proposed general testing framework $\mathcal{G}_S$ is instantiated to DNN programs of a classification task, and studies how the internal indices are adequate for the software testing of training programs $\mathcal{L}_f$.

4.1   MNIST Classification Problem

MNIST dataset is a standard problem of classifying handwritten arabic numbers. It consists of a training dataset LS of 60,000 sheets, and a testing dataset TS of 10,000. Both LS and TS can be selected randomly from a pool of sheets, and thus are considered to follow the same data distribution. The machine learning task is to classify an input sheet, or a vector data, into one of ten categories from 0 to 9. A sheet is presented as 28×28 pixels, each taking a value between 0 and 255 to represent gray scales. Pixel values represent hand-written strokes, and each number appears as specific patterns of these pixel values.

In the experiments, the learning model is a classical fully-connected neural network [13] with a hidden middle layer and an output layer. The activation function of neurons in the hidden layer is $ReLU$; its output is linear for positive input values and a constant zero for negatives. A *softmax* activation function is introduced so that the inference program $\mathcal{I}_f$ returns probabilities that an incoming data belongs to each of the ten categories. This choice is consistent with the discussion regarding to π and $\mathcal{O}_{prob}$ in Sect. 3.3.

4.2   Overview of Testing Method

Testing of a deep neural networks (DNN) training program $\mathcal{L}_f$ is difficult in general. A resultant trained learning model Y_{W^*}, that $\mathcal{L}_f$ is searching for, is not only unknown prior to the development, but also unable to be validated directly. The validation can be conducted only with a prediction program $\mathcal{I}_f$ of which behavior the model Y_{W^*} defines. Furthermore, the prediction results are not decisive, and are accompanied with uncertainties (*softmax* values).

Because of these, testing $\mathcal{L}_f$ is conducted with an instance of the proposed framework introduced in Sect. 3.1.

Fig. 1. Synthesized data with semantic noises

$$\mathcal{G}_S(\ \underline{\mathcal{L}_f(Y)(LS)},\ \underline{\mathcal{L}_f(Y)(T_f(LS))}\ )$$

In particular, it is based on the metamorphic testing method.

Note that $\mathcal{L}_f$ solves a non-convex optimization problem [13] to search for an optimal solution. The solution is, indeed, a trained machine learning model. Therefore, identifying an appropriate metamorphic property would be key to adopting the testing framework successfully. It involves to find a follow-up test generation function T_f with a metamorphic relation that the hypothesis testing procedure $\mathcal{H}_S$ refers to.

The details are the subjects of the rest of this section. Briefly, T_f is so chosen to build up the dataset diversity [21,22], and the metamorphic relation is identified by means of studying the characteristics of the optimization problem [23].

4.3 Semantic Noises

A test input to $\mathcal{L}_f$ is a kind of training dataset. Since the dataset may be regarded as *implicit* specifications of $\mathcal{I}_f$ or Y_{W^*} under development, any test input dataset must serve to train the same machine learning task. In the experiment, a dataset used as the test input is similar to, but different from the training dataset LS of the MNIST classification task. Such datasets for software testing of $\mathcal{L}_f$ show the dataset diversity [21], and each data-point in them is synthesized with semantic noises.

Let $\mathcal{S}_f$ be a function to generate a data vector augmented with semantic noises.

$$\mathcal{S}_f \in (V \rightarrow T) \rightarrow (V \times T \rightarrow V)$$

Given a trained learning model Y_{W^*} and a data-point $\langle x_c, t_c \rangle$, $\mathcal{S}_f(Y_{W^*})(x_c, t_c)$ returns a new data vector X^* to build a new data-point $\langle X^*, t_c \rangle$. $\mathcal{S}_f$ is essentially a program to solve a constrained optimization problem below [22]; its formulation is based on the L-BFGS [27].

$$X^* = \underset{X}{argmin}\ \ell(Y_{W^*}(X),\ t_c)\ +\ \lambda \cdot \ell'(X,\ x_c)$$
$$\text{s.t.}\ \ 0 \le X_j \le 1\ \wedge\ \Psi(X, x_c)$$

where X_j is a j-th component of a vector X. In the above, $\ell(\_,\_)$ and $\ell'(\_,\_)$ are appropriate loss functions, defined, for example, with the L_2 norm. The first term enforces that a prediction for X with Y_{W^*} must reconstruct the tag t_c. The second term specifies that X is close to x_c measured in terms of the chosen norm. Selecting a right value for the hyper-parameter λ will produce an optimal solution being added semantic noises such that X^* is indistinguishable from x_c for human eyes. Figure 1 shows a portion of a synthesized dataset with semantic noises. Each obtained graphical image mostly preserves the original patterns, and thus the dataset serves to train the same machine learning task as MNIST.

With a trained learning model Y_{W^*} obtained from the MNIST training dataset that $LS = \{\langle x^{(n)}, t^{(n)} \rangle\}$, a new dataset LS' is so constructed as below.

$$LS' = \{\langle x^{*(n)}, t^{(n)} \rangle \mid x^{*(n)} = \mathcal{S}_f(Y_{W^*})(x^{(n)}, t^{(n)})\}$$

The expression can be rewritten compactly with a new function $\mathcal{T}_x$,

$$\mathcal{T}_x \in (V \to T) \to (\mathbb{P}(V \times T) \to \mathbb{P}(V \times T))$$

and that $LS' = \mathcal{T}_x(\mathcal{L}_f(Y)(LS))(LS)$ because $Y_{W^*} = \mathcal{L}_f(Y)(LS)$.

Another function $\mathcal{T}_Y$, so defined that $\mathcal{T}_Y(LS) \overset{def}{=} \mathcal{T}_x(\mathcal{L}_f(Y)(LS))(LS)$, is a dataset transformer,

$$\mathcal{T}_Y \in \mathbb{P}(V \times T) \to \mathbb{P}(V \times T).$$

It shows that the functional behavior of $\mathcal{T}_Y$ is dependent on the given $Y(W; \_)$.

A series of datasets $LS^{(K)} = \mathcal{T}_Y(LS^{(K-1)})$ is systematically synthesized with $\mathcal{T}_Y$ where $LS^{(0)}$ is equal to LS of the MNIST training dataset. The series constitute a set building up the dataset diversity; $\varXi_Y(LS) = \{LS, LS^{(1)}, \ldots, LS^{(N)}\}$. The MNIST testing dataset TS leads to $\varXi_Y(TS)$ as well.

4.4 Solving Two Optimization Problems Interleaved

Two basic ingredients of the metamorphic testing method are a follow-up test generation T_f and its accompanying metamorphic relation Rel_T. Now, T_f refers to the function $\mathcal{T}_Y$ or $\mathcal{T}_x$ generating the diverse datasets $\varXi_Y$. The next question is what properties Rel_T looks at. The discussion here depends on the view in which the training machine learning model (Sect. 3.2) and the semantic noise generation (Sect. 4.3) are both formulated as optimization problems. Two solutions of optimization problems are involved; $Y_{W^{(K-1)*}} = \mathcal{L}_f(Y)(LS^{(K-1)})$, and $LS^{(K)} = \mathcal{T}_x(Y_{W^{(K-1)*}})(LS^{(K-1)})$.

Because of the second equation concerning to the semantic noises, $LS^{(K)}$ is more fitted to $Y_{W^{(K-1)*}}$ than $LS^{(K-1)}$ is. In a sense, the data distribution in $LS^{(K)}$ is more biased towards $Y_{W^{(K-1)*}}$ than $LS^{(K-1)}$ is. Owing to this, the degree referring to how much $LS^{(K)}$ is biased towards $Y_{W^{(K)*}}$ is smaller than the degree arising from $LS^{(K-1)}$ towards $Y_{W^{(K)*}}$. Repeatedly solving the two optimization problems, in an interleaving manner, leads to an index M at which $LS^{(M)}$ and $LS^{(M+1)}$ are not distinguishable, because each resultant trained machine learning model returns almost the same computation results for a fixed set of evaluation data ES; $\mathcal{O}_f(Y_{W^{(M)*}})(ES) \approx \mathcal{O}_f(Y_{W^{(M+1)*}})(ES)$. This implies that the metamorphic relation is simply the equality between some indices obtained from the M-th and $M+1$-th executions.

If a test target program $\mathcal{L}_f$ has faults in it, the interleaving process may not reach such a stable index M. Therefore, $\mathcal{G}_S$ is introduced as a test oracle making use of the hypothesis testing procedure,

$$H'_S(\ \mathcal{U}(\ \mathcal{O}_f(\underline{\mathcal{L}_f(Y)(LS^{(M)})})(ES)\ ),\ \ \mathcal{U}(\ \mathcal{O}_f(\underline{\mathcal{L}_f(Y)(\mathcal{T}_Y(LS^{(M)}))})(ES)\ )\ )$$

with a certain observer function $\mathcal{O}_f$ (see Sect. 3.3).

4.5   Controlled Experiment

The controlled experiment concerns with two machine learning programs, $\mathcal{L}_f^{PC}(Y)$ and $\mathcal{L}_f^{BI}(Y)$. The symbol PC is an abbreviation of *Probably Correct*, and $\mathcal{L}_f^{PC}$ is a faithful implementation of a standard machine learning algorithm to adopt well-known methods such as the back-propagation and stochastic gradient decent [13]. The BI stands for *Bug-Injected*, and $\mathcal{L}_f^{BI}$ is a modification of $\mathcal{L}_f^{PC}$. The machine learning model $Y(W; \_)$, common to both programs, is a classical fully-connected neural network, in which the activation function of neurons at the hidden layer is $ReLU$. The two test target programs are collectively denoted as $\mathcal{L}_f^{MD}$ where MD is either PC or BI.

The data used in the training process are MNIST training dataset LS and its testing dataset TS. The experiment, as explained below, consists of two series, one with $\mathcal{L}_f^{PC}(Y)$ and another with $\mathcal{L}_f^{BI}(Y)$ in parallel, and the derived information is decorated similarly as $LS_{MD}^{(K)}$ or $TS_{MD}^{(K)}$. The MNIST datasets are indexed as $LS_{MD}^{(0)}$ and $TS_{MD}^{(0)}$. In particular, $LS_{PC}^{(0)} = LS_{BI}^{(0)} = LS$ by construction, and similar relationships hold for $TS_{MD}^{(0)}$. Note that, for $K \geq 1$, $LS_{PC}^{(K)}$ may not be the same as $LS_{BI}^{(K)}$ and, neither is the case between $TS_{PC}^{(K)}$ and $TS_{BI}^{(K)}$. Note that $LS_{MD}^{(K)}$ is used training in the process of searching for solutions while $TS_{MD}^{(K)}$ plays a role to check whether the search proceeds appropriately [13]. Thus, both $LS_{MD}^{(K)}$ and $TS_{MD}^{(K)}$ are employed in obtaining $Y_{W^{(K)*}}^{MD}$.

Below are the steps of the experiment starting with $K = 0$.

1. Training conducted with $LS_{MD}^{(K)}$ and $TS_{MD}^{(K)}$,
   $Y_{W^{(K)*}}^{MD} = \mathcal{L}_f^{MD}(Y)(LS_{MD}^{(K)})$
2. Using the original MNIST test dataset TS as a set of evaluation data to measure indices, $Acc(Y_{W^{(K)*}}^{MD})(TS)$, $\mathcal{O}_{prob}(Y_{W^{(K)*}}^{MD})(TS)$ and $\mathcal{O}_{act}(Y_{W^{(K)*}}^{MD})(TS)$,
3. Generating a pair of datasets augmented with semantic noises,
   $LS_{MD}^{(K+1)} = \mathcal{T}_x(Y_{W^{(K)*}}^{MD})(LS_{MD}^{(K)})$ and $TS_{MD}^{(K+1)} = \mathcal{T}_x(Y_{W^{(K)*}}^{MD})(TS_{MD}^{(K)})$
4. Repeating the process so that $K := K + 1$ if not finished,

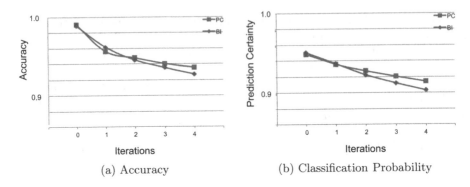

(a) Accuracy　　　　　　　(b) Classification Probability

Fig. 2. External indices

The statistical test oracle $\mathcal{G}_S^{MD}$ is evaluated at the end of each cycle above,

$$\mathcal{G}_S^{MD}(\ \mathcal{L}_f^{MD}(Y)(LS_{MD}^{(K)}),\ \mathcal{L}_f^{MD}(Y)(LS_{MD}^{(K+1)})\ )$$

It basically employs the hypothesis testing procedure referring to the observer function for the internal states $\mathcal{O}_{act}$,

$$H_S^{MD}(\mathcal{U}(\mathcal{O}_{act}(\underline{\mathcal{L}_f^{MD}(Y)(LS_{MD}^{(K)})})(TS)),\ \mathcal{U}(\mathcal{O}_{act}(\underline{\mathcal{L}_f^{MD}(Y)(LS_{MD}^{(K+1)})})(TS)))$$

Since the evaluation data TS is common, the sample sizes are the same ($N = M$), for which the t-value can be as simple as

$$t^{(K)} = \frac{\overline{y_{(K)}} - \overline{y_{(K+1)}}}{\sqrt{(s_{(K)}^2 + s_{(K+1)}^2)/N}}$$

The $t^{(K)}$ is in accordance with the identified metamorphic relation, namely the equality between indices obtained from two executions. Furthermore, $|t^{(K)}|$ is compared with $t_{\alpha/2}(\infty)$ because the sample size N is almost $10,000$ and can be large enough.

4.6   Results and Discussions

External Indices. Figure 2 shows graphs concerning with the external indices. The x-axis is common, and indicates the number of iterations K. The y-axis in Fig. 2(a) denotes the accuracy Acc, and that in Fig. 2(b) refers to the average of classification probability of $\mathcal{O}_{prob}$. For simplicity, let $Acc_{(K)}^{MD}$ be $Acc(Y_{W(K)*}^{MD})(TS)$, and $Prob_{(K)}^{MD}$ be the average of $\mathcal{O}_{prob}(Y_{W(K)*}^{MD})(TS)$.

Two graphs in Fig. 2 are monotonically decreasing. It is consistent with the method of constructing $LS^{(K)}$. As K increases, semantic noises are repeatedly added such that the empirical distribution of $LS^{(K)}$ is shifted from that of $LS^{(0)}$ whose distribution may be the same as TS. In summary, the data shift TS with respect to $LS^{(K)}$ is large as K increases, and thus the accuracies become lowered.

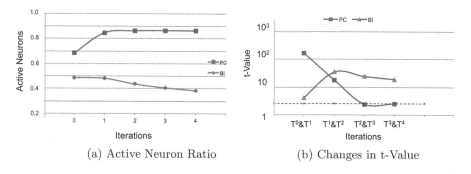

(a) Active Neuron Ratio   (b) Changes in t-Value

Fig. 3. Internal indices

The accuracies at K being 0 in Fig. 2(a), $Acc_{(0)}^{PC}$ and $Acc_{(0)}^{BI}$, are almost the same nearly to be 99%. This ensures a previous observation in [21] that the accuracy is not appropriate to check whether the test target program $\mathcal{L}_f$ may contain faults.

As K increases, the accuracies decrease, both $Acc_{(K)}^{BI}$ and $Prob_{(K)}^{BI}$ decrease faster than $Acc_{(K)}^{PC}$ and $Prob_{(K)}^{PC}$. This indicates that the degrees of the data shift in $LS_{BI}^{(K)}$ against TS are larger than those in $LS_{PC}^{(K)}$. In addition, $Y_{W^{(K)*}}^{BI}$ is less robust than $Y_{W^{(K)*}}^{PC}$ because $Prob_{(K)}^{BI}$ is smaller than $Prob_{(K)}^{PC}$.

Internal Indices. Figure 3 shows graphs concerning with the internal indices. In Fig. 3(a), the x-axis is the same as those in Fig. 2, but the y-axis refers to the neuron coverage at the penultimate layer, indeed, to the average of $\mathcal{O}_{act}$. Let $Act_{(K)}^{MD}$ be the average of $\mathcal{O}_{act}(Y_{W^{(K)*}}^{MD})(TS)$.

The values of $Act_{(K)}^{PC}$ and $Act_{(K)}^{BI}$ are quite different. $Act_{(K)}^{PC}$ reach a stable value just below 0.9 for $K>1$, while the values of $Act_{(K)}^{BI}$ are below 0.5 and decrease down to below 0.4. These show that $Y_{W^{(K)*}}^{PC}$ employ more neurons than $Y_{W^{(K)*}}^{BI}$ to make predictions for classifying data, but may imply that many neurons in the machine learning model are void in $Y_{W^{(K)*}}^{BI}$. However, the difference in the $Act_{(K)}^{MD}$ values is not usable for software testing of $\mathcal{L}_f$, because the threshold value to discriminate $\mathcal{L}_f^{PC}$ from $\mathcal{L}_f^{BI}$ is not apparent in general.

The discussion in Sect. 4.4 indicates that $\mathcal{L}_f$, if free from faults, derives trained machine learning models $Y_{W^{(K)*}}$, for which the average of $\mathcal{O}_{act}$ is converged. This is in accordance with the $Act_{(K)}^{PC}$ graph in Fig. 3(a), but it is still not clear from the graphs alone whether the $Act_{(K)}^{BI}$ graph is similar or not. It needs a detailed statistical analysis, which will be studied below.

Hypothesis Testing. As mentioned previously, the statistical oracle $\mathcal{G}_S^{MD}$ is essentially the two-sample hypothesis testing, $\mathcal{H}_S^{MD}$.

Figure 3(b) shows the $t^{(K)}$ values. The dotted line depicts the t-value at a confidence level of 0.001, $t_{0.001/2}(\infty)$. The graph concerning with $\mathcal{L}_f^{BI}$ is well above the dotted line for all the measured K. Thus, the hypothesis testing method rejects the null hypothesis. It implies that the statistical averages of $Act^{BI}_{(K)}$ and those of $Act^{BI}_{(K+1)}$ are not equal. Therefore, $\mathcal{L}^{BI}_f$ does not satisfy the metamorphic property discussed in Sect. 4.4, which is consistent with the fact that $\mathcal{L}^{BI}_f$ is so implemented as to inject faults in it.

Although the graph for $\mathcal{L}^{PC}_f$ goes below the $t_{0.001/2}(\infty)$ value, it does not ensure that $\mathcal{L}^{PC}_f$ accepts the null hypothesis (equivalently satisfies the metamorphic property), and thus that the program is free from faults. It is because the oracle uses the hypothesis testing method, which is usable for rejecting the null hypothesis, but is not appropriate to provide a positive support for it. Namely, the hypothesis testing is a methodology to find faults, if any, which is the same as software testing in general, as is argued in [7], "program testing can be a very effective way to show the presence of bugs, but is hopelessly inadequate for showing their absence".

5   Related Work

Adopting the statistical hypothesis testing method to software testing is not new. Such statistical oracles are known effective, as presented in Sect. 2.2, for testing of programs showing probabilistic behavior [11,17,26]. However, applying the method to testing of machine learning software, particularly deep neural networks, is new in this work.

Metamorphic Testing (MT) [4,5] is a standard approach to machine learning testing [32], and identifying Metamorphic Properties (MPs) is a primary concern for the successful application of the methodology. The work [30] introduces six MPs for machine learning classifiers. Each MP is concretized to more than one follow-up test generation functions, T_j.

Consider an example of supervised machine learning classifiers, Support Vector Machines (SVM) [25]. SVM is formulated as a Lagrangian-based optimization problem, and the obtained Lagrange multipliers are employed to define the separating hyper-planes. The test oracle therein may be considered to take the form of $\mathcal{G}^{[M]}_T(\mathcal{C}_f(LS), \mathcal{C}_f(T_j(LS)))$ for such T_js, if $\mathcal{C}_f$ represents the SVM results. The work [19] further studies the MT for SVM, and discusses a systematic method to derive the follow-up test generation function, each of which is so identified as to make the Lagrangian invariant. This view is based on a fact that the obtained hyper-planes are the same when the Lagrangian is not changed with invariant-preserving transformations. Furthermore, the method proposes to apply such a $T_f(\_)$ successively to obtain $T^K_f(\_)$ for the application of K times. The test oracle is $\mathcal{G}^{[M]}_T(\mathcal{C}_f(T^K_f(LS)), \mathcal{C}_f(T^{K+1}_f(LS)))$ to compare the results, one with $T^K_f(LS)$ and another with $T^{K+1}_f(LS)$ for a series of Ks. This view is generalized to the notion of the dataset diversity [21]; the dataset diversity is also a basis of the testing method that this paper presents (Sect. 4.3).

Some recent works [28,31,33] illustrate how the MT is effective in machine learning software testing. Their focus is testing of $\mathcal{I}_f(Y_{W^*})$, namely testing whether a trained machine learning model Y_{W*} behaves as expected. The test oracle takes a form of $\mathcal{G}_T^{[M]}(\ \mathcal{I}_f(Y_{W*})(a),\ \mathcal{I}_f(Y_{W*})(T_j(a))\ )$, and the metamorphic relation is defined on the application properties such as the steering angles of the auto-driving cars. Each work makes use of a different method for implementing a set of follow-up test generation functions $\{T_j\}$. DeepTest [28] adapts a classical data augmentation method [15], which is referred to as the test-time augmentation. DeepRoad [31] uses a GAN-based data synthesis method UNIT [16]. As GAN [9] ensures that the synthesized data follow the data distribution of the original test data $\{a\}$, the method enlarges the coverage of positive testing. On the other hand, negative testing, to study exceptional cases, is desirable as well, and the follow-up generation function T_f in [33] adapts the idea of fuzz [18].

The approach proposed in this paper is best summarized as a statistical test oracle to take a form of $\mathcal{G}_S(\ \mathcal{L}_f(Y)(T_f^M(LS)),\ \mathcal{L}_f(Y)(T_f^{M+1}(LS))\ )$ for some M where R_T is the statistical equality as the null hypothesis indicates. The rationale behind the testing method is the identified MR (Sect. 4.4). Although the testing method to use the statistical hypothesis seems complicated, it is more general than the approach in [21]. This previous work adopts a runtime monitor for execution of training programs $\mathcal{L}_f$, which may be dependent on some heuristics to solve the machine learning optimization programs. On the other hand, because the function T is also defined in terms of an optimization problem (Sect. 4.3), the method in this paper does not need to monitor program executions.

The group $\Xi_Y(LS)$ (Sect. 4.3) is diverce enough to be used either positive or negative testing. Choosing $\mathcal{O}_{act}(Y_{W*})(TS)$ as the observer is based on the preliminary studies in [23]. It follows the observation that the ratio of active neurons at the penultimate layer converges as the semantic noises, added to the test input dataset, are large (Sect. 4.3). The function $\mathcal{S}_f$ to augment semantic noises [22] is based on the L-BFGS [27], and builds up the dataset diversity that $\Xi_Y(LS)$ exhibits.

Last, the neuron coverage (NC) is introduced in [24] as the test suite adequacy criterion, and NC is calculated for all neurons in a trained machine learning model Y_{W*}. DeepTest [28] uses NC values as a guide to control the test data generation process. The usefulness of NC is, however, questioned [12] in view of efficiency in identifying hidden faults. The primary discussion is that NC has little correlation with certain correctness criteria in regard to the external indices. The view in [12] does not contradict with the key idea of the present paper in that the internal indices based on NC are employed as the test indices. Particularly, the results in Sect. 4.6 illustrate that the internal indices are appropriate to discriminate the bug-injected program from the probably correct one, but the accuracy, one of the standard correctness criteria, is inappropriate.

In summary, the notion of neuron coverages are used, in this paper, as test indices for the quality assurance of DNN software, while the existing works, including the original proposal [28], regard the NC as adequacy criteria of test input data.

6   Concluding Remarks

Major contributions of the present paper are two fold: (1) to introduce a general testing framework to account for machine learning software. Testing of such software is conceptually complicated because two programs, a training program $\mathcal{L}_f(Y)$ and a prediction program $\mathcal{I}_f(Y_{W^*})$, are involved, (2) to show a concrete case of applying the proposed method to testing of a training program with neural network models $\mathcal{L}_f(Y)$. Currently, the machine learning model is classical fully-connected neural networks. Extending the approach to cases of other DNN models, such as CNN or RNN [10], might be necessary to show the usefulness of the proposed method.

Last, some might argue that testing of $\mathcal{I}_f$ is more important than of $\mathcal{L}_f$, because $\mathcal{I}_f$ is the entity to make predictions for data at the operation time. We conjecture that the proposed method will be usable to test the machine learning frameworks provided as an open source platform. As in the case of component-based software development, where black-box open source components are often integrated into a software system, the system integrator is responsible for the reliability of the whole system, and thus testing of the black-box platform is mandatory.

Acknowledgment. The work is supported partially by JSPS KAKENHI Grant Number JP18H03224, and is partially based on results obtained from a project commissioned by the NEDO.

References

1. Ammann, P., Knight, J.C.: Data diversity: an approach to software fault tolerance. IEEE TC **37**(4), 418–425 (1988)
2. Ammann, P., Offutt, J.: Introduction to Software Testing. Cambridge University Press, Cambridge (2008)
3. Barr, E.T., Harman, M., McMinn, P., Shahbaz, M., Yoo, S.: The oracle problem in software testing: a survey. IEEE TSE **41**(5), 507–525 (2015)
4. Chen, T.Y., Chung, S.C., Yiu, S.M.: Metamorphic Testing - A New Approach for Generating Next Test Cases, HKUST-CS98-01. The Hong Kong University of Science and Technology (1998)
5. Chen, T.Y., et al.: Metamorphic testing: a review of challenges and opportunities. ACM Comput. Surv. **51**(1), 1–27 (2018). Article no. 4
6. Davies, M., Weyuker, E.: Pseudo-oracles for non-testable programs. In: Proceedings of the ACM 1981, pp. 254–257 (1981)
7. Dijkstra, E.W.: The humble programmer. Comm. ACM **15**(10), 859–866 (1972)
8. Elbaum, S., Rosenblum, D.S.: Known unknowns - testing in the presence of uncertainty. In: Proceedings of the 22nd FSE, pp. 833–836 (2014)
9. Goodfellow, I.J., et al.: Generative adversarial nets. In: Advances in NIPS 2014, pp. 2672–2680 (2014)
10. Goodfellow, I., Bengio, Y., Courville, A.: Deep Learning. The MIT Press, Cambridge (2016)

11. Guderlei, R., Mayer, J.: Statistical metamorphic testing - testing programs with random output by means of statistical hypothesis tests and metamorphic testing. In: Proceedings of the QSIC 2007, pp. 404–409 (2007)

12. Harel-Canada, F., Wang, L., Gulzar, M.A., Gu, Q., Kim, M.: Is neuron coverage a meaningful measure for testing deep neural networks? In: Proceedings of the 28th ESEC/FSE, pp. 851–862 (2020)

13. Haykin, S.: Neural Networks and Learning Machines, 3rd edn. Pearson India (2016)

14. Howden, W.E.: Theoretical and empirical studies of program testing. In: Proceedings of the 3rd ICSE, pp. 305–311 (1978)

15. Krizhevsky, A., Sutskever, I., Hinton, G.E.: ImageNet classification with deep convolutional neural networks. In: Advances in NIPS 2012, pp. 1097–1105 (2012)

16. Liu, M.Y., Breuel, T., Kautz, J.: Unsupervised image-to-image translation networks. In: Advances in NIPS 2017, pp. 700–708 (2017)

17. Mayer, J., Guderlei, R.: Test oracles using statistical methods. In: Proceedings of the SOQUA 2004, pp. 179–189 (2004)

18. Miller, B.P., Fredricksen, L., So, B.: An empirical study of the reliability of UNIX utilities. Comm. ACM **33**(12), 32–44 (1990)

19. Nakajima, S., Bui, H.N.: Dataset coverage for testing machine learning computer programs. In: Proceedings of the 23rd APSEC, pp. 297–304 (2016)

20. Nakajima, S.: Generalized oracle for testing machine learning computer programs. In: Cerone, A., Roveri, M. (eds.) SEFM 2017. LNCS, vol. 10729, pp. 174–179. Springer, Cham (2018). https://doi.org/10.1007/978-3-319-74781-1_13

21. Nakajima, S.: Dataset diversity for metamorphic testing of machine learning software. In: Duan, Z., Liu, S., Tian, C., Nagoya, F. (eds.) SOFL+MSVL 2018. LNCS, vol. 11392, pp. 21–38. Springer, Cham (2019). https://doi.org/10.1007/978-3-030-13651-2_2

22. Nakajima, S., Chen, T.Y.: Generating biased dataset for metamorphic testing of machine learning programs. In: Gaston, C., Kosmatov, N., Le Gall, P. (eds.) ICTSS 2019. LNCS, vol. 11812, pp. 56–64. Springer, Cham (2019). https://doi.org/10.1007/978-3-030-31280-0_4

23. Nakajima, S.: Distortion and faults in machine learning software. In: Miao, H., Tian, C., Liu, S., Duan, Z. (eds.) SOFL+MSVL 2019. LNCS, vol. 12028, pp. 29–41. Springer, Cham (2020). https://doi.org/10.1007/978-3-030-41418-4_3. arXiv:1911.11596

24. Pei, K., Cao, Y., Yang, J., Jana, S.: DeepXplore: automated whitebox testing of deep learning systems. In: Proceedings of the 26th SOSP, pp. 1–18 (2017)

25. Platt, J.C.: Fast training of support vector machines using sequential minimal optimization. In: Advances in Kernel Methods - Support Vector Machine, pp. 185–208. The MIT Press, Cambridge (1999)

26. Servcikova, H., Borning, A., Socha, D., Bleek, W.-G.: Automated testing of stochastic systems: a statistically grounded approach. In: Proceedings of the ISSTA 2006, pp. 215–224 (2006)

27. Szegedy, C., et al.: Intriguing properties of neural networks. In: Proceedings of the ICLR 2014. arXiv:1312.6199 (2013)

28. Tian, Y., Pei, K., Jana, S., Ray, B.: DeepTest: automated testing of deep-neural-network-driven autonomous cars. In: Proceedings of the 40th ICSE, pp. 303–314 (2018)

29. Weyuker, E.J.: On testing non-testable programs. Comput. J. **25**(4), 465–470 (1982)

30. Xie, X., Ho, J.W.K., Murphy, C., Kaiser, G., Xu, B., Chen, T.Y.: Testing and validating machine learning classifiers by metamorphic testing. J. Syst. Softw. **84**(4), 544–558 (2011)
31. Zhang, M., Zhang, Y., Zhang, L., Liu, C., Khurshid, S.: DeepRoad: GAN-based metamorphic testing and input validation framework for autonomous driving systems. In: Proceedings of the 33rd ASE, pp. 132–142 (2018)
32. Zhang, J.M., Harman, M., Ma, L., Liu, Y.: Machine Learning Testing: Survey, Landscapes and Horizons. arXiv:1906.10742 (2019)
33. Zhou, Z.Q., Sun, L.: Metamorphic testing of driverless cars. Comm. ACM **62**(3), 61–67 (2019)

Formalizing Spark Applications with MSVL

Meng Wang$^{(\boxtimes)}$ and Shushan Li

Cyberspace Security and Computer College, Hebei University, Baoding 071000, China
wangmenghbu@hbu.edu.cn

Abstract. Distributed computing framework Spark is widely used to deal with big data sets efficiently. However, it is more demanding implementing in Spark than coming up with sequential implementations. Thus, formal verification is needed to guarantee the correctness of Spark applications. In order to verify Spark applications using verification tool *UMC4M*, this paper presents an approach to formalizing Spark applications with Modeling Simulation and Verification Language (MSVL). We first implement Spark operations with MSVL functions, then formalize a Spark application with MSVL based on its directed acyclic graphs (DAGs). As a case study, the word count application is used to show the process.

Keywords: Spark · DAG · Big data · Formal verification

1 Introduction

As the volume of data to analyze grows rapidly, parallel computing frameworks such as Hadoop [16], Spark [12], and Flink [1] are gaining significant momentum for processing data on terabyte and petabyte scales. In simple terms, these frameworks split a large computing task into smaller computing tasks on several machines.

Hadoop MapReduce is widely used in the industry as a distributed computing framework, and the programming process includes two stages: Map and Reduce. A MapReduce job can only deal with data sets for one-pass computation, then save results to a disk for a next job. However, if the data processing is complex, it is often necessary to execute a series of MapReduce jobs in sequence. This leads to a high time cost since each job must load data from a disk. In contrast, Spark introduces an abstraction called resilient distributed datasets (RDDs) to solve the problem. Users can explicitly cache an RDD in memory

This research is supported by Advanced Talents Incubation Program of the Hebei University (No. 521000981346) and Hebei Natural Science Foundation under grant No. F2020201018.

© Springer Nature Switzerland AG 2021
J. Xue et al. (Eds.): SOFL+MSVL 2020, LNCS 12723, pp. 193–204, 2021.
https://doi.org/10.1007/978-3-030-77474-5_13

across machines and reuse it in multiple MapReduce-like parallel operations. Moreover, Spark processes data through a more general directed acyclic graph (DAG) of operators using rich sets of transformations and actions. Spark inherits the map and reduce operators provided by Hadoop and adds operators filter, groupByKey, distinct etc. for parallel programming by developers. In order to deal with different distributed tasks such as streaming analysis, graph analysis, SQL interactive query and machine learning, Spark provides different components, including Spark Streaming, Spark GraphX, Spark SQL and SparkMLib. In addition, Spark supports several programming languages such as Scala, Java and Python.

Spark exploits a master/worker architecture and the master is responsible for the work scheduling of each node in the entire cluster. As the main abstraction in Spark, RDD supports two kinds of operations: transformation operations and action operations, where transformation operations includes map(), flatmap(), filter(), reduceByKey(), groupByKey(), combineByKey, etc., while action operations includes collect(), count(), countByValue(), reduce(), foreach(), etc. The actual calculation of Spark takes place when an RDD action operation is called. Before that, for all transformations, Spark just records the trajectory generated by RDD without triggering the actual calculation. The Spark kernel draws a DAG of the computational path at the moment when it needs to compute. A node in a Spark DAG is called stage, which is divided according to the wide dependence. Then the DAG is used to organize the operations that compose a Spark application.

It is of great importance to guarantee the correctness of big-data batch applications especially Spark applications. However, little research has been done in this area. Grossman et al. [7] propose an SMT-based approach for verifying the equivalence of interesting classes of Spark programs, and show that it is complete under certain restrictions. Beckert et al. [3] prove the equivalence between imperative and deterministic MapReduce algorithms by partitioning the proof into a sequence of equivalence proofs between intermediate programs with smaller differences, and demonstrate the feasibility by evaluating it on k-means and PageRank algorithms. Baresi et al. [2] just focus on the verification of evaluating execution time of Spark applications. They abstract each specific execution of a Spark application as a DAG and formulate the identification of the global execution time as a reachability problem. However, these efforts do not verify temporal properties which Spark applications should be satisfied. In [15], we formalize Hadoop Mapreduce with MSVL. Here, we focus on how specify Spark applications in a formal way in order to verify temporal properties of the programs.

Modeling, Simulation and Verification Language (MSVL) [4,5] is a formal language which is used for verifying properties of software. Support tools including compiler *MC* [10], runtime verification tool *PPTLCheck* [11] and model checker *UMC4M* [8] have been developed by researchers. Thus, we prefer to formalize Spark applications using MSVL programs. To do that, we first implement the two kinds of RDD operations using MSVL functions. Then we abstract a specific execution of a Spark application as a DAG. After that, we model the Spark application according to its DAG using MSVL programs.

The following are the three main contributions of the paper: (1) The principle for formalizing RDD transformation operations and action operations using MSVL is summarized. (2) The principle how to formalizing a Spark application with the help of its DAG is proposed. (3) A unified model checking approach at code level [6,8,14] to verifying Spark applications is demonstrated.

The paper is organized as follows. Section 2 briefly presents the syntax and semantics of MSVL. Section 3 provides an overview of Apache Spark. In Sect. 4, we summarize the principle for formalizing Spark applications with MSVL programs; then, a unified model checking approach at code level to verifying these programs is demonstrated. In Sect. 5, as a case study, a word count problem is given to show how a Spark application can be modeled and verified with MSVL. Section 6 concludes the work.

2   Preliminaries

2.1   MSVL

As an executable subset of Projection Temporal Logic (PTL) [5], MSVL [4,5] can be used to model, simulate and verify programs. The arithmetic and boolean expressions in MSVL can be inductively defined as follows:

$$e ::= c \mid x \mid \bigcirc e \mid \ominus e \mid g(e_1,\ldots,e_m) \mid ext\ f(e_1,\ldots,e_n)$$
$$b ::= \mathsf{true} \mid \mathsf{false} \mid \neg b \mid b_0 \wedge b_1 \mid e_0 = e_1 \mid e_0 < e_1$$

where c is a constant, and x a variable. $\ominus e$ and $\bigcirc e$ stand for the value of a variable at the previous state and the next one, respectively. The $g(e_1,\ldots,e_m)$ is a call of a state function g. Each usual arithmetic operation $(+ \mid - \mid * \mid \%)$ can be viewed as a two-arity function call $g(e_1,e_2)$. $ext\ f(e_1,\ldots,e_n)$ is an external call of MSVL function f, which means we concern only the return value of function f but not the interval over which the function is executed. These expressions can be treated as terms in PTL. The statements of MSVL can be defined by PTL formulas as follows.

NAME	SYNTAX	SEMANTICS
1. Termination:	empty	$\stackrel{\text{def}}{=} \varepsilon$
2. Unit Assignment:	$x := e$	$\stackrel{\text{def}}{=} \bigcirc x = e \wedge \text{len}(1)$
3. Assignment:	$x <== e$	$\stackrel{\text{def}}{=} x = e \wedge p_x$
4. State Frame:	$\text{lbf}(x)$	$\stackrel{\text{def}}{=} \neg\text{af}(x) \rightarrow \exists b : (\ominus x = b \wedge x = b)$
5. Interval Frame:	$\text{frame}(x)$	$\stackrel{\text{def}}{=} \Box(more \rightarrow \bigcirc\text{lbf}(x))$
6. Next:	$\text{next } \phi$	$\stackrel{\text{def}}{=} \bigcirc\phi$
7. Always:	$\text{always } \phi$	$\stackrel{\text{def}}{=} \Box\phi$
8. Conditional:	$\text{if } b \text{ then } \phi_0 \text{ else } \phi_1$	$\stackrel{\text{def}}{=} (b \rightarrow \phi_0) \wedge (\neg b \rightarrow \phi_1)$
9. Local Variable:	$\text{exist } x : \phi(x)$	$\stackrel{\text{def}}{=} \exists x : \phi(x)$
10. Sequential:	$\phi_0 ; \phi_1$	$\stackrel{\text{def}}{=} \phi_0; \phi_1$
11. Conjunction:	$\phi_0 \text{ and } \phi_1$	$\stackrel{\text{def}}{=} \phi_0 \wedge \phi_1$
12. While:	$\text{while } b \{ \phi \}$	$\stackrel{\text{def}}{=} (b \wedge \phi)^* \wedge \Box(\varepsilon \rightarrow \neg b)$
13. Selection:	$\phi_0 \text{ or } \phi_1$	$\stackrel{\text{def}}{=} \phi_0 \vee \phi_1$
14. Parallel:	$\phi_0 \parallel \phi_1$	$\stackrel{\text{def}}{=} \phi_0 \wedge (\phi_1; \text{true}) \vee (\phi_0; \text{true}) \wedge \phi_1 \vee \phi_0 \wedge \phi_1$
15. Projection:	$(\phi_1, \ldots, \phi_m) \text{ prj } \phi$	$\stackrel{\text{def}}{=} (\phi_1, \ldots, \phi_m) \, prj \, \phi$
16. Await:	$\text{await}(c)$	$\stackrel{\text{def}}{=} \text{frame}(x_1, x_2, \ldots, x_n) \wedge \Box(\varepsilon \leftrightarrow c)$

MSVL supports not only some basic control flow statements such as sequential, conditional and while-loop statements, but also non-determinism and concurrent programming including selection, conjunction, parallel and projection statements. The termination statement empty indicates that the current state is the final state of an interval. next ϕ means that at the next state ϕ will be executed. More details refer to [5]. In addition, MSVL supports plenty of data types including integer, float, char, string, array, pointer and structure [9], and a mechanism for internal and external function calls [13]. Further, an MSVL compiler MC [10] and a model checker $UMC4M$ [8] have been developed to execute and verify MSVL programs, respectively.

3 Spark Framework

Spark is usually deployed on a cluster of servers and exploits a master/worker architecture. Multiple slave nodes and one master node are used to form the cluster. The master node needs to schedule all tasks to complete a job, while each slave node only completes tasks published by the master node. The basic framework of Spark is as shown in Fig. 1.

In order to describe how Spark works, some Spark terminology definitions are given as follows:

(1) Application: a spark application written by users, containing codes running on Driver and Executor. An application consists of one or more jobs.
(2) Job: produced by executing an action operation. Each action in a Spark application will be scheduled as a job by Spark.

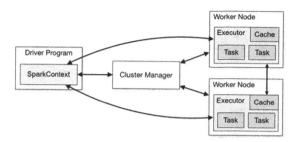

Fig. 1. Spark basic framework diagram

(3) Task: the smallest unit of work, which is responsible for performing and completing specific tasks on an Executor.

(4) Stage, TaskSet: a set of related tasks that do not have Shuffle dependencies on each other. Each job is split into stages.

(5) SparkContext: a process responsible for communication with Cluster Manager, resource application, task allocation and task monitoring, etc.

(6) Driver Program: the host process executing the main function of an application and creating SparkContext. It transforms an application into tasks and coordinates the scheduling of tasks between Executor processes.

(7) Cluster Manager: responsible for resource allocation. It acts as the master node in the Standalone mode of Spark. It controls the whole cluster and monitors all workers.

(8) Worker Node: acting as a slave node. It is responsible to start an Executor or a Driver.

(9) Executor: a process running on Work Node which is responsible for running tasks and storing data to memory or disks. Each application has a separate set of Executors.

(10) TaskScheduler: responsible for the actual physical scheduling of each specific task. It submits Taskset to Executor to run and report the results.

The detailed operation process of Spark is as follows:

(1) The running environment of a Spark application is built. That is a Spark-Context is created and initialized. After that, SparkContext submits registration to the Cluster Manager and requests to run Executors.

(2) Cluster Manager assigns Executors required for application execution, and starts these Executors on Worker Nodes. Executors send heartbeat to the Cluster Manager.

(3) The SparkContext builds a DAG and divides it into stages. A stage can been seen as a TaskSet. The SparkContext sends TaskSets to TaskScheduler.

(4) Executors request Tasks from SparkContext, then the TaskScheduler issues tasks to Executors for running. At the same time the SparkContext issues application code to Executors.

(5) Tasks run through Executors. When the tasks are completed, all the resources are released.

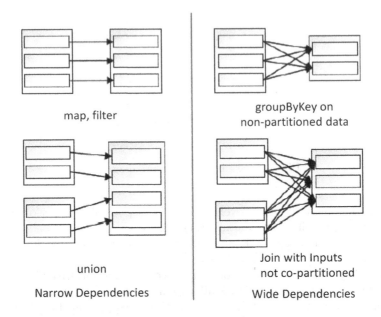

Fig. 2. Dependency types

Each operation in Spark generates an RDD. The calculation of Spark takes place when an action operation of an RDD executes, while for all transformation operations before the action operation, Spark just records the trajectory generated by RDDs, without triggering the real calculation. Spark kernel will draw a DAG about the calculation path when the calculation needs to take place. After that the DAG is divided into stages according to narrow dependencies and wide dependencies. As shown in Fig. 2, narrow dependencies require that a partition of each parent RDD is used by at most one partition of each child RDD, while for wide dependencies, a partition of each parent RDD may be used by more than one partion of each child RDD and a partition of each child RDD usually uses all partitions of parent RDDs.

4   Principle for Formalizing Spark Applications

Spark can be used to deal with large data sets effectively. However, it is more demanding implementing in Spark than coming up with sequential implementations. Thus, checking the correctness of Spark application is of great importance. In this paper, we concentrate on formalizing a Spark application with MSVL and present the principle of formalization.

4.1   Data Storage System

Usually, large data sets to be processed are stored on external storages. Spark can call a textFile operation to read data from a file to RDD, and call a saveAs-

TextFile operation to write data to a file. Whereas MSVL supports C functions as external functions. We can call these functions on external file management such as fopen(), fgets(), fputs(), fclose(), etc. to read and write data. In addition, in order to store data in local memory, MSVL supports multi-types to build various data structures. When data are read from a file, they can store to lists or arrays in MSVL. If data are complicated consisting of several components, type struct in MSVL can be used to store the data.

4.2 Spark Operations

Spark supports two kinds of operations, namely transformation operations and action operations, where transformation operations include map(), flatmap(), filter(), reduceByKey(), groupByKey(), combineByKey, etc., while action operations include collect(), count(), countByValue(), reduce(), foreach(), etc. Whereas MSVL supports function definitions and statements similar to imperative languages such as assignment, conditional, sequential and while statements. We can write the corresponding functions using MSVL statements and add them to the MSVL function library.

4.3 DAG-Based Formalization

Each operation in Spark generates an RDD. Connect RDDs with an edge, then these RDDs and edges form a DAG. A DAG can be generated after a series of transformations of original RDDs. The next task of Spark kernel is to divide computation into task sets, namely stages, according to the DAG diagram, so that tasks can be submitted to the computation node for real computation. Two stages are connected if one uses the data produced by the other. A stage can only be executed if and only if all of its predecessors are completed. The intermediate result of default is kept in memory. When a DAG is divided into stages, Spark considers which parts can be calculated pipelined in distributed computing in order to improve the efficiency. That means operations in the same stage are executed in a pipeline way. For different stages of a DAG, if there are no direct or indirect connections between them, they can be calculated in parallel.

As you can see from Sect. 2, MSVL is a parallel programming language with sequential construct $P; Q$, several parallel or concurrent constructs such as P and Q, $P\|Q$ and $(P_1, \ldots, P_m)$ prj Q. For one stage in RDD, parallel construct $P\|Q$ can be used to formalize the pipeline calculation on a series of executors. For two stages which have direct connection between them, sequential construct $P; Q$ can be used to formalize the relation. For two stages which have no direct or indirect connections between them, parallel construct $P\|Q$ can be used to formalize it.

4.4 Verifying Programs

A compiler MC and a model checker $UMC4M$ have been developed for MSVL. These enable us to execute and verify properties of MSVL programs translated from Spark applications automatically.

5   Case Study: Word Count

In this section, we use the word count application as a case study to show our work. The following subsections show the details of formalization.

5.1   Spark Application

Figure 3 shows Scala code of the word count Spark application that performs a simple aggregation over a dataset read from a text file where each line contains some English words. The variable $fileRDD$ contains multiple lines of text content after Spark $textFile$ operation is executed. Then $fileRDD.flatMap(line => line.split(""))$ traverses each line of text content in $fileRDD$. As it traverses the text content in one line, the text content is assigned to variable $line$ and $line => line.split("")$ is executed. $line => line.split("")$ is a Lamda expression where the left side is an input parameter and the right side is the processing logic executed in the function. Here executing $line.split("")$ means that for a line of text content, using blank space as a delimiter to do the word segmentation, we can get a set of words separated from the line of text context. In this way, for each line in $fileRDD$, a word set can be obtained. The $fileRDD.flatMap()$ operation flattens the multiple word sets into one large word set. Then, for this large set of words, Spark performs the map operation, namely $map(word => (word, 1))$. The map operation iterates through each word in the set. When iterating through one of the words, it assigns the current word to variable $word$ and executes the Lamda expression $word => (word, 1)$, which means that for the input $word$, a tuple $(word, 1)$ is build, where $word$ is the key, and 1 is the value indicating the word appears once. Then an RDD can be obtained and each element of this RDD is a tuple in the form of (key,value). Finally, for this RDD, $reduceByKey(\_ + \_)$ operation is executed. Reduce operations will be conducted on multiple values with the same key and return the (key,value) after reducing. Thus the word frequency of this word can be obtained.

Figure 4 is a DAG of the word count application in Fig. 3 and it shows how the application is executed by Spark. Each blue rectangle in a stage is an RDD that is produced by the associated operation; the arrows define the ordering relation between the transformations in Stage 0 and Stage 1. Due to the lazy evaluation of transformations, nothing happens until $saveAsTextFile$ is executed. At that moment, Spark creates the DAG as in Fig. 4. Since $flatmap$ and map do not require data shuffling, the first three operations are grouped in a single stage (Stage 0). Conversely, $reduceByKey$ requires shuffling because tuples with the same key are not guaranteed to be all in the same partition. For this reason, Stage 1 is created and depends on Stage 0. Thus, it can be scheduled only when Stage 0 has completed its execution.

```
package com.hx.spark
import org.apache.spark.{SparkConf, SparkContext}
import org.apache.spark.rdd.RDD
object WordCount {
  def main(args: Array[String]): Unit = {
    val sparkConf=new SparkConf().setAppName("WordCount")
    val sc = new SparkContext(sparkConf)
    val fileRDD: RDD[String] = sc.textFile(args(0))
    val wordRDD: RDD[String] = fileRDD.flatMap(line =>line.split(" "))
    val mapRDD: RDD[(String, Int)] = wordRDD.map(word=>(word,1))
    val wordToSumRDD: RDD[(String, Int)] = mapRDD.reduceByKey(_+_)
    wordToSumRDD.saveAsTextFile(args(1))
    sc.stop()
  }
}
```

Fig. 3. Scala Code of Word Count

5.2 Formalization

According to the DAG of word count, we can obtain that two stages are executed in a sequential way. Thus, we can formalize the whole application as follows:

$$WordCount \overset{\text{def}}{=} Stage0; Stage1$$

where $Stage0$ reads all words from the file, then performs *flatmap* and *map* operations to rewrite each word to a key-value pair. $Stage1$ reduces the record with the same key together and saves the result in a file.

Formalization of Stage 0. In this stage, the application reads records from the file line by line, separates words from records and rewrites each record to $(word, 1)$, where *word* is the word string and 1 means the word appears once. In order to do that, two structure types *struct* **Words** and *struct* **KeyValue** are defined as follows.

```
1   struct Words
2   {
3       char *data and
4       int idle
5   };
6   struct KeyValue
7   {
8       char *key and
9       int value
10  };
```

In the *struct* **Words**, the component **data** stores words and **idle** represents the state of this memory block, where **idle = 1** indicates the memory block is idle, **idle = 2** means that entries are being processed and **idle = 3** represents that the processing of entries are completed. To store original records

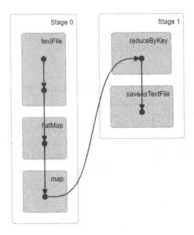

Fig. 4. DAG of Word Count

read from the file, **struct Words lineData[N]** are defined, where **N** is an integer constant and **lineData[i].data** ($0 \leq i < $ **N**) is used to store a line of words, while to store records after $flatmap()$, **struct Words word[M]** is defined, where **M** is an integer constant and **word[i].data** ($0 \leq i < $ **M**) is used to store a word. In the $struct$ **KeyValue, key** stores the word and **value** represents the number of times the word appears. We define an array **struct KeyValue wordcount[T]** to store the pairs $(word, value)$. With MSVL, $Stage0$ can briefly be specified as follows:

$$Stage0 \stackrel{\text{def}}{=} ReadWords()||(flatmap(1)|| \cdots ||flatmap(n))||$$
$$||(map(1)|| \cdots ||map(n))$$

$ReadWords$ reads entries of a line from the file into the memory when there is an idle memory block **lineData[i]** (**lineData[i].idle=1**). Function $flatmap$ separates all entries stored in **lineData[i]** (**lineData[i].idle=2**) into words and stores each word in an idle memory block **word[j]** (**word[j].idle=1**). After processing, **lineData[i].idle** is reset to 1 and **word[j].idle** to 3. Thus, n $flatmap$ processes execute in parallel. Function map rewrites each word in **word[i]** (**word[j].idle=3**) into a key-value pair $(word, 1)$ and stores it in $wordcount$.

Formalization of Stage 1. We reduce the records with the same key together and obtain the number of times each word appears in the file. To do that, we define a structure type $struct$ **OutData** as follows:

```
1  struct OutData
2  {
3      struct   KeyValue wordcount and
4      int idle
5  };
```

In the *struct* **OutData**, the component **wordcount** stores the word and its appearance number, and **idle** has the same meaning with **idle** in **struct Words**. An array *struct* **OutData result[P]** is defined to store results after *reduceByKey*, where **P** is an integer constant. The reduce process can be defined as follows:

$$Stage1 \stackrel{\text{def}}{=} shuffle(); ((reduceByKey(0)|| \cdots ||reduceByKey(n))|| \\ WriteRecord())$$

Function *shuffle* puts all records with the same key together. Function *reduceByKey* computes all entries with the same key to obtain final entries. For a word that is not counted, an idle memory (**result[i].idle=1**) $(0 \leq i < $ **P**$)$ is used to store data (**result[i].idle=2**). If the count for a word (**result[j].wordcout.key**) is finished, **result[j].idle** is set to 3. *WriteRecord* writes the processed records (**result[j].idle = 3**) into another file.

6   Conclusion

In this paper, we present an approach to formalizing a Spark application with an MSVL program. We first formalize Spark operations using MSVL functions, and then based on DAGs of the application, we can formalize the whole application using an MSVL program. In the future, we will further study properties these Spark applications should satisfy and verify them using model checker $UMC4M$.

References

1. https://flink.apache.org/
2. Baresi, L., Bersani, M.M., Marconi, F., Quattrocchi, G., Rossi, M.: Using formal verification to evaluate the execution time of spark applications. Formal Aspects Comput., 1–38 (2020)
3. Beckert, B., Bingmann, T., Kiefer, M., Sanders, P., Ulbrich, M., Weigl, A.: Relational equivalence proofs between imperative and MapReduce algorithms. In: Piskac, R., Rümmer, P. (eds.) VSTTE 2018. LNCS, vol. 11294, pp. 248–266. Springer, Cham (2018). https://doi.org/10.1007/978-3-030-03592-1_14
4. Duan, Z.: An extended interval temporal logic and a framing technique for temporal logic programming. Ph.D thesis. University of Newcastle Upon Tyne (1996)
5. Duan, Z.: Temporal Logic and Temporal Logic Programming. Science Press (2005)

6. Duan, Z., Tian, C.: A unified model checking approach with projection temporal logic. In: Liu, S., Maibaum, T., Araki, K. (eds.) ICFEM 2008. LNCS, vol. 5256, pp. 167–186. Springer, Heidelberg (2008). https://doi.org/10.1007/978-3-540-88194-0_12

7. Grossman, S., Cohen, S., Itzhaky, S., Rinetzky, N., Sagiv, M.: Verifying equivalence of spark programs. In: Majumdar, R., Kunčak, V. (eds.) CAV 2017. LNCS, vol. 10427, pp. 282–300. Springer, Cham (2017). https://doi.org/10.1007/978-3-319-63390-9_15

8. Wang, M., Tian, C., Duan, Z.: Full regular temporal property verification as dynamic program execution. In: Proceedings of the 39th International Conference on Software Engineering Companion, pp. 226–228. IEEE Press (2017)

9. Wang, X., Tian, C., Duan, Z., Zhao, L.: MSVL: a typed language for temporal logic programming. Frontiers Comput. Sci. 11(5), 762–785 (2017)

10. Yang, K., Duan, Z., Tian, C., Zhang, N.: A compiler for MSVL and its applications. Theor. Comput. Sci. 749, 2–16 (2017)

11. Bin, Yu., Duan, Z., Tian, C., Zhang, N.: Verifying temporal properties of programs: a parallel approach. J. Parallel Distrib. Comput. 118, 89–99 (2018)

12. Zaharia, M., Chowdhury, M., Franklin, M.J., Shenker, S., Stoica, I.: Spark: cluster computing with working sets. HotCloud 10(10-10), 95 (2010)

13. Zhang, N., Duan, Z., Tian, C.: A mechanism of function calls in MSVL. Theor. Comput. Sci. 654, 11–25 (2016)

14. Zhang, N., Duan, Z., Tian, C.: Model checking concurrent systems with MSVL. Sci. China Inf. Sci. 59, 118101 (2016)

15. Zhang, N., Wang, M., Duan, Z., Tian, C., Cui, J.: Implementing MapReduce with MSVL. In: Tian, C., Nagoya, F., Liu, S., Duan, Z. (eds.) SOFL+MSVL 2017. LNCS, vol. 10795, pp. 148–167. Springer, Cham (2018). https://doi.org/10.1007/978-3-319-90104-6_10

16. Zikopoulos, P., Eaton, C., et al.: Understanding Big Data: Analytics for Enterprise Class Hadoop and Streaming Data. McGraw-Hill Osborne Media, New York (2011)

Author Index

Printed in the United States
by Baker & Taylor Publisher Services